COLLECTIVE BARGAINING PREPARATION ESSENTIALS

THE HANDBOOK
SECOND EDITION

HUGH J. FINLAYSON

FriesenPress

Suite 300 - 990 Fort St
Victoria, BC, V8V 3K2
Canada

www.friesenpress.com

Copyright © 2020 by Hugh J Finlayson
Second Edition — 2021

All rights reserved.

No part of this publication may be reproduced in any form, or by any means, electronic or mechanical, including photocopying, recording, or any information browsing, storage, or retrieval system, without permission in writing from FriesenPress.

Every effort has been taken to ensure that these materials comply with the requirements of copyright clearances and appropriate credits. The author will attempt to incorporate in future printings any corrections that are communicated to the author in writing

ISBN
978-1-5255-5423-0 (Hardcover)
978-1-5255-5424-7 (Paperback)
978-1-5255-5425-4 (eBook)

1. *Business & Economics, Negotiating*

Distributed to the trade by The Ingram Book Company

"I sure hope the negotiations go well."

Used with permission, The New Yorker Collection/The Cartoon Bank, 2020 by Jason Patterson (2008).

CONTENTS

Preface	IX
Overview of the Structure	XI
A Note about the Statutory Framework:	XIV
Chapter 1: Collective Bargaining Concepts and Constructs	**1**
Stages of Collective Bargaining	6
Bargaining Configurations and Philosophy	8
Your Role	11
Your Role and Understanding the *Real* Organization	12
Consider Your Organization: What do I know, how do I know it, and why does it matter?	16
Terms	17
Objectives, Positions, and Interests	17
Chapter 2: Why We Bargain the Way We Bargain	**22**
Understanding Union-Employer Relationships	26
Evolving Union-Employer Relationships	30
Attitudinal Relationship Factors	32
Predetermined Factors or Antecedent Determinants	32
Emergent Relationships	34
Testing the Propositions: An Emergent Relationship Quick Test	37
Organizing Concepts	37
Dual Concerns and Collective Bargaining: Conflicts per se	39
Orientations	42
Positions and Positioning	43
The Difference Between the Three: An Attitude as Much as an Approach	51
Without a Full Appreciation: A Word of Caution	56
Collective Bargaining and Continuous Improvement	57
A Place to Start	57
Interests and a *Good* Agreement or Settlement?	61
Win-Win = Good?	62
Elements of Good	63
Fairness	63
Efficiency	64

Wisdom	64
Stability	65

Chapter 3: In Support of Informed Decisions — 67

The Importance of Information	67
Foundations and the Importance of Understanding	68
The Organization	69
The Existing Collective Agreement	70
Benchmark Settlements	71
The Organization's Objectives and Limits	71
The Other Negotiating Team	72
Summarizing the Last Negotiations	73
Outreach to Inform	74
Understand the Issues, Understand Your Audience	76
Considering Probable Demands and Costs	77
Developing Bargaining Objectives	78
Developing Bargaining Proposals: For what problem is this the solution?	82
Do You Really Need to Make a Proposal?	83
Assessing the Bargaining Climate	84

Chapter 4: Choosing a Negotiating Team — 86

Number of Team Members	86
Personal Attributes of Team Members	87
Qualities of the Spokesperson	88
Bargaining Roles	88

Chapter 5: Organizing Information During Bargaining — 90

CB Resource 1: Contextual Data/Information Resource	90
CB Resource 2: Historical Clause Development	92
CB Resource 3: Proposal-Counter Proposal-Agreed in Principle Resource (P-CP-AiP)	93
CB Resource 4: Working Resource	93
CB Resource 5: Bargaining Status Worksheet	94
CB Resource 6: Bargaining Notes or Minutes	95
Points to Remember When Taking Notes	96

Chapter 6: Costing Proposals and Determining Wage Criteria — 97

Costing the Proposals	97
Determining Wage Criteria	98
Comparability of Wage Rates	98
Productivity	99
Ability to Pay	99
Cost of Living	100

How do you cost proposals or an agreement? An approach to consider:	100
Have a Standard Set of Definitions	100
Develop Costing Principles	101

Chapter 7: Crafting Collective Agreement Language — 103

Subjects of Collective Bargaining	103
Mandatory Provisions	104
Other Articles	104
Drafting Collective Agreement Language	105
General Guidelines	106
This Doesn't Need to be in the Collective Agreement, Does It?	109
Interpretation of Language	110
The Meaning of the Provisions	110
Ordinary Meaning	110
Other Interpretive Issues	112
Summary	113

Chapter 8: Establishing a Bargaining Protocol — 114

Bargaining Protocol: Considerations	114
Location, Timing, and Length of Meetings	115
Wages for Employee Members	116
Negotiation Proceedings	116
Other Protocol Considerations	117
Confirm Authority	117
Roles and Responsibilities	117
Draft Collective Bargaining Protocol	118
Exchanging Initial Proposals	120

Chapter 9: To the Table: Considerations — 121

To Start: Is this a First Collective Agreement?	121
Putting Collective Bargaining in Context: Reflections on the Alternatives Chosen	123
Are You Ready? Reflections on Process	123
Make a Considered Assessment: Options and *Best Alternatives*	123
Do You Have a Contingency Plan?	128
Strikes and Lockouts: Rules and Regulations	129
Plan Manager	129
Continuation of Operations	129
Communications Plan	129
Security Implications	129
Approaches to Interactions at the Table	130
Clarifying Interests and Concerns	130

    Listening and Checking Assumptions 130
    Managing the Process 131
    Deciding When a Caucus is Needed 131
    Taking Care of the Relationship 131
    Working Effectively, Ethically and Constructively 131
    Ensuring the Desired Outcomes 132
At the Table: Guidelines for Bargaining 132
    Preparing for the Initial Negotiating Session 132
    Developing Your Initial Meeting Strategy 133
    Questions and Questioning 134
    Opening the Negotiations 135
    Building Understanding 136
    Improved Problem Solving 137
    To Facilitate Movement Toward Agreement 137
    Closing the Negotiations 138
Learning from Results: Checklist for Reviewing Your Negotiation 139

Chapter 10: Good Faith in Collective Bargaining   **141**

Guidelines: The Duty to Bargain in Good Faith 142
    The Parties Must Meet 142
    The Parties Must Engage in Rational, Informed Discussion 143
    The Parties Must Intend to Enter into a Collective Agreement 144
Remedies for Failure to Bargain in Good Faith 145

Chapter 11: At an Impasse: Strikes and Lockouts   **147**

Strikes, Lockouts, and Picketing 147
Preconditions to a Strike or Lockout 148
What are the Consequences of an Unlawful Strike or Lockout? 149
Continuation of Benefits 149
Picketing 149
Strikes, Lockouts, and Essential Services 150
Causes of Strikes and Lockouts 151

Chapter 12: Bargaining Assistance: Conciliation, Mediation, Arbitration and Inquiry   **153**

Conciliation and Mediation 154
Why Mediate? 154
    Mediation Process Guidelines and Suggestions 155
Other Alternatives 156
    Inquiries and Statutory Commissions 156
Mediation-Arbitration (Med-Arb) 157
Final Offer Selection (FOS) 157

    Final Offer Selection Variants   158
    Interest Arbitration   159

Conclusion: Preparing to Constructively Engage on Things That Matter   **161**

    1. Consider You and *Them*   162
    2. From Now to Understanding   162
    3. Awareness in preparation: Unconscious Biases, Perceptions, and the Matters at Issue   163
        Confirmation Bias   164
        False Consensus Effect   164
        Self-serving Bias   165
        Fundamental Attribution Error   165
        One Way Forward   165
    4. Consider Your Approach and the Pursuit of Constructive Alternatives   166
        As a General Proposition   166
        Before the *Intractables* Become Irreconcilable: Preparation Focussed on Potentials   166
    5. What Stands in the Way   172
    6. Where to Start and When   172
    In Summary: Building a Framework for Thinking, Understanding, and Action   173

In Closing: Credits and Final Observations   **175**

Resource One: CB Statutes and Rules Test: *What do I need to confirm?*   **177**

Resource Two: Collective Bargaining Process (CPB) Checklist   **180**

Resource Three: How to Draft a Memorandum of Agreement   **190**
    Sample A   191
    Sample B   191

Glossary   **193**

References   **209**

Index   **212**

About the Author   **231**

Notes   **232**

PREFACE

> "There is, and will continue to be, a natural conflict of interests between labour and management . . . however, the two parties have common interests, including the state of the economy as a whole and the continuing welfare of the enterprise from which they both earn their living."
>
> —Economic Council of Canada, 1967

Something is essential if it is of the utmost importance: basic, indispensable, necessary. This book is just that, essential.

Collective Bargaining Preparation Essentials: The Handbook is about collective bargaining—the negotiation or renegotiation of employees' terms and conditions of employment—and alternatives. What emerges from your planning, negotiation, and implementation efforts is a codification of what the union and the employer agree on to regulate their conduct and dealings over a certain period. All based on the parties' choice of alternatives.

Negotiation, in simple terms, is the basic means of getting what you want from others. It is back and forth communication designed to reach an agreement when you and the other party have some interests that are shared and others that are opposed. At its core, negotiation is really about persuasion—how you present your ideas to others in a way that moves them to agree with you, reach meaningful accommodations or to take action.

> We are all negotiators. Whether you sometimes disagree with a colleague or spouse, buy a car, lead a project or work group, you negotiate and need to know how to do it given the specific circumstance and nature of the interactions. In people centric institutions it takes the form of a search for the terms and conditions of the parties' co-existence.
>
> While we may negotiate in many forums and have a variety of negotiating experiences, we don't bargain collectively all the time!

Collective bargaining between unions and employers constitutes a specialized area in the field of negotiations. The underlying legal and relationship aspects make it distinct. Unlike general negotiations, a specific statutory regime governs the practice and process of collective bargaining and further, the ongoing relationship between the parties makes it different from many of the other types of bargaining interactions.

The agreement that results from collective bargaining has a term with specific provisions, and the parties must continue to deal with each other as the terms and conditions of the agreement are applied to the employment aspects of the workplace. Union and management representatives must resolve disagreements that occur with respect to the interpretation, application, and administration of the agreement's provisions.

At the end of the day, negotiators, including collective bargainers have three universal concerns: substance, process, and relationships.

- Substantive, the concrete content directly related to the matters at issue—the *what*.

- Procedural, related to the manner, process, and procedures used to settle the matters at issue and are how we talk to and treat each other—the *how*.

- Relationship or relational, subjective in nature (intangible, qualitative, and emotional); pertaining to the strength, nature, and type of both individual relationships (between individuals or groups of individuals) and institutional relationships (between, for example, representatives of the employer and representatives of the union).

At the centre are their interests, defined as the things that people want to satisfy or achieve in a negotiation situation. Unlike people's positions—which are simple statements purportedly that represent their interests—the interests underlying a position answers the question, "Why do you want that?" or "Why do you feel that way?"

Figure 1: A Negotiator's Universal Concerns: Issues and Interests

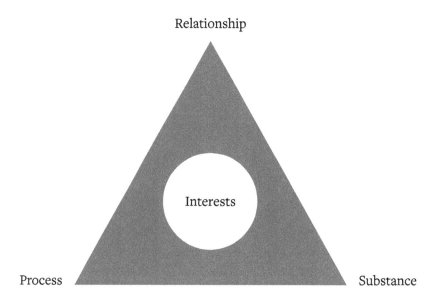

Overview of the Structure

Before negotiating any collective agreement, negotiators must have a firm philosophy to guide them in developing both their own proposals and their stance when considering the other team's proposals. For negotiators and who they represent, it is a question of alternatives—a course or courses of action, the selection of which precludes any other possibility.

Collective Bargaining Preparation Essentials: The Handbook is divided into twelve topical chapters and supplemented by additional resources and a comprehensive glossary. It begins by setting a conceptual foundation that serves to frame the resources, tools, and best practices guidelines that follow. While a sound foundation, *Collective Bargaining Preparation Essentials: The Handbook* is not a substitute for informed professional advice in particular situations. When it comes to advice we stress informed. Remember that advice—guidance or recommendations concerning prudent future action, typically given by someone regarded as knowledgeable or authoritative—can **inform but not decide** for you. After all, those who provide advice won't be around to implement it and certainly won't be around to experience the direct result of the choices made in a particular circumstance. The alternatives may be many but the **decisions are yours**.

> The goal of *Collective Bargaining Preparation Essentials: The Handbook* is to help you make wise choices. Wise choices can only result from informed preparation and a considered approach to bargaining collectively. Given the dynamic nature of negotiations generally and collective agreement negotiations in particular, readers are encouraged to continue their best practices inquiry.

Collective Bargaining Preparation Essentials: The Handbook is written with the assumption that the parties intend to bargain in good faith in an effort to conclude a collective agreement.

Chapter 1 – Collective Bargaining Concepts and Constructs. Collective bargaining between unions and employers constitutes a specialized area in the field of negotiations. Chapter 1 introduces an organizer or *framework for thinking* about union-employer collective bargaining. It describes the three major phases of collective bargaining and includes a flowchart illustrating the bargaining stages within the three phases. Within the context of the framework, roles as a member of a negotiating team are detailed.

Chapter 2 – Why We Bargain the Way We Bargain. The process and practice of collective bargaining takes many forms in workplaces. When unions and employers bargain collectively to determine the terms of their continuing relationship why do they bargain the way they do? The concepts of bargaining, negotiation, positions vs. interests and distributive vs. integrative approaches central to understanding negotiations generally and collective bargaining in particular are examined.

Chapter 3 – In Support of Informed Decisions. Collective bargaining is a research and data informed exercise. The approach and processes for assembling the necessary information about the organization, the other negotiating team, the existing agreement, benchmark settlements, and objectives and limits of the negotiating teams are examined. Chapter 3 also addresses topics including how to summarize a round of negotiations as soon as it is completed, consider probable demands and potential costs, develop bargaining objectives and proposals, and assess the bargaining climate.

Chapter 4 – Choosing a Negotiating Team. To have optimal negotiation outcomes a team that understands the organization and is representative of it is essential. Chapter 4 provides guidelines for selecting a negotiating team—for example, the number and personal attributes of team members—and deciding on a spokesperson. Team roles are also discussed.

Chapter 5 – Organizing Information During Bargaining. Collective bargaining can be information intensive. Tools, systems, and processes for organizing data are necessary. Chapter 5 provides one approach that includes a series of resources that can be adapted for a particular round of bargaining.

Chapter 6 – Costing Proposals and Determining Wage Criteria. The determination of employee compensation is a central feature of collective bargaining. Chapter 6 examines the processes for costing proposals and for determining wage criteria that take account of comparable wage rates, productivity, ability to pay, and cost of living.

Chapter 7 – Crafting Collective Agreement Language. Collective agreements are codified terms and conditions of employment. Chapter 7 reviews the subjects of collective bargaining including mandatory provisions and details drafting best practices.

Chapter 8 – Establishing the Bargaining Protocol. Describes issues to consider when establishing the bargaining protocol including the location, timing, and length of meetings, wages for employee members, negotiation proceedings, and contains a sample protocol agreement. Chapter 8 also discusses the exchange of initial proposals once the protocol is determined.

Chapter 9 – To the Table: Considerations. Whether bargaining a first agreement or the renegotiation of an existing one, collective bargaining is a dynamic, fluid process. Chapter 9 is an introduction to bargaining dynamics, providing thoughts and ideas to guide participants at the table.

Chapter 10 – Good Faith in Collective Bargaining. Collective bargaining occurs within a legal framework that requires the parties "bargain in good faith." Considerations and legal principles concerning the duty or requirement to bargain in good faith are examined.

Chapter 11 – At an Impasse: Strikes and Lockouts. Negotiating parties are entitled to advance proposals or adopt positions that represent their particular interests, to stick firmly to their respective bargaining positions and, where necessary, to rely on economic sanctions—strike or lockout—to force the other side to make concessions. Chapter 11 examines strikes and lockouts and the associated statutory parameters.

Chapter 12 – Bargaining Assistance: Conciliation, Mediation, Arbitration, and Inquiry. There are a variety of forms of bargaining assistance that can be accessed by the parties in the event of a bargaining impasse. Consensual and adjudicative processes are examined and contrasted.

Conclusion – Preparing to Constructively Engage on Things That Matter. This conclusion poses the question *is this the best we can do?* And provides some concluding thoughts to inform your search for constructive alternatives that help build productive and sound working relationships.

There are three resources:

- **Resource One: CB Statutes and Rules Test: *What do I need to confirm?*** This resource challenges you to test your knowledge concerning the statutes, regulations and rules that govern collective bargaining in your specific jurisdiction. *What do you know* and *what do you need to confirm* that will inform your preparations and ultimately negotiations?

- **Resource Two: Collective Bargaining Process (CBP) Checklist**. Given the complexity of collective bargaining preparation a process checklist can be of assistance. The CBP Checklist is a framework that can be adapted for a particular round of negotiations.

- **Resource Three: How to Draft a Memorandum of Agreement**. This resource provides guidance for the preparation of a Memorandum of Agreement, the document signed by the union and the employer setting out the terms of the negotiated settlement.

Chapter 5 provides **six tools** (CB Resources 1-6) for organizing data and associated information to support bargaining.

A Note about the Statutory Framework:

Effective management and leadership in a unionized workplace requires an understanding of the legal framework within which the workplace functions. Each province and territory in Canada—and the federal government, in federally-regulated industries—has its own legislation to regulate union-employer relations.[1] The statutes establish:

- The right of employees to join the union of their choice and be represented by that union in the determination of terms and conditions of employment through collective bargaining;

- An administrative agency responsible for the statute. Typically referred to as the *Labour Board* or *Labour Relations Board;* for the purposes of this resource, the agency will be referenced as the LRB;

- A duty on both parties to "bargain in good faith" and a prohibition on "unfair labour practices."

For illustrative purposes, the British Columbia Labour Relations Code (the Code) will be referenced. The principles, approaches, and practices are evident in the other Canadian jurisdictions. See Resource One: CB Statutes and Rules Test: *What do I need to confirm?* to evaluate your knowledge concerning the statutes, regulations and rules that govern collective bargaining in your specific jurisdiction.

---

1   Based on the 1935 U.S. *National Labor Relations Act* also known as the *Wagner Act*. The *Wagner Act* model was subsequently adopted by Canadian jurisdictions and is the origin of collective bargaining and grievance procedures.

CHAPTER 1
Collective Bargaining Concepts and Constructs

Chapter 1 is based on the following ideas:

- Collective bargaining is **multi-dimensional**: Two parties. Two constituent groups. Two cultures. Two sets of problems. Engaged in a singular process of negotiation on a recognizable four step path of preparation, information exchange, explicit bargaining, and commitment.

- Collective bargaining is a **representative process**. One party represents the union and the union's members (the employer's employees) and the other the employer. Negotiators represent these larger organizations and are acting on behalf of someone else, not for themselves. In other words, they are acting as agents, not principals—with the result the interests of who they represent, their constituents, become critically important.

- When parties bargain collectively there is a **tension between behaviours**: those that are competitive and those that are cooperative/collaborative. In any negotiation, the parties must decide whether to be competitive, cooperative, or some aspect of both.

- There is a **natural conflict of interests** between an employer and the union that represents the employer's employees. The two parties do however **have common interests**, including the continuing welfare of the enterprise from which they both earn their living. Collective bargaining is the process, codified by statute, to reconcile the associated conflicts.

- Negotiating is **essentially a voluntary activity** in the sense that either party can break away from or refuse to enter into discussion at any time during the process, subject to the duty imposed by law. The parties are not required to enter into "endless" discussions, nor are they required to put forward or accept particular proposals.

- A negotiation on a particular issue usually starts because at least one of the parties wants to **change the status quo**. To varying degrees, one of the parties believes that a mutually satisfactory agreement is possible.

- Entering negotiations **implies acceptance** by both parties that agreement between them is required or is desirable. If a matter can be decided unilaterally by one of the parties, or could be achieved outside the process, there may be no point in committing to negotiate on that matter.

- Timing is a **critical factor** in collective agreement negotiations. It influences the overall climate of the negotiation process and directly affects the negotiation outcomes, both substance and relationship. Timing and the **notion of *ripeness*** are interrelated. A matter is said to be "ripe" for settlement when it has reached a point where the parties have determined that their alternatives to negotiation will not get them **what they want or need**. They are prepared to negotiate a form of settlement that will attain **at least a measure of their interests**, more than they are getting otherwise or stand to get if they pursue their current strategy including force-based ones further

- A successful outcome in collective bargaining is not "winning at any cost," or even the ill-defined and often overused "win-win" agreement. A successful outcome involves the **satisfaction of the interests** of both parties, the outcome of their engagement.

    You want to satisfy:

    - Your interests **well**—that's why you're negotiating in the first place.

    - Your negotiating counterpart's **acceptably**, because a measure of their interests must be satisfied also if an agreement is to be concluded.

    - Others **tolerably**, because as interested parties or constituents, they influence their negotiators and may ratify the resulting agreement.

- The progress of a negotiation, even when it is assisted by a third party, is **strongly influenced** by the frames of reference,[2] personal values, skills, perceptions, attitudes, and emotions of the people at the bargaining table. It is also affected by the respective organizational cultures.

---

2   **Frame of reference:** *The context, viewpoint, or set of presuppositions or of evaluative criteria within which a person's perception and thinking seem always to occur, and which constrains selectively the course and outcome of these activities. They govern how we think and who we are. Our behavior can be traced to these fundamental values.* I.M. Hunter, *Harper Dictionary of Modern Thought* (New York: Harper and Row, 1988), 330.

- Your personal allegiances and objectives may lead you to have **strong opinions about the best result** in terms of substance, what your bargaining effort is seeking to achieve and process, how to achieve that best result. You will be challenged to resist the temptation of using your default styles and approaches and of being influenced by your biases. Those who are participants in or responsible for a collective bargaining initiative must recognize that the alternatives chosen, decisions made, or agreement reached must **satisfy the interests of the broader organization** as well as those central to the matters at issue.

"Employee relations" refers to the direct employer-employee relationship, and "labour relations" refers to the workings of the continuous relationship between a group of employees (represented by a union) and an employer. The terms and conditions of employment, and the consequent processes or practices that define these terms, exist in both union and non-union workplaces.

With those two terms as the backdrop, consider how the three-way terms and conditions of employment are determined:

- Unilateral Determination: Employers **unilaterally define** the terms and conditions of employment (employee relations).

- Collective Bargaining: Unions and employers **collectively bargain** the terms and conditions of employment (labour relations) under rules codified in labour relations statutes. With bargaining comes the mechanisms to compel the other side to move: the union can strike, and the employer can lock out. If the organization is operating in an industry that delivers what are considered essential services, in some jurisdictions labour code provisions modify the strike/lockout concept.

- Third-Party Processes: The terms and conditions are **determined by a neutral** third party through a process codified in a collective agreement, at the direction of government or with the agreement of a union and employer to resolve a bargaining impasse (labour relations).

Collective bargaining is defined as a process whereby a union and an employer seek to negotiate a collective agreement, or the renewal or revision of an existing collective agreement; labour relations statutes require the parties to bargain in good faith with a view to concluding a collective agreement.

Beyond this basic definition, collective bargaining is also a process of "applied politics," a means to reach a result, namely, the resolution or suspension of competing interests for the length of time covered by the collective agreement.

It is an opportunity for an employer and a union to discuss mutual problems, issues, concerns, and priorities, and to fashion appropriate solutions whether through problem solving efforts, accommodations, or compromises.

Given the nature of this form of negotiation, relationships are central and understanding relationships in the context of collective bargaining is essential.

> Collective agreements define and redefine the rewards employees receive for their services, and the conditions under which these services are rendered.

Negotiated periodically, collective agreements define and redefine the rewards employees receive for their services, and the conditions under which these services are rendered. Negotiations vary in terms of employer representation, union representation, occupations involved, and geographical areas covered. They vary to the extent they influence or are influenced by other negotiations.

Collective agreements are also affected by:

- The size, structure, systems, resources, and respective organizational cultures of the union and the employer;

- The statutory framework—for example, statutes governing:
    - Union-employer relations, labour relations
    - Minimum or basic employment standards
    - Human rights
    - Occupational health and safety
    - A particular industry, sector, or profession;

- The parties' experiences with negotiations and the agreements that arise from them;

- The assumptions people have about how organizations work, developed through a combination of experience and education that influence their interactions;

- Individual's frames of reference concerning power, authority, and the organization of work;

- The relationship between the parties generally and between individuals specifically. Those who have influence or have the potential to influence organizational life.

Figure 2: Employer, Union, and the Statutory Framework

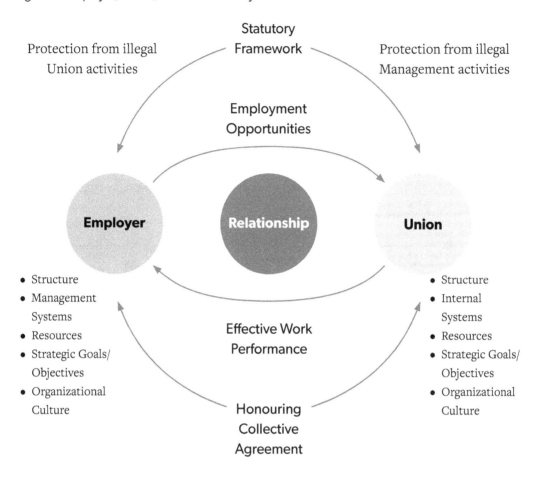

Each round of collective agreement negotiations has outcomes that make it unique. Through the process and practice of collective bargaining they can be generally grouped as either substantive or relationship outcomes.

Substantive outcomes include the specific contractual terms contained in the new collective agreement (for example, terms and conditions of employment, wage and benefit provisions, and codified work rules). The substantive outcomes also refer to the consequences or results of the terms and conditions in the agreement. How will the agreement affect the effectiveness and operating efficiency of the organization? What will be required to implement the new agreement (for example, systems changes, or increases to wages/salaries and benefits)? Implementation of the new collective agreement invariably results in changes to workplace practices—to how work is done—and possibly to productivity or how services are delivered/provided.

The negotiation process also affects the relationship between the parties, producing relationship outcomes. Since negotiations do not occur in isolation, the manner in which the agreement is achieved and the process and the substance of what is achieved impact the ongoing relationship between the parties. This impact or effect can be termed the spillover effect.

Specifically, whether the negotiations can be characterized as adversarial and highly conflictual or as more cooperative and focused can affect the level of cooperation and harmony between the parties during the organization's day-to-day operations. Naturally, problems that develop over the term of the collective agreement often set the stage for the type of issue and level of adversity that the parties bring to the bargaining table when they renegotiate the agreement.

Stages of Collective Bargaining

Collective agreements in workplaces establish the basic rules that govern the day-to-day relationship between an employer and a union representing the employer's employees. Negotiated through the process of collective bargaining, the collective agreement represents what can be characterized as a meeting of the minds—a crystallization and codification of what the parties have agreed on to regulate their conduct and dealings over a certain period. The collective agreement does the following:

- **Defines** the respective rights of the employer and the union.

- **Fixes** the terms and conditions of employment for employees covered by its provisions.

- **Sets** wage rates or salary levels and benefits.

- **Determines** the standards for eligibility to the benefits of the agreement.

- **Establishes** procedures for settling disputes that arise during the agreement's term concerning the application, administration, or interpretation of the agreement.

Collective agreements are broad, complex instruments that touch on almost every aspect of employers' dealings with their employees and union representatives.

Figure 3 illustrates the three phases of collective bargaining—preparation, bargaining, and implementation/administration, and the stages within each phase. As you can see from the figure, several steps are required before actual negotiations begin.

Figure 3: Phases and Stages Typical of Collective Bargaining

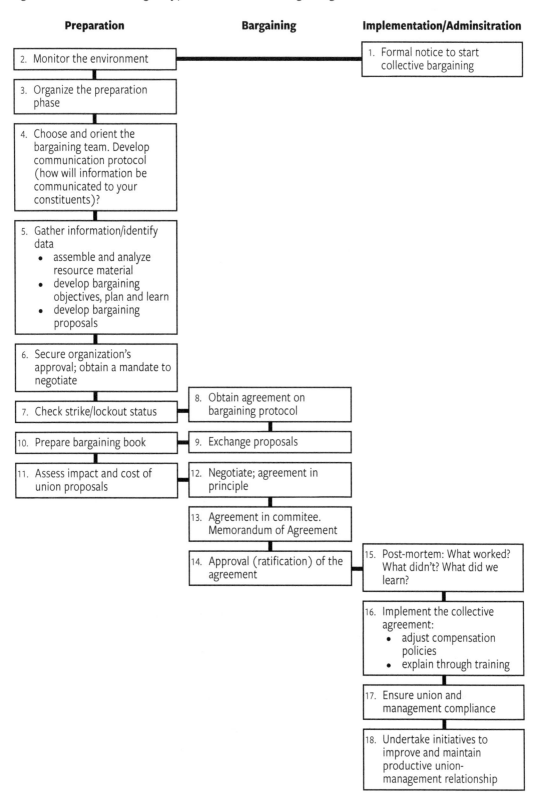

CHAPTER 1 COLLECTIVE BARGAINING CONCEPTS AND CONSTRUCTS | 7

Bargaining Configurations and Philosophy

Collective bargaining involves a number of negotiating or bargaining configurations. Although agreements may seem to be negotiated only at the bargaining table, they are also negotiated in other ways. In difficult negotiations, arguably very little bargaining is actually done at the bargaining table. However, what is negotiated across the table is by no means unimportant. Activities across the table may include information sharing, exploration, clarification, identification of interests, and in some cases, posturing, positioning, and position taking.

> Active negotiations are constantly being conducted within each team—referred to as intra-organizational bargaining—where the expectations of principals/constituents are brought into alignment with those of the chief spokesperson. This alignment is essential if the team, through the spokesperson, is to properly represent the matters at issue to the other bargaining team. Internal bargaining of this nature often takes place in caucus meetings or in meetings with constituents—in the union's case, the membership, and in the employer's case, management representatives—but in all cases is done away from the bargaining table.

Therefore, members of both bargaining teams must not only bargain internally with members of their team, but also work with their constituents and with the interests those constituents represent. Understanding the particular bargaining configuration is necessary because the parties' respective constituents must accept the proposed agreement by ratification.

> Different bargaining configurations make the process of negotiating a collective agreement a dynamic one.

Under some circumstances, representatives of each bargaining team—in many cases, the spokespersons—meet privately to see if bargaining table processes can be made more productive or, at a critical point in negotiations, whether a deal is possible. Bargaining team members may or may not fully authorize these meetings. These different bargaining configurations make the process of negotiating a collective agreement a dynamic one.

Figure 4 illustrates the relationship between spokespersons and their negotiating teams, and the parties' respective constituents. As you move out from the centre, each party's constituents grow in complexity with varying degrees of internal influence. Put another way, you don't think alone—what to do, how to do it and when—and you are never alone. You are working with the complexities of a bargaining team with a broad constituent group looking on.

- **Primary** constituents are those who are most affected or influential. They usually have the greatest dependency on the matter(s) in question and/or are the most affected by the outcomes (negotiation outcomes affects their basic interests).

- Important but **secondary** constituents are those who are more indirectly or less affected by the outcome of the negotiation. For example, the matters negotiated do not affect their basic interests, but they may influence or be influenced by the reconciliation process.

- **Others** are those who have a connection with the primary and secondary groups but have limited influence.

It is important to remember that the union and employer come to the bargaining table with an approach and expectations that enjoys a measure of general acceptance by their constituents. This general acceptance may take the form of a formal ratification of their bargaining agenda. This ratification is based on the information provided including the stories and characterizations of the matters at issue and the bargaining challenges faced. The stories and characterization form a defining narrative. When this narrative emerges at the bargaining table you will be challenged to suspend judgement, assume positive intent, and focus on the matters at issue. Recognize that individuals are probably doing the best they can with what they have or what they know. Engagement and considered inquiry will help to identify relevant considerations and potential motives. Be prepared to constructively test your assumptions and theirs.

> Recognize that individuals are probably doing the best they can with what they have or what they know.

Figure 4: Relationship between Spokespersons, Bargaining Teams, and the Concept of Constituents

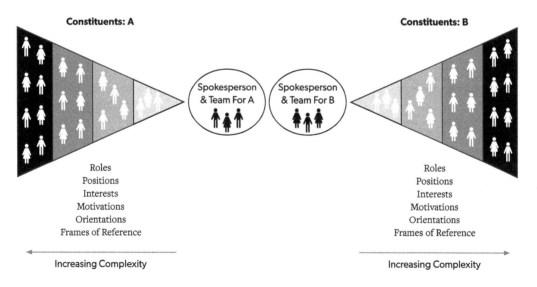

With the concept of constituents in mind, the challenge is to create a solution that satisfies both those present at the table and those at the back table(s) (area specific influencers/decision makers, boards of directors, the board executive, members, and the like) by creating sometimes unlikely coalitions and mapping that crucial territory at the outset.

There is an inherent complexity of individuals and groups of individuals that comprise a constituent group. Consider **what you see and hear**—words and language, descriptive metaphors, behaviour and **what you don't**—frames of reference, motivations, understandings and interpretations, skills and knowledge, values and beliefs, self-image. That which is not seen drives decisions!

Further consider the potential for internal **coalitions**—a combination or alliance, often a temporary one between persons, factions etc.—resident in constituent groups. When such groups come together they form the makings of "a single body of authority" to push through their preferred proposals, or block those they find unacceptable. There are two types of coalitions:

- **Natural coalition**: allies who share a broad range of common interests.
- **Single-issue coalition**: parties with differing issues unite to support or block a single issue (often for different reasons).

The project leader or spokesperson has the responsibility of making sense of this *what you see and hear/what you don't* and coalition complexity. It consists both of representing constituents' interests and trying to shape their expectations and secure their approval. Central to this is clarity and coherence of message in representing their team, its objectives and the processes they have adopted to achieve those objectives.

Sometimes teams take for granted that members understand what the team is attempting to accomplish and why they adopt the approaches they do. They fail to discuss is the importance of staying "on message" – that is, making sure that statements by individual members don't contradict the group's agreed-upon positions and goals. If you want your constituents to understand and appreciate what you are doing, clarity of message is essential.

> **Remember!** You are seeking to satisfy your interest well, your primary constituents' interests acceptably, and your secondary and other constituents' interests tolerably.

Considering these variables and other circumstances unique to a particular round of bargaining, there is obviously no one way to prepare and negotiate a collective agreement. What is true however, is that every round of collective bargaining requires detailed planning and preparation.

Your Role

Regardless of your assignment on the bargaining team, you must clearly understand your role. As team members, you and the rest of your team are negotiating on behalf of someone else, not for yourselves. In other words, you are acting as "agents," not "principals."

An organization's managers are the principals of the employer negotiating team. Senior management, board members, or an executive committee may articulate the organization's direction. Those who provide direction to the team are considered the management team's contacts during negotiations.

For the union negotiating team, the employees in the bargaining unit are the principals. The members' views are articulated by the union executive, which is the union negotiating team's contact with respect to the interests of the principals.

Although different constituents may make up the principals, at some point each organization comes together to provide its negotiating team with a mandate to negotiate a collective agreement.

As agents, you have a duty to be honest and direct in your dealings, and to provide your principals (through your contacts) with the information needed to give appropriate direction or instructions and to assess the consequences of a given course of action.

Since the principals (represented by your contacts) may take the form of a committee or board, their views may not always be the same. You must work with them to develop:

- General agreement on what **needs to be accomplished** in the round of bargaining;

- An **understanding and appreciation** of the collective bargaining process, the matters at issue, and the consequences of a particular course or courses of action.

> If, as a bargaining team member, you are to provide useful advice to your constituents, you need to begin negotiations with an end in mind. Ask these questions:
> - As a result of this round of negotiations, what do we want to achieve?
> - Why is this achievement important to us? What interests do they satisfy?
> - What will achieving this agreement help us to do?
> - What will happen if we do not achieve what we want to achieve?
> - Bargaining can be protracted. How will we keep our constituents informed and engaged?

As you go through the clarification process and begin to formalize the objectives on which your proposals will be based, do not promise more than you can deliver. In clarifying objectives, you will have greater chance for success if you formulate your objective as a direction you would like to go, rather than as a narrow statement or a fixed position.

Be candid with your constituents about your objectives and proposals. Objectives, even if ambitious, should be **conceivably achievable**. Aggressive promises can lead to unrealistic expectations and long-term problems; in particular, unrealistic expectations that invariably go unfulfilled. Make sensible, realistic, and reasonable predictions or forecasts about the negotiations, and keep your principals informed as the negotiations progress.

The bargainer's role consists both of representing constituents' interests and trying to shape their expectations and secure their approval. Central to this is clarity and coherence of message in representing the negotiating team, its objectives and the processes they have adopted to achieve those objectives. Sometimes teams take for granted that members understand what the team is attempting to accomplish and why they adopt the approaches they do. They fail to discuss is the importance of staying "on message"—that is, making sure that statements by individual members don't contradict the group's agreed-upon positions and goals. If you want your constituents to understand and appreciate what you are doing, clarity of message is essential.

Your Role and Understanding the *Real* Organization

Your role requires that you be *historically alert* (understand the organization's history and how relationships have evolved[3]) and *contextually grounded* (the frame in which events occur).

We live our lives in context with the reality that we bargain terms and conditions in that context. How do you begin to understand the real organization . . . and the influence this reality has on union-employer relationships and the determination of terms and conditions of employment?

> Our values are based on what we believe
> to be true about the world.

Whether we are aware of it or not, we live our lives according to a philosophy, a set of values that guide our everyday thoughts and behaviours. These values tend to remain

---

3 Although parties can develop trust over time, there are also countless examples of protracted feuds that developed as a result of conflicting interpretations and invocations of history. Shilio Rea, *Carnegie Mellon University News*, July 17, 2015.

constant. They govern how we think and who we are. Our behaviour can be traced to these fundamental values.

Our values are based on what we believe to be true about the world. These perceptions shape our attitudes, which in turn shape our behaviours. Over time, these attitudes and behaviours, reinforced through repeated use, shape our habits. Eventually, our habits shape our lives.

Organizations also have philosophies—sets of fundamental values that define how they operate and do business. These philosophies are central to shaping an organization's and an individual's frame of reference. These fundamental values are evident in each individual's words and actions, as well as in the systems developed by the organization.

Many people, however, dismiss these concepts as theoretical and without meaning. In fact, they provide insight into everything we think and do.

An organization's philosophy is the foundation of its operations and should serve as the basis for understanding its actions.

> The beliefs, perceptions, attitudes, and values of all the people in an organization form a culture that makes it unique. However, the attitude of any particular member of an organization may deviate from the institutional pattern. If this perspective lacks sufficient power or political support within the organization, it will not affect the institutional attitude. As a result, while individuals may act differently, in general the organization can be characterized by its central tendency.

The organizational culture is central to understanding the values and beliefs about the legitimacy of managerial authority and the distribution of power in an organization. Each individual is socialized by experiences, which result in values and attitudes that come to be regarded as "the way we do things around here." These values are reinforced by the groups that the individual moves within, such as people in like positions and other employees.

The frame of reference individuals have affects their response to the problems they face—it determines their criteria for making judgements and filters information they receive. The frame of reference is grounded in their beliefs about how the workplace should be organized.

Gibson Burrell and Gareth Morgan, in *Sociological Paradigms and Organisational Analysis*, identify three types of ideological frames—unitary, pluralist, and radical—central to an individual's approach to power and authority.[4] This classification represents the three main theories of workplace organization:

- **Unitary or Unitarist**: Society is seen as an integrated whole where the interests of the individual and society are one. Power can be largely ignored and assumed to be used benevolently by those in authority to further the mutual goals of all parties.

- **Pluralist**: Society is viewed as a place where different groups bargain and compete for a share in the balance of power; it realizes a negotiated order that creates unity out of diversity.

- **Radical** (also referred to as Critical or Marxist): Sees society as made up of antagonistic class interests held together as much by coercion as by consent.

Note that each of the three frames reflects a particular set of values and assumptions about the proper extent and form of management control in the workplace, as well as about the proper place and scope of collective bargaining.

> The frames also provide an account of how management control is viewed and collective bargaining operates in practice. They are, however, a generalization of viewpoints, and consequently do not necessarily represent in their entirety the perspectives of those persons and groups who would nonetheless fit within a particular frame. In other words, one cannot presume an exact homogeneity of views within each frame. Nor should it be assumed that there is no overlap between some frames. This reality helps illustrate the complexity of both bargaining team and constituency leadership and management.

Workplaces are an amalgam of perspectives. Although a unitarist manager may work alongside a radical union official or employee, usually one perspective dominates to form the common culture of the organization. The concept of central tendency is in evidence—the inclination to particular approaches or courses of action.

The authors observe that each distinct ideological frame engenders its own "structures and expectations" about how individuals respond to issues of power and conflict. These ideological frames or theories of workplace organization can be used as a framework for understanding why employers approach unionization and unions in the workplace differently. The theories also provide insight into why it can be difficult to resolve workplace disputes and why collective bargaining can be challenging.

---

4 See also Gareth Morgan, *Images of Organization*. Newbury Park, CA: Sage Publications, 2006.

Table 1: Assumptions about the Three Ideological Frames

Assumptions About...	Unitarism	Pluralism	Radicalism
Workplace relations	• management and employees share common interests • one source of legitimate authority: management	• managers and employees have different objectives • multiple sources of legitimate authority	• reflects a wider class conflict between capital and labour • reflects coercion of working class into dominant capitalist values
Workplace conflict	• abnormal: aberration, destructive, to be avoided • caused by poor management, communication, or dissidents/agitators	• inevitable: caused by different opinions and values; benefit to an organization • can be avoided by accepting union legitimacy and including union in decision making	• inevitable: capital seeks to reduce costs; workers seek fairer price for labour • will only cease by revolutionary change in the distribution of wealth/property
Unions	• competing and illegitimate source of authority • an unwarranted intrusion in the workplace • create conflict where none would otherwise exist	• not the cause of conflict • are expressions of diverse workplace interests that always exist • legitimate part of workplace relations	• should raise revolutionary consciousness of workers • should not limit improving material lot of workers • union leaders who accommodate management betray workers
Role of collective bargaining	• creates and institutionalizes unnecessary divisions of interest • serves to generate workplace conflict rather than resolve it • sows the seeds of and results in inefficiency and bureaucracy	• deals with problems on a collective basis • most efficient means of institutionalizing employment rules • fairer outcomes by balancing employee and employer power	• merely offers temporary accommodations • leaves important employer power intact • poor substitute for real change

From a union-employer relationship and in particular a collective bargaining perspective another way to view these frames is as ideologies of management control.[5] The predominance of a particular frame determines:

---

5 U.K, Royal Commission on Trade Unions and Employers' Associations *Industrial Sociology and Industrial Relations,* (Research Paper no. 3) by A. Fox (London: H.M.S.O., 1966) at 1.

1. one's **perceptions** of existing employer-union relations in the workplace.

    - Identify the authentic relationship between the employer and the union and how that affects bargaining. Review the Walton and McKersie Emergent Relationship Model (see Figure 8) in Chapter 2. Pay special attention to the Predetermined Factors also referred to as Antecedent Determinants. When you look at the other party and consider yourself through the lens of the model, how are you informed?

    - Consider the five Emergent Relationship categories. What are your goals for a working relationship and are those goals aligned with the other party?

2. one's **evaluation** of the status quo—the current state of things—in the workplace.

    - Consider the rights and responsibilities of the parties. What is the division of decision-making rights and responsibilities, if any, envisaged between management and employees? How is this division determined? Are the allocations of decision making to joint determination via collective bargaining substantial or marginal?

3. one's **responses to the status quo** when (if at all) it is sought to change the balance of power in employer-union relations.

Points 1, 2, and 3 influence how parties develop bargaining objectives, positions and how they choose to conduct themselves.

Consider Your Organization: What do I know, how do I know it, and why does it matter?

Every organization has a culture that makes it unique with at least two variants: one that we speak about and one that we don't. Top executives often talk about their organization's vision, values, and organization charts, as well as offer publicity, advertising, and policy manuals about what is most important.

With carefully crafted key messages, headlines, and stories, the "visible" organization is especially clear and apparent to outsiders and the external public. What lies beneath the visible organization is what can be characterized as the "shadow" organization. Frequently invisible to outsiders and often filled with "unwritten rules," this version of the organization is usually more powerful than the first. Written and unwritten rules and individuals' frames of reference profoundly influence the preparation and practice of collective bargaining.

> Constructive collective bargaining practitioners seek to understand their organization, the **real** organization—its culture and shadow culture and its written and unwritten rules.

Constructive collective bargaining practitioners seek to understand their organization, the real organization—its culture and shadow culture and its written and unwritten rules—and are historically alert (they understand the organization's history and how relationships have evolved) and contextually grounded (the frame in which events occur). You may discover longstanding, built-in assumptions and role definitions that frame the organizational view of collective bargaining and the parties to the agreement.

Terms

The words bargaining and negotiation are used to describe the process of collective bargaining. While some may use bargaining to describe a competitive process akin to haggling over a price in a commercial transaction, and negotiation to reflect a more civilized process of two parties seeking a mutually acceptable solution to the matters at issue, here the terms are used interchangeably.

Despite workplace specific changes in how collective agreements are reached, the adversarial process that characterizes traditional or conventional collective bargaining remains predominant. Collective bargaining is still the cornerstone of the Canadian system of union-employer relations. It has a profound impact on the climate in the workplace, which in turn influences an organization's productivity and effectiveness.

Collective bargaining occurs within a legal framework that requires the parties to "bargain in good faith." Chapter 10 contains the considerations and legal principles concerning the duty or requirement to bargain in good faith.

Both parties are entitled to advance proposals or adopt positions that represent their particular interests, to stick firmly to their respective bargaining positions and, where necessary, to rely on economic sanctions—strike or lockout—to force the other side to make concessions. However, the party advancing a proposal must be prepared to explain the rationale for the proposal, and to enter into a discussion about it with a view to concluding an agreement.

Objectives, Positions, and Interests

The terms objectives, positions, and interests are used throughout this book. Within the collective bargaining context, each term has a particular meaning and application.

- An **objective is a description** of your desired outcome. It is not your position but rather your goal, something aimed at.

- **Positions are developed** to represent a party's demands at the bargaining table. A position is an attitude toward, opinion on, or statement on a subject; a particular stand or stance on an issue or subject. Positions are developed to represent a party's demands and are focused on "what" or "how," whereas an interest is focused on "why." Positions are something that you decide upon. Interests are what caused you to so decide.

- The term **interests refers to an underlying reason** for a party taking a particular stand or adopting a certain position—that party's aspirations, needs, concerns, hopes, or fears. When you define the matters at issue in a negotiation, you need to identify and consider the underlying interests and needs. Asking the question "why" usually surfaces critical values, needs, or principles that a party wants to achieve in the negotiation. The *5 Whys*[6] technique is helpful. An iterative interrogative technique, it serves to focus on revealing the root cause of a problem or concern by repeating the question "Why?" Each answer forms the basis of the next question.

- Interests can be classified as:

    - Substantive: directly related to the matters at issue—the "what"

    - Process based: related to the manner, process, and procedures used to settle the matters at issue—the "how"

    - Subjective: based on principles or standards as a guideline for desires and expectations about how the negotiating relationship will be established, conducted, and continued. Principles or standards help classify behaviours, procedures, and outcomes as acceptable or unacceptable. Principles and standards include:

        - A commitment to tell the truth, maintain integrity, and be polite and civil to each other.

        - Beliefs about when a competitive or collaborative approach is appropriate; and

---

[6] *5 Whys Root Cause Analysis* technique, Sakichi Toyoda (1867-1930) Japanese industrialist, inventor, and founder of Toyota Industries. The "five" in the name derives from an anecdotal observation on the number of iterations needed to resolve the problem.

- Beliefs about the degree to which each side should take care of itself and not be concerned with how the other side is doing.

Each type of interest may also be intrinsic, in that the parties value the interest for its essence—its properties, attributes, or ultimate nature—or may be instrumental in that the parties value the interest because it helps them achieve their objectives or other outcomes in the future.

Consider the substantive, subjective, or procedural nature of interests and whether they can be categorized as:

1. **Financial, economic**
2. **Ethical**, pertaining to or dealing with morals, rules, or standards of right conduct or practice.
3. **Experiential**, relating to experience, observation, and learning.
4. Instrumental in that it helps achieve objectives or other outcomes in the future.
5. **Procedural**, relating to process and/or due process.
6. **Relational**, concerning the way, manner and nature in which people are connected; can also include the concept of **affiliation**—the desire/need to be connected or associated with a person or group.
7. **Reputational**, respecting a reputation or concept of self that a party wishes to protect or promote.
8. **Representational**, relating to felt responsibility to those a party represents.
9. **Recognitional**, concerning feelings of respect, identity, legitimacy, standing.
10. **Security**, respecting yours (personal) and others (you have a measure of responsibility for)

Do other categorizations emerge when assembling your list?

In *Essentials of Negotiation*, Roy Lewicki, David Saunders, Bruce Barry, and Kevin Tasa[7] make several instructive observations about interests that help define the concept:

1. There is almost always **more than one type of interest** underlying a negotiation. Parties can have more than substantive interests about the issue—they can also

---

7   Adapted from Lewicki, Saunders, Barry, and Tasa in *Negotiation Essentials*, Third Canadian Edition (Toronto: McGraw-Hill Education, 2017), 64.

care deeply about process, the relationship, or the principles at stake. Note that "interests as principles" effectively cuts across substantive, procedural, and relationship interests as well, so that the categories are not necessarily exclusive.

2. Parties **can differ on the type** of interests at stake (substance, process, relationship). One party may care deeply about the specific issues under discussion. Others may care about how the issues are resolved, questions of principle or process. Bringing these different interests to the surface may enable the parties to see that in fact they care about quite different things. This provides opportunities to invent solutions that address the interests of both sides.

3. Interests can change including their relative priorities. Like positions on issues, **interests can change over time**. What was important to the parties last week—or even earlier in the day—may not be important now. Interaction between the parties can put some interests to rest, but it may raise others. As a result, the parties must continually be attentive to changes in their own interests and the interests of the other side. As noted, when parties begin to talk about things in a different way—when the language or emphasis changes—it may indicate a change in interests or in the relative priority of a specific interest.

4. Surfacing interests. There are **numerous ways to get** at interests. Sometimes we are not even sure of our own interests. In these cases, we should be asking ourselves not only "What do I want (from this negotiation)?" but also "What do I really want?", "Why is that important to me?", "What will achieving that help me do?", "What will happen if I don't achieve my objective?" The *5 Whys Root Cause Analysis* technique noted earlier is an essential tool for helping to reveal interests. Listening to your own inner voices concerning fears, aspirations, hopes, and desires animates and helps make explicit your interests and their relative priority.

5. The same **dialogue is essential** in clarifying the other party's interests. Asking probing questions and paying careful attention to the other party's language, emotions, and nonverbal behaviour are essential keys to the process. You might also want to distinguish between intrinsic interests that need to be satisfied as ends in themselves and instrumental interests, which help us get other outcomes. In both cases, once these interests are understood, it may be possible to invent a variety of ways to address them. The result is a mutually satisfactory solution.

6. Surfacing interests is **not always easy** and to your best advantage. Critics to the "interest approach" to negotiation have identified the difficulty of defining interests and taking them into consideration. Provis suggests that it is often difficult to define interests and that trying to focus on interests alone often oversimplifies or conceals the real dynamics of conflict. In some cases, parties do not pursue their

own best objective interests but focus on one or more subjective interests, which may mislead the other party.

7. Focussing on interests **can be harmful**. There are situations where focussing on interests can impede negotiations. For instance, with a group of negotiators whose consensus on a particular issue is built around a unified position rather than a more generalized set of interests, a focus on interests may not help achieve a solution. If a coalition is held together by a commitment to pursue a specific objective in negotiations, then encouraging the lead negotiator (spokesperson) to discuss interests rather than push for the specific objective is clearly encouraging him or her to deviate from the coalition's purpose.

CHAPTER 2

Why We Bargain the Way We Bargain

The process and practice of collective bargaining takes many forms given the parties' history, experiences, and, as discussed in Chapter 1, their frames of reference. When unions and employers bargain collectively to determine the terms of their continuing relationship why do they bargain the way they do?

> Listen to the language,[8] in particular, the metaphors[9] people use to illustrate union-employer relations generally and collective bargaining specifically. The choice of metaphor has an influence on the behavior of the participants because it sets the tone for any proceedings.

As noted earlier, consider **what you see and hear**—words and language, descriptive metaphors, and behaviour—and **what you don't**—frames of reference, motivations, understandings and interpretations, skills and knowledge, values and beliefs, self-image.

---

8 Language is descriptive. It describes events, people, scenes, ideas. Each of these—except ideas—have physical qualities. The event took place physically, at a specific location with specific actors in a specific way. In describing these events our language is clear and generally precise.

9 Ideas do not have physical qualities. No specific location, no specific actors describe an idea. We do not have a language of ideas, but rather use metaphors and apply them to the ideas we wish to convey. Metaphors are used constantly to give physical qualities—which are understood from daily experience—to non-physical things such as ideas. The listener, hopefully, hears our description and translates it into a conceptual understanding.

That which is not seen or heard drives decisions.

Figure 5 What We See and Hear and What We Don't

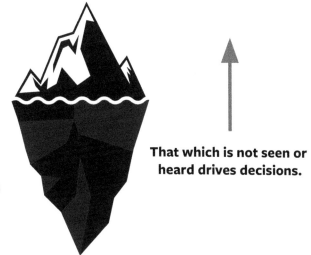

What you see and hear...
Words and Language
Descriptive Metaphors
Behaviour

What you don't see and hear...
Frames of reference
Motivations
Understandings and Interpretations
Skills and Knowledge
Values and Beliefs
Self-image

That which is not seen or heard drives decisions.

Every person we encounter engages in *meaning-making* through stories and metaphors. In an effort to describe the orientations in action metaphors are used to give physical qualities to non-physical things such the ideas and concepts resident in the orientations. The metaphors we use reveal deeper meaning beneath the explicit words regarding how we view the process and the relationship to one another.

The dominant negotiation metaphors are competitive ones, from games, sports, and war where you either win or lose. A second set are more cooperative in nature like dance, cooking, or a journey where working together is the essential feature. How one sees negotiations and bargaining relationships is revealed by the choice of metaphor to describe it. That choice has an influence on the behavior of the participants because it sets the tone for the interactions.

While no two negotiations are exactly the same, from what you have come to know about union-employer negotiations, does this sound familiar? In his book, *Front Stage, Backstage: The Dramatic Structure of Labor Negotiations*, Raymond Friedman describes what is often referred to as traditional or conventional collective bargaining:

> What, exactly, is the "traditional" process of negotiation whose persistence has to be explained? While no two negotiations are exactly the same, there is a pattern of behavior that is known and expected by experienced negotiators. As a local union president at International

Harvester put it: "There was a formula for it. It's no big secret." A labor relations manager at the same company pointed out: "The script was written, and you could just about predict what was going to be said, what the union's list would look like, what our list would look like, how the meetings would go, and how the adjournments would happen."

Based on field research, this "script" begins with each side collecting its thoughts and rallying its troops. Often the union reminds members of management's past deeds—their own management's or management in general. Both sides set goals and objectives and develop a bargaining strategy. Then, in the first meetings, each side presents an exhaustive list of changes that it would like, called a "laundry list," and broadly explains the requests. The company says that it needs to be competitive and cannot afford much more; the union explains that its members are angry and demand just treatment. After these preliminary steps, negotiations begin in earnest.

At first the negotiators stand tough. Then slowly each side signals what it really cares about by expressing their rejections in softer or harder terms and mentioning their own proposals more or less often. Stock phrases, with well-known meanings, are used to indicate where they really stand. Some issues just "fall off the table" and are forgotten. There is some horse trading, as proposals from each side are simultaneously accepted or dropped.

Throughout this process the conversations across the table are usually brisk and contentious, and the mood is one of anger and apprehension. Negotiators are careful to say only what is planned and reveal only what they must: they rarely admit that the other side has a good point. The lead bargainer usually coaches his or her team on what to say and when to say it, and when negotiators do improvise, they still maintain their roles—their comments display anger and distrust toward the opponent, as well as solidarity with their teammates. Negotiators rarely let down their guard during negotiations; both their words and their attitude are highly controlled.

During caucuses negotiators try to discern their opponent's true position and to clarify any disagreements on their own goals. The lead bargainer stands apart from the others, showing that he or she knows what the opponents really meant by their last move, and what the team should do in response. In many cases he or she has met with the opponent in private to clarify some elements of each side's proposals.

As negotiations proceed, angry exchanges continue, while negotiators narrow the number of unresolved issues and begin to seriously consider each other's financial proposals. Near the deadline the frequency of moves and countermoves increases; with each move the negotiating teams recede from the main table to meet alone. Meanwhile, on the side, lead bargainers meet more often in private. In the final flurry of activity before the contract expires, the two sides settle on an economic plan, complex or unresolved issues are dropped, and the final agreement is rushed to members, hot off the presses after all-night bargaining.

Chances are that all or elements of this description properly capture the negotiation dynamic from your perspective. The above passage was written by Raymond Friedman over twenty-five years ago. Not all negotiations follow Friedman's script but despite workplace-relationship specific approaches in how collective agreements are reached, the adversarial process that characterizes traditional collective bargaining remains predominant.

> To start, we do not assume positive intent on the part of the other party. We falsely assume that our interests are incompatible with theirs. A negative bias causes us to react more strongly to negative information, such as actions perceived as threats, than to positive information, such as revelations about possible opportunities, trade-offs and the like.

This creates a self-fulfilling prophecy: the belief that this is more than likely a zero-sum situation—a gain for you represents a loss for me, both in terms of process and substance—causing us to behave in ways that creates a competitive atmosphere. Consequently, our approach to reconciling matters at issue leads to a focus on position taking and positioning characterized by zealous advocacy of each party's positions.

The bargaining stance and approach is further animated by how the employer's employees came to have union representation in the first place, the employers continuing reaction to it and the union's response.

The passage of time plays a role. The transition from employee relations to labour relations may be a relatively new phenomenon, necessitating that employees grapple with the change to their current state and the negotiation of a first collective agreement. However, unionization may date back decades with current employees largely unfamiliar with the workplace events and circumstances that gave rise to unionization. Collective bargaining is viewed as a periodic event with varying degrees of importance given the environment. Later in this section organizational philosophies and how union-employer relations evolve are examined.

In preparing to negotiate a collective agreement, whether a first agreement or the renewal of an existing one, you must reflect on and consider during all three phases of the process (preparation, negotiation, and implementation/administration) what you are trying to achieve and what constitutes a good negotiation—the basis on which success is measured.

Understanding Union-Employer Relationships

Collective bargaining is defined as a process whereby a union and an employer seek to negotiate a collective agreement, or the renewal or revision of an existing collective agreement; labour relations statutes generally require the parties to bargain in good faith with a view to concluding a collective agreement.

As noted earlier collective bargaining is also a process of applied politics, a means to reach a result, namely, the resolution or suspension of competing interests for the length of time covered by the collective agreement.

Given the nature of this form of negotiation, relationships are central and understanding relationships in the context of collective bargaining is essential.

This section makes core assumptions about union-employer relationships—specifically, that they emerge over time, based on a particular set of factors and further, that relationships are influenced by the mixed-motive nature of the relationship—in other words, a mixed-motive dynamic.

The mixed-motive dynamic is largely driven by the "who" of it all. Who plays what role, who has influence, and who leads what and for what purpose? The interactions among those that comprise this composite are complex, multi-dimensional, and with the negotiated terms, subject to ratification.

> While the mixture of common and competing interests can be most evident in the relationship between the union and employer, there are multiple interest groups within the union (for example, groups representing specific skills or types of work, internal political structures) and within the employer (for example, line vs. staff functions, board members).

Others with an interest in the workplace or sector (for example, associations of like groups or organizations, government, the public) also bring a mix of common and competing interests to their interactions with the union and the employer.

As we examine relationships and collective bargaining structures, it is important to keep in mind the fluid nature of the mixed-motive dynamic and the influence it has on how the relationship emerges. This includes the functional consequences experienced by the workplace—operational implications, nature of conflict, disputes, and their disposition—that flow from the relationship.

The close personal interaction between a union and an employer that occurs during the bargaining process provides the opportunity for the parties to either build trust (and therefore move towards a more constructive, cooperative, and less conflict-laden relationship) or reinforce a traditional, predominantly unitarist view of union-employer relations (a relationship seen as inherently conflictual with a large measure of what are believed to be irreconcilable differences). This latter perspective has emerged as the default response given their perspectives concerning workplace authority, and it can be partly attributed to what we have come to believe negotiations are about: a competitive, positioning exercise.

In the seminal work on unions-employers and collective bargaining *A Behavioral Theory of Labor Negotiations: An Analysis of a Social Interaction System*, Richard Walton and Robert McKersie provide a useful framework to examine collective bargaining and employment relationships.

The authors offer the proposition that collective bargaining is a form of social negotiations—the deliberate interaction of two or more multi-faceted social units attempting to define or redefine the terms of their interdependence and which are comprised of four sub-systems, each with its own function for the interacting parties, internal logics, and identifiable set of instrumental acts or tactics. In social negotiations, the resolution goal can relate to the reconciliation of several values and can involve allocation of resources such as economic resources, power, or status symbols. The sub-systems described by the authors help us understand the complexity of collective bargaining and the employer-employee/union relationships that result after bargaining.

The first, **distributive bargaining**, functions to resolve pure conflicts of interest. Position based, the process focuses on dividing up a resource or array of resources that parties have identified. It is the system of activities central to the attainment of one party's goals when they are in basic conflict with those of the other party. Characterized by position taking and positioning, it is bargaining in the strictest sense of the word.

Figure 6: Distributive Bargaining

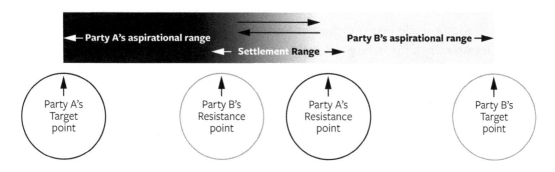

One way to view the negotiation process is one where each party moves along a continuum in opposite directions to an area of potential overlap called the bargaining zone. The bargaining zone model—described as a distributive goal-setting model—assumes that tangible (measurable) goals are easier to understand and deal with. Maximalist and equitable positioning are variants of distributive goal-setting approaches with:

- an initial position (in the case of the maximalist positioner, usually extreme) that is the opening offer to the other party,

- a target (the desired outcome) that is the realistic goal or expectation for a final agreement, and

- a resistance or reservation point, which is the bottom line the party is extremely reluctant to go beyond, based on resource constraints, other available options, and personal preferences. No further concessions will be made beyond this point. It is the point in negotiation when the highest price at which someone is willing to buy an item is established, and the lowest price at which a seller will sell the item is confirmed, and the back and forth that occurs between these two negotiators. It's an attempt at reconciling these two, often hidden, goals in negotiation.

The second seeks to reconcile matters through integration. ***Integrative bargaining*** functions to find common or complementary interests and solve problems confronting both parties. It is instrumental in attaining objectives that are not, upon examination, in fundamental conflict with those of the other party. There is a potential for the parties' interests to be combined or elements incorporated in ways that create joint value. In other words, parties could join forces to achieve something together that cannot be achieved independently. While there will be a division of resources or selection of options at some point the debate and decision occurs only after the creation of options, alternatives. In other words claiming value follows the creation of value.

Integrative bargaining and distributive bargaining are both joint decision-making processes. These processes, however, are quite different and yet rational responses to different situations. A distributive negotiation involves dividing identified resources and is most often associated with a single issue in which one gains at the expense of the other. Integrative potential exists when the nature of a problem permits solutions that benefit both parties, or at least when the gains of one party do not represent equal sacrifices of the other.

A matter is said to have integrative potential when it meets this test:

- The parties **cannot achieve** what they need to achieve **independent of one another**. There is a measure of interdependence.

- It is **multi-dimensional. More than one** issue is involved.

- It is possible **to add more** issues to the mix.

- The parties' interactions **will recur** over time.

- The parties have **varying preferences** across issues.

When parties bargain collectively, there is more than one matter at issue. To varying degrees, each party values the issues differently, necessitating a measure of creative problem-solving to develop solutions. The solutions are not comparable to a fixed pie to be divided between the parties; rather, given the issues, interests, and options identified through discussions, an agreement can be crafted that is better for both parties than what they would have achieved through distributive bargaining.

However, some bargainers approach collective bargaining as essentially a distributive exercise. It is characterized by position taking, positioning, and back and forth concession making until a deal is reached. This orientation may be grounded in their ideologies or social belief systems, bargaining experiences, or "just the way we see how negotiations are done!"

This approach leads negotiators to interpret bargaining interactions as inherently competitive and the dominant bargaining approach to be positional and distributive. They assume that their interests directly conflict with those of the other party ("if it's good for them, it must be bad for us") with the result that the negotiation becomes a debate over who gets what in relation to the fixed positions advanced.

Walton and McKersie identify the dilemmas inherent in reconciling the requirements of the two polar, yet interdependent, decision-making processes of distributive and integrative bargaining:

> The test of time has confirmed the usefulness of conceptualizing the dilemmas that arise between distributive and integrative bargaining because the tactical requirements of one sub-process are opposite of the other sub-process.
>
> If distributive bargaining is pursued too vigorously and/or at the wrong time, then a negotiator may gain a greater share, but a smaller set of joint gains, or worse, may generate an outcome in which both parties lose. Similarly, if the negotiator pursues integrative bargaining in a single-minded manner; for example, being totally candid and completely forthcoming with information, he or she can be taken advantage of by the other party. In practice, collective bargaining is a hybrid of sorts influenced by perspectives, personalities, and practices. That said, wise negotiators realize that bargaining is about identifying or creating value and claiming value.[10]

---

10 Value is the regard that something is held to deserve; the importance, worth, or usefulness of something. The notion of value goes beyond the monetary or monetary nature to include such things as time, resources, re-purposed resources, contacts, access, support, logistics, components, structured packages,

The third approach, **attitudinal structuring**, refers to the activities of the union and the employer that affect the general attitude one party has towards the other—events and circumstances experienced by union and management and their reactions to them. The attitudes of each party towards the other, taken together, define the attitudinal relationship. Attitudinal structuring aims to influence the attitudes of the participants towards each other and to affect the basic bonds that relate the two parties they represent.

The three processes of distributive bargaining, integrative bargaining, and attitudinal structuring impact the reconciliation process that takes place between the union and the employer. During negotiations, another system of activities is in motion—**intra-organizational bargaining**. This form of internal negotiations is designed to achieve consensus within the union and within the employer with respect to the "what" and "how" of the negotiations.

Intra-organizational bargaining brings the expectations of the principals into alignment with those of the bargaining team and chief spokesperson so that bargaining between the union and the employer bargaining teams can occur. This approach has the function of achieving consensus within each of the interacting constituent groups on courses of action.

Intra-organizational bargaining is bargaining in a broader context. In a sense, the bargaining team, and, in particular, the chief spokesperson, is the recipient of two sets of demands—one from across the table and one from his or her own organization.

This circumstance results from conflict at two levels: differing aspirations about issues and differing expectations about behaviour and the conduct of negotiations.

Constituents hold a variety of interests and motivations. While they are not present during negotiations they are, to varying degrees, concerned with what happens at the bargaining table. The union negotiator faces unique challenges and is arguably subject to more organizational constraints than their employer counterpart.

Evolving Union-Employer Relationships

Union-employer relationships develop over time. The attitudinal relationship between union and management is exclusive to those particular parties; given the nature of union-employer relations, it is a continuing relationship. Does the relationship provide a foundation for productive bargaining through constructive dialogue and exchange of views?

Attitudes are fluid, changing with the dynamics of the union-employer relationship. Given the sometimes-volatile nature of the relationship, however, and the potential for adversity, it usually takes considerable time to develop an attitude of confidence and mutual respect. Trust and confidence can collapse quickly, given a particular set of circumstances and the parties' actions and reactions to those circumstances.

Figure 7: Emergent Employment Relationships in a Unionized Environment

Four Major Factors (Attitudinal Relationship Factors)
- Acceptance of legitimacy of other party
- Degree of trust
- Degree of friendliness or hostility
- Degree of competitiveness, individualism, cooperation

Pre-determined Factors (Antecedent Determinants)
- Basic personality disposition
- Union-employer ideologies
- External factors

Events/Circumstances (Attitudinal Structuring Activities)
- How the employees came to have union representation
- Grievance and arbitration history
- Administration of the collective agreement
- Ongoing relations
- Approach to workplace issues and dispute resolution

Emergent Relationship
- Conflict
- Containment-Aggression
- Accommodation
- Cooperation
- Collusion

Functional Consequences
- Operational implications
- Nature of workplace disputes and their disposition
- Implications for collective bargaining

Attitudinal Relationship Factors

Many factors shape the union-employer relationship. Some factors are matters the parties have little or no control over. Others are variables that the parties do have some control over, and which parties might attempt to vary so as to change their relationship.

Four main factors affect the relationship between a union and an employer and can help us understand "why things are as they are."

Acceptance of legitimacy: The willingness of one party to accept the legitimacy of the other party in fulfilling the roles and objectives of the organization; the degree to which one party believes and demonstrates, through thought, word, and action, that the other party has a legitimate role to play.

Degree of trust: The degree to which the parties have a firm belief in the other party's honesty, integrity, reliability, and competence.

Prevailing attitude of friendliness, respect, or hostility: The degree to which the parties have cordial feelings towards one another; whether the parties, although not necessarily friendly towards one another, respect each other as individuals and the job they must do; or the degree to which the parties' relationship is one of hostility and bitterness—the parties develop an actual dislike or hatred for each other.

Prevailing attitude or motivational orientation and action: Tendencies towards each other, the degree of competitiveness, individualism, cooperation; whether the parties' attitudes are competitive—they evaluate each encounter as one of winning or defeating the other party and each side seeks to maximize their relative advantage over the other, even though in the process they may incur some sacrifice to their own interests. May be individualistic—each party pursues its own goals and objectives and ignores the other party in their pursuit of their objectives—or may be characterized as cooperative, where the parties actually work together in pursuit of common goals and objectives and each party is concerned about the other's welfare in addition to their own.

Predetermined Factors or Antecedent Determinants

Certain predetermined factors, also referred to as antecedent determinants, also influence the existing relationship pattern.

Basic personality of the key individuals in the relationship. This is the frame of reference the individuals hold that informs their decisions, actions, and reactions. Union and management leaders may have personalities that make them more or less friendly, trusting, and cooperative. Authoritarian personality types are typically more competitive, have lower levels of trust, and are less tolerant to the views of others.

The union-employer ideologies or social belief systems. The prevailing social belief reflected in the organization. Review the unitarism, pluralism, and radicalism frames of reference presented in Chapter 1. The social beliefs of union and management leaders may also be important. Some employers have a predominance of individuals who do not believe in the legitimacy of unions (a unitarist ideology). Some union leaders may have a basic mistrust of the market system, which extends to resentment towards those in management positions.

External factors, including market forces, legislative initiatives, and technological developments. The implications that arise from the economic environment the employer faces might affect the relationship with the union. If the employer faces an economic downturn, increased competition, or demands for increased services without increased resources, there will be pressure to be more demanding of the union. The evolving legislative environment might affect the relationship. Technological innovation might also lead to hostility when the employer seeks to implement changes that threaten job security.

Actual bargaining experiences that the parties have shared, including how the parties negotiate resolution to workplace disputes. The relationship might also be affected by past experiences with collective bargaining. If either of the parties has had a negative experience with previous negotiations or the administration of a collective agreement, the relationship could be more hostile.

Someone who has had a decision challenged *through the grievance process and experienced cross-examination at an arbitration hearing* may have a particular view of what they see as the consequences of collective bargaining.

Events and circumstances experienced by both parties will also affect the nature of the relationship. These include the actions and reactions of the parties to workplace issues, how the parties resolve issues and disputes, collective bargaining experiences, and both what was achieved (the outcomes of bargaining) and how the outcomes were achieved (the process of bargaining). Experiences such as strikes or lockouts, legislatively imposed agreements, and the parties' reactions to them also contribute to shaping the relationship.

Emergent Relationships

Attitudinal relationship factors, certain predetermined factors (antecedent determinants), and the parties' actions/reactions in response to events (attitudinal structuring activities) taken together influence the relationship. Defined as the emergent relationship, it is a general characterization of the relationship between the parties.

The emergent relationship is illustrated through five models that help explain how parties approach collective bargaining, dispute management, and day-to-day relationships.

- **Conflict:** In the conflict model, the parties are in constant competition. The union vilifies the employer as a way of building itself up and the employer competes for the hearts and minds of its employees by disparaging, undermining, or ignoring the union.

  Each party denies the legitimacy of the other party—the union's role as the exclusive representative of its members and the employer's responsibility for the management of the enterprise. The relationship is typified by distrust and, in some cases, even hatred. Management refuses to deal with the union whenever possible, and the union sees management as the enemy.

- **Containment-Aggression:** In the containment-aggression model, the presence of the union and its legitimacy is accepted grudgingly by the employer—the law permits unionization and management accepts it but does not necessarily like it! The parties have little respect for each other and are suspicious and mutually antagonistic. The union is determined to extend its scope of influence, and the employer is determined to limit it believing that any change represents an erosion of their management rights.

- **Accommodation:** In the accommodation model, while each party fully recognizes the legitimacy of the other party, they are still individualistic in their orientation in that they pursue their own goals, giving no thought or consideration to the goals of the other party. The parties have adjusted to each other and have evolved routines for performing functions and settling disputes.

  Each party has a moderate amount of respect for the other party's officials and adopts a hands-off approach to the other's internal affairs. There is little competition for the allegiance of employees. Although they do not adopt an alarmist approach to every demand, the parties adopt what is described as "alert watchfulness." The parties go about their business, interacting in a courteous but informal manner.

The adoption of an accommodation approach is generally an instrumental choice anticipating reciprocity—response to constructive gestures or actions with corresponding ones.

- **Cooperation:** In the cooperation model, both parties completely accept the other's legitimacy, and have developed a mutual trust and respect. While some interests of the parties are different, some are not.

When faced with a problem or negotiation, the parties engage in discussions in an attempt to clarify the matter at issue or enlarge the range of alternatives so that the needs of both parties are addressed and met to the greatest extent possible. Discussions extend beyond typical issues such as wages and working conditions to issues such as productivity, organizational efficiency, and use of technology.

There is full respect for each other's organization and officials. The union accepts managerial success as being of concern to the union; the employer recognizes its stake in stable, effective unionism. The parties, while pursuing their own objectives, act in ways that strengthen the other organization. There is mutual trust and a friendly attitude between the parties.

- **Collusion:** In the collusion model, the parties form a coalition to pursue common, often illegitimate goals, inconsistent with their true mandate and statutory responsibilities. At times, the union will conspire with management in violation of the rights of their members. Collusion, depending on the degree, could constitute a breach of the statutory duty of fair representation and be considered a conflict of interest.[11]

When you examine the evolving union-employer relationship, dominant bargaining and issues management approaches are often in evidence. In relationships characterized by conflict and containment-aggression, a positional, distributive bargaining stance is dominant.

As you move to relationships of accommodation, a greater degree of integrative bargaining is in evidence, and in relationships where the cooperation approach dominates, parties predominantly adopt an integrative approach.

Figure 8 provides a useful summary of the emergent relationship model and its interrelated components.

---

11 **Conflict of interest.** A situation that has the potential to undermine the impartiality of a person because of the possibility of a clash between the person's self-interest and professional interest or public interest.

Figure 8: Emergent Relationship Model

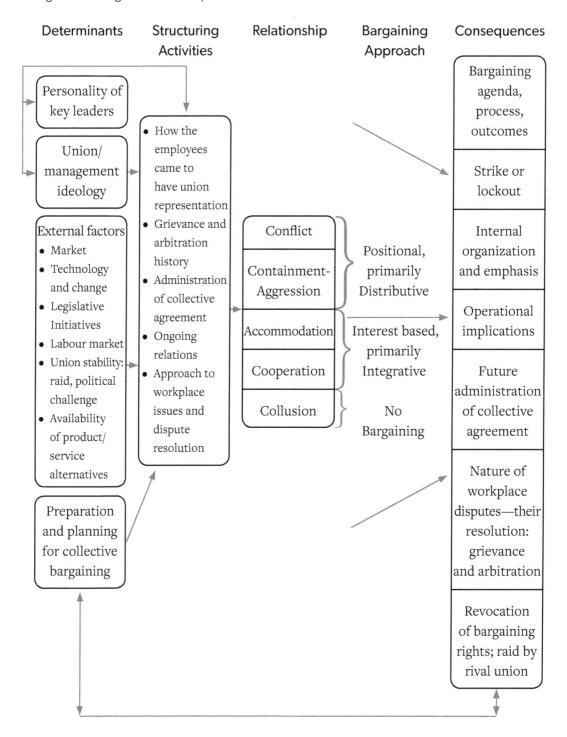

Testing the Propositions: An Emergent Relationship Quick Test

Consider a union-employer relationship you have been part of or are familiar with. To evaluate the relationship:

1. Assess each of the four Main Factors in the first column—Legitimacy, Trust, Attitude and Respect, Motivational Orientation. Determine a rating for each factor on a scale of 1–4 that best describes the relationship. Use the descriptions to assist your analysis.

2. Sum these numbers and divide by four to determine an overall score.

In the example below, a rating for each factor has been circled, resulting in an overall rating of 2.75.

- What does the resulting score tell you about the central tendency of the relationship?

- Would the analysis differ when applied to individual vs. institutional relationships? Why?

- Would the analysis have produced a different result five years, three years, or one year ago?

- Remember, this is your perspective. How would your counterpart rate the relationship?

Organizing Concepts

Figure 9: Emergent Relationship Quick Test

Note: This is an adaptation of the Walton-McKersie Emergent Relationship Model. The use of a numerical scoring system is not part of the model and is used for discussion purposes only.

Main Factors	Conflict	Containment–Aggression	Accommodation	Cooperation
Legitimacy	Denial 1	Grudging acknowledgement 2	Acceptance of status quo (3)	Complete 4
Trust	Extreme distrust 1	Distrust 2	Limited trust (3)	Extended trust 4
Attitude and respect	Hatred 1	Antagonism (2)	Neutralism courteousness 3	Friendly and respectful 4
Motivational orientation	Competitive tendencies to destroy or weaken 1	Competitive tendencies to destroy or weaken 2	Individualistic (3)	Cooperative tendencies to assist or preserve 4
		(2.75)		

The following organizing concepts are used to help discern why we bargain collectively as we do.

- **Dual Concerns**: Negotiators have dual concerns. Concern **for substance—self** (as represented by our constituents) and concern **for relationship—others** (the other party as you see them and what they stand for).

  Note: Your personal allegiances and objectives may lead you to have strong opinions about the best result. The decisions that are made or agreements reached must satisfy the interests of the broader organization as well as those central to the matters at issue.

- **Orientations**: We are influenced by our frames of reference and how we see the world, our view of power, authority, and what we believe specific interactions to be about. Taken together, a general orientation emerges that informs our approach to potentially contentious discourse, as well as the approach we adopt to reconcile matters at issue. Orientations can be placed in one of three general frames—**maximalist** positioning, **equitable** positioning, or the **integrative** approach.

- **Approach**: The three orientations give rise to one of two approaches to reconciling matters at issue: **distributive**—dividing up a resource or array of resources that parties have identified—or **integrative**, integrating across multiple issues to identify and create new sources of value. Often, what looks distributive is in fact integrative, as there may be additional issues that can be added to the discussion.

Dual Concerns and Collective Bargaining: Conflicts per se

With interests in common and those that are opposed in union-employer relationships, the dual concerns model can help us understand conflict responses. We use the dual concerns model to frame the approaches negotiators and bargaining teams adopt to reconcile the differences that emerge in the collective bargaining process. It is important to keep in mind that this reconciliation takes place at a number of levels with a variety of people, who themselves are reconciling matters at issue.

Conflict—a clash between individuals arising out of a difference in thought processes, attitudes, understanding, stated positions, interests, and sometimes even perception—is often best understood by examining the consequences of various behaviours at moments in time. These behaviours can be usefully categorized according to conflict styles. The dual concerns model provides that categorization. It suggests that conflict requires balancing the concern of meeting one's own goals with concern for other people and maintaining healthy relationships when reconciling matters at issue.

The dual concerns model is a two-dimensional framework that advances the idea that parties in conflict have two independent types of concerns:

- Concern for substance (self): The degree to which you attempt to satisfy your own interests, which is embodied in the quality of being self-assured and confident without being aggressive (assertiveness).

- Concern for relationship (others): The degree to which you attempt to satisfy the interests of others as embodied in the ability to see the world through the eyes of another person; to share and understand the other's feelings, needs, concerns, and interests (empathy).

Figure 10: Dual Concerns Model

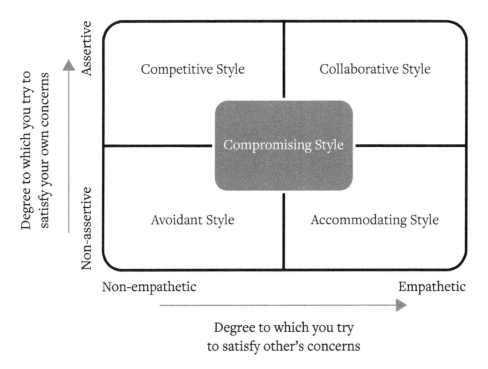

Conflicts and the consequent negotiations are situationally specific. Some situations require a considerate or cooperative approach while others benefit from either a competitive or passive approach. The Dual Concerns Model two-dimensional framework yields five conflict styles that can be adopted based on what you are seeking to achieve. The adoption of a style should be a considered choice rather than a default to what is comfortable.

Table 2: The Five Conflict Styles

Conflict Style	Description
Competitive Contending, Competing, Forcing, Directing	Maximizes assertiveness and minimizes empathy; can involve using your formal authority or power to satisfy your concerns, without regard to the other party's concerns.
Accommodation Accommodating, Yielding, Smoothing, Obliging	Maximizes empathy and minimizes assertiveness, allowing the other party to satisfy their concerns while neglecting your own temporarily with the expectation of in-kind responses to your behavior (seeking a measure of reciprocity).
Avoidant Avoiding, Withdrawing	Low in assertiveness and low in empathy; not paying attention to the conflict and not taking any action to resolve it.
Compromising	Intermediate on both the assertiveness and empathy dimensions; attempting to resolve the conflict by identifying a solution that is partially satisfactory to both parties but completely satisfactory to neither.
Collaborative Collaborating, Integrating, Problem Solving	Highly assertive and highly empathetic at the same time; co-operating with the other party to understand their concerns in an effort to find a mutually satisfying solution.

By understanding each style and its consequences, we may normalize the results of our behaviours in various situations and better appreciate the expected consequences of each approach. Ask yourself what is more important—the substantive outcome or the relational outcome?

Table 3: Conflict Styles and Outcomes

Conflict Style	Outcome
Competitive	We might force others to accept "our" solution, but this acceptance may be accompanied by dissatisfaction and resentment.
Accommodation	The relationship may proceed smoothly in the immediate term setting the stage for constructive actions, but there may be lingering dissatisfaction and building frustration that "our" needs are going unmet if nothing emerges from the accommodation.[12]
Avoiding	Both parties may remain unaware and uninformed about the real underlying issues and concerns, only to be dealing with them in the future.
Compromising	We may feel okay about the outcome, but still have resentments for goals not achieved.
Collaborative	We may not gain a better solution than a compromise might have yielded, but we are more likely to feel better about our chances for future understanding and goodwill.

---

12 Expecting reciprocity: the practice of exchanging things with others for mutual benefit; a social norm of responding to a positive action with another positive action, rewarding like actions.

A note on compromise: Some scholars argue[13] that compromise is not a viable conflict management strategy because it results from either lazy problem-solving involving a half-hearted attempt to satisfy the two parties' interests, or simple yielding by both parties.

Orientations

We are influenced by our frames of reference—how we see the world, our view of power and authority. Further by what we believe union-employer relations and collective bargaining to be about and the specific negotiation concerns in terms of process, substance, and outcome. Taken together, a general orientation emerges. This informs our approach to potentially contentious discourse such as collective bargaining, as well as the approach we adopt to reconcile matters at issue.

Orientations can be placed in one of three general frames. Two of the orientations can be characterized as focussing on positions and positioning (maximalist positioning and equitable positioning) and the third focussed on integration. Forming, organizing, ordering, coordinating, combining, packaging, or blending parties' ideas, suggestions, and resources in ways that creates something of value for both consistent with their respective interests. (integrative approach). These general orientations, or stances, then becomes our reality and we live within it, subject to imprisoning assumptions and the reinforcing influence of confirmation bias.

- **Maximalist positioning** is characteristically competitive and position based. This approach assumes a zero-sum game (any gain for one party is offset by an equal or opposite loss by the other). From the maximalist position, participants assume they maximize their outcomes by making extreme initial demands.

- **Equitable positioning** is characteristically position-based, yet through interactions there is a potential to be more cooperative. The central concerns are equity and fairness through compromise. From the equitable position, participants assume they can best respond to one another's needs by making equal concessions on their positional demands and accepting lesser than proposed outcomes.

    While a maximalist sets extreme demands an equitable positioner advances positions that, in their mind, are *conceivably achievable*. The positions fall within what they believe to be a reasonable zone of potential agreement and cast what they are seeking in a way that *gives them room* to adjust, trade or otherwise modify their initial position(s) or stance during negotiations.

---

13   Including D. Pruitt and J. Rubin, *Social Conflict, Stalemate and Settlement* (New York: Random House, 1986).

- The **integrative approach**, characteristically cooperative and interest-focessed, is driven by its interest-based aspects, seeking to reconcile the underlying needs, concerns, and problems to achieve an efficient solution.

Maximalist positioners, equitable positioners, or those who adopt an integrative approach all seek to solve problems. The first two start from set, established positions and the third starts with the identification of interests, generation of options, and the selection of an option based on objective criteria or standards.

Figure 11: Interrelationship of Orientations

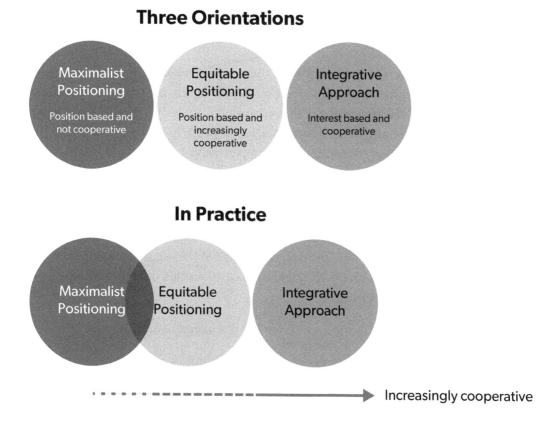

Positions and Positioning

The position-framed, positioning approach views negotiation as an adversarial, zero-sum exercise focused on claiming rather than creating value. Typically, one party will stake out a high (or low) opening position (demand or offer) and the other a correspondingly low (or high) one. Then a series of, usually reciprocal, concessions are made until an agreement is reached somewhere in the middle of the opening positions, or no agreement is reached at all.

Positioners believe that when approaching a negotiation, the starting position should be more ambitious than where one is willing to settle. But when the starting position is so far outside the realm of possibility, it doesn't help that side's negotiating position. In fact, it could have the opposite effect.

> Maximalist positioning and equitable positioning are the primary forms of typical or traditional negotiations. In position-based negotiations, parties typically focus on some plan of action or objective to fulfil their sets of needs. Positioners craft a set of positions that are advanced and argued for during negotiations. These positions are motivated by and purportedly represent the proposer's interests—positions being something that you decide upon, and interests that caused you to so decide.

The effort to secure an agreement focusses on these objectives, or positions, and not on the parties' overall concerns or interests. Position-based negotiators typically view differences as fixed; they see the agreement as the conclusion of a concession based, zero-sum contest and focus on obtaining some desired portion of gains. In position-based negotiations, parties can work either cooperatively or competitively.

Positioners adopt the main tenets of distributive bargaining to varying degrees and employ tactics that include:

- Adversarial and advocacy stance: *You do your job, I'll do mine. You give me your proposals, and I'll give you mine*, and out of the clash of these positions will come the reconciliation of what we both want (and possibly a clearer definition of the problem(s) or matters at issue).

- Making a tactical decision concerning opening discussions, making a first offer.

- Starting with an extremely aggressive position (if adopting a maximalist positioning stance) to anchor the other person's expectations.

- Advancing positions that the proponent believes are *conceivably achievable* (if adopting an equitable positioning stance). The positions fall within what they believe to be in a reasonable zone of potential agreement casting what they are seeking in a way that *gives them room* to adjust, trade or otherwise modify their initial position(s) or stance during negotiations.

The concept of "anchoring" refers to the tendency to attach (or "anchor") our thoughts to a reference point—even though it may have no logical relevance to the decision at hand. It is a cognitive bias that describes the common human tendency to rely too heavily on the first piece of information offered (the "anchor") when making decisions and is considered a bias because it distorts our judgement, especially when matters are unclear or otherwise unexplored.

> Anchoring is the attempt to establish a reference point (anchor) around which a negotiation will revolve.

The tactic of anchoring is the attempt to establish a reference point (anchor) around which a negotiation will revolve and use this reference point to make subsequent adjustments. The initial value, or starting point, may be suggested by the formulation of the problem, or it may be made as the result of a partial computation. In either case, different starting points yield different estimates, which are biased toward the initial values.

Anchoring is inevitable because one of the parties must open discussions and negotiations first. Opening offers are anchors whether you intend them as a tactical move or not because the opening offer often has the psychological effect of framing what each side will view as the possible outcomes in the ensuing negotiation. The best way to avoid anchoring in negotiations is to engage in rigorous critical thinking.

When you believe the other party likely knows more than you do about the size of the zone of potential agreement (ZOPA), you will have difficulty anchoring effectively. Before *dropping* an anchor in such situations, arm yourself with as much information as possible.

You will recognize the maximalist approach as having the following features:

- **Not disclosing** their underlying interests, related information, or asserting that they have limited alternatives;
- **Concealing** or misrepresenting relevant settlement information;
- **Repeating** their initial position again and again;
- **Not acknowledging** the other person's perspective;
- **Not engaging** in problem solving that requires them to change their position;
- Making **very small moves** and taking a long time between moves;
- Making **take-it-or-leave-it** demands, stating that no additional movement is possible;
- Engaging in **doubt-creation** behaviours such as theatrics, threats, exaggerations, distortions, or bluffs;
- Getting up and walking out or **threatening** to walk out, if demands are not met.

The positional approach, whether maximalist or equitable positioning, has its limitations. Disadvantages of positional bargaining:

- **Locks** participants into positions that make movements difficult;
- Can lead to a **polarizing** kind of impasse on specific issues or on an agreement generally;
- **Conceals** the parties' underlying concerns, needs, and interests;
- Can result in parties becoming **angry or entrenched** in their positions;
- Encourages **continued positioning** and positional bargaining;
- **Interferes** with reaching an agreement efficiently;
- Tests, if not potentially **endangers**, relationships.

Figure 12: Traditional, Positional Negotiations

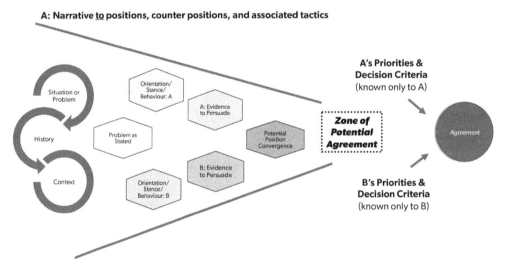

Traditional, positional negotiations are illustrated in Figure 12. Depending on the degree to which you adopt a maximalist stance or are more to the centre of the equitable positioner approach determines how negotiations flow. The emergent relationship model illustrated in Figure 7 and 8 illustrates the rationale and consequences of the alternative chosen.

The integrative approach is a means of decision making that conceptualizes the actions and contingencies of all possible outcomes, options, and scenarios with the intention of incorporating the goals and aims of the parties to create maximum value[14] through collaboration.

It can be seen as problem-solving dialogue. Parties cooperate by pooling efforts to uncover information, develop alternatives independent of the degree to which outcomes serve self-interests, and then agree on the alternatives that are best for each party and for the relationship as a whole. This approach is characteristically cooperative but is also distinguished by aspects that are not essential to a cooperative negotiation.

The integrative approach:

- Observes the **principles of the dual concerns** model: the concern for self and the concern for others balance.

- Respects the three **elements of good faith**: the willingness to meet, to engage in rational discussions with a mind open to persuasion. Through words and action **demonstrates** good faith behaviour:

    - acts honestly, openly, and without hidden or ulterior motives

    - raises issues in a fair and timely way

    - is constructive and cooperative

    - is proactive in providing others with relevant information and consider all information provided

    - responds promptly and thoroughly to reasonable requests and concerns

    - keeps an open mind, listen to others and is prepared to change an opinion about a particular situation or behaviour, and

    - treats others respectfully.[15]

- Seeks to identify, understand, and focus on **underlying interests.**

- Directly examines sets of **needs and concerns** (position-based seeks need fulfilment by achieving certain stated desired positions).

---

14 Value is the regard that something is held to deserve; the importance, worth, or usefulness of something. It is said to be in the eye of the beholder with the result that it varies from person to person. In negotiation value can take a variety of forms: $'s, time, resources, re-purposed resources, contacts, access, support, logistics, components, structured packages, recommendations, referrals.

15 Adapted from New Zealand Ministry of Business, Innovation and Employment (MBIE) (http://employment.govt.nz/er/solvingproblems/keyprinciples/goodfaith.asp)

- Exhibits **mutual problem-solving** behaviour.

- Reframes the problem in **non-positional terms** and avoids specific outcome engendering words.

- Does **not advocate** positions/outcomes to serve self-interest in early stages (distinguishes creating value from claiming value).

- Stresses **seeking, assembling, and sharing** information.

- Adopts an **analytic frame**[16] to examine specific matters at issue that could be or are contentious and create a common *knowledge base* in support of rational collective engagement on matters at issue.

- Establishes **points of comparison** (objective criteria).

- Places emphasis on **developing new** alternatives/use of dialogue.

- Acts assertively in selecting **favourable alternatives**; good for self and relationship.

- Proceeds **independent of trust.**

- Takes a **long-term view**: As Fisher and Brown advise in *Getting Together, Building Relationships As We Negotiate,* "we either look out for both parties, or we don't proceed; we won't risk an adversarial future."

An integrative approach seeks the potential for parties' interests to be combined, or elements incorporated, in a way that creates joint value. If both parties can independently satisfy their interests, there is no need for an integrative approach. If however they are interdependent, then there is no other way to find a fair, effective, wise, and sustainable (stable) path forward.

An integrative approach is as much an attitude as an approach. It also requires particular skills such as:

- **Active** listening.

- Assuming positive intent and **suspending judgement** in order to achieve an understanding of all parties' interests.

---

16 An evidence-based framework that informs the issues being addressed and determines what information or research is available and what additional information is required to support informed decision making. Developed collaboratively before formal deliberations or negotiations begin, the analytic frame makes explicit the categories and multiple sub-categories that comprise the issue(s) at hand.

- **Constructively** managing the tension of opposing ideas and, instead of choosing one at the expense of the other, generating a creative resolution of the tension in the form of a new idea that contains elements of each of the opposing ideas but is superior to either alone;[17]

- Curiosity and **informed** inquiry: what do I (we) know and what do I (we) need to know to make an informed decision? What might be contentious?

The approach is more than opening demands, offers, counter offers, and back and forth concession making. It describes an attitude and approach that carries through to the other stages of the interaction and is an alternative to pure position-based discourse (maximalist positioning and equitable positioning).

All those involved should be explicitly committed to the search for integrative potential and willing to refine the personal skills necessary for it to succeed.

> As identified earlier the following factors indicate the potential for integration:
> - The parties cannot achieve what they need to achieve independent of one another;
> - Is multi-dimensional. More than one issue is involved.
> - It is possible to add more issues to the mix.
> - The parties' interactions will recur over time.
> - The parties have varying preferences across issues.

Integrative solutions are based on a shared understanding of an evidentiary base that includes relevant facts and research. This includes an appreciation of the contested aspects of an issue and the beliefs and desires of each party that are the root cause of the disagreement. Therefore, the use of an analytic frame to develop those shared understandings is an important preparation.

> To increase the integrative potential, it is useful to develop a shared statement of the challenge or opportunity using neutral, non-positional language.

As the analytic frame is developed, factual foundations, areas of agreement, and areas of difference become clarified. The original problem statement often shifts as a result. To increase the integrative potential, it is useful to develop a shared statement of the

---

[17] Concept of integrative thinking introduced by Roger Martin in *The Opposable Mind: How Successful Leaders Win Through Integrative Thinking* (Brighton, Mass.: Harvard Business Review Press, 2007).

challenge or opportunity using neutral, non-positional language. The analytic frame can begin the process of assembling objective criteria that will serve as a point of comparison to inform any final agreement.

Mutual understanding of technical or detailed subjects will be required in any negotiation. It is advantageous for the parties to identify *what we need to know* and *what is contentious or potentially contentious* as a preparatory matter at the outset, before bargaining table discussions begin. Those matters can be the subject of an analytic frame with a shared knowledge base developed. This allows for more constructive, informed negotiations on an issue. The creation of an analytic frame is a negotiation in and of itself.

> Nothing exists in isolation and action on any matter
> both affects and is affected by other matters.

Integrative potential is also increased by standing back from the specific issue to view it in a broad systemic way. Nothing exists in isolation and action on any matter both affects and is affected by other matters. Considering an issue from a systemic point of view complicates it of course, but that very complexity also adds variables that can be used to create value. A narrow focus on an issue, particularly when it is defined as a problem to be solved, limits possible action and thus limits creative response.

Figure 13: Integrative Negotiations[18]

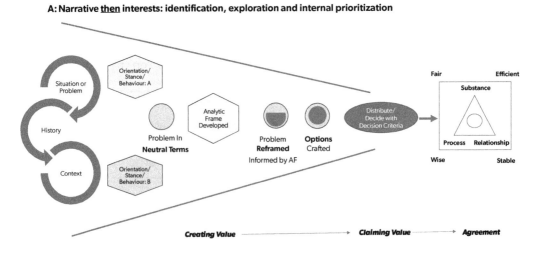

---

18   For a description of fair, efficient, wise and stable see Table 6 and for substance, process, relationship see Figure 1.

The Difference Between the Three: An Attitude as Much as an Approach

One might argue that at a practical level, these orientations represent a continuum of strategies. In other words, you could start out positional and see how the other party responds, with the goal of becoming generally integrative.

On the journey to a collective agreement, the story goes, you can employ various forms of equitable positioning, increasingly introducing your more *integrative action*.

Figure 11 illustrates the three orientations that one has or adopts at the outset of a situation, maximalist position, an equitable position, or an integrative approach. The maximalist position is characteristically competitive and position-based and makes extreme initial demands.

The equitable position is characteristically position-based, yet increasingly cooperative as positions are clarified and concessions made. The integrative approach is cooperative and interest based. It seeks to resolve the underlying concerns and problems to reconcile the matters at issue.

Note that there is a degree of overlap between the position-based approaches and the cooperative approach. This results because some negotiations (the equitable position) can be characterized as both position-based and cooperative. The part of the position-based sphere outside the cooperative sphere represents the most competitive region (the maximalist position), where cooperation is low and differences in positions are seen as fixed. Conversely, the part of the cooperative sphere outside the position-based sphere represents the most integrative region (the integrative approach), where cooperation is high, and differences are not seen as fixed to positions.

In answering the question as to whether this is a continuum, one argument is that negotiations can take on hybrid forms. Negotiations are not either/or propositions and they are not interest-focused or position-focused. Rather, negotiations are characterized by certain qualities that can be shown along a continuum, generally reflecting purely position-based approaches on one end versus purely interest-based approaches on the other.

Another argument is that the integrative approach has principles and associated strategies. It focusses on the long-term relationship—one of acknowledged interdependence. The back and forth of negotiations serves to better define that interdependence.

However, starting from a position—whether from a maximalist or an equitable position—and moving to a more integrative approach has its limitations, including:

- Your **motivations can't be seen** only your actions. What you intend to do is only known to you.

- What **message do your actions send** to the other party, their constituents, and to your constituents?

- Actions are **subject to interpretation**. What's to stop you from cycling in and out of approaches, and then are you really seeking to be interest-based and cooperative?

- It is difficult to avoid the **anchoring effect.**

- You can't control the **other party's responses** or their reactions in the face of your actions.

- It is inefficient; the so-called hybrid is **equitable positioning labelled** as an integrative approach.

- You are **more likely than not to become hostage** to the norm. It is easier to retreat to the position-based traditional approach that represents the status quo.

- It **relieves you** from being prepared: you go with what you've done before and what you've come to know. The emphasis is on positioning and reaction rather than a process of engagement and information exchange to identify interests.

- How the negotiation process **is framed will influence** whether a positioning/distributive or integrative approach is pursued. The stereotype of negotiation is a contentious win-lose process, not the exercise of collaborative problem-solving. Simply labelling the task at hand as a negotiation or bargaining can drive the assumption of a fixed-pie, distributive, positional approach.[19]

- It is **questionable what you are seeking**, whether in terms of process or substance, long term versus short term.

Table 4 compares the two approaches, position based, and interest based. Integrative-Interest Based negotiation is a distinct subset of cooperative discourse or negotiation. It involves a high degree of informational exchange aimed at mutual problem-solving and uses objective criteria as points of comparison. It is characterized by interactions that facilitate relatively higher levels of trust than would be found in other negotiations. Trust is not a requirement of an integrative approach; however, those actions typical in integrative initiatives generally promote trust.

---

19 C.C. Smith, *Moving from Distributive to Integrative Negotiation* (Garland, TX: Amberton University, 2012).

Cooperative negotiations that are position based, in contrast, entails a broad set of negotiations where parties accommodate their counterparts' efforts to explore their own needs rooted in the positions advanced. Characterized by position taking and back and forth concessions, the parties are more open to persuasion.

In position-based negotiations, parties can work either cooperatively or competitively. Cooperative position-based negotiators typically view differences as fixed: they focus on securing objectives to meet end goals, allow for their counterparts' efforts to pursue their own objectives, and expect that fair agreements can be achieved through compromise.

Competitive position-based negotiators' focus, and view of differences are the same as those of cooperative negotiators. However, competitive position-based negotiators see the agreement as one dimensional, the conclusion of a zero-sum contest.

Table 4: In Comparison: Position-Based and Integrative/Interest-Based Negotiations

	Traditional, Position-Based Negotiations	**Integrative, Interest-Based Negotiations**
Key Concepts	Positioning and position taking: Positions are developed to represent a party's demands. A position is focused on "what" or "how." See maximalist and equitable positioning. Management rights preservation: every change represents an erosion of *our right to manage*.	Objectives, positions and interests distinguished. Interests: Why a party takes a particular stance on an issue, the reasons a party is demanding something; a party's needs, concerns, hopes, or fears. An interest is focused on "why." Note the difference: maximalist and equitable positioning and the integrative approach.
Pre-bargaining	Internally focused preparation. Research and data for strategic presentation, internal communication and as necessary media purposes.	Internally focused preparation and the development of analytic frames with the other party for technical/complex issues and ones that are contentious or potentially contentious to create a common *knowledge base*.
Preparation for Bargaining	Observing the basic tenets of distributive bargaining, prepare a target (reasonable) and a resistance point (backup) for each issue that you and the other side are likely to raise.	Identify your core interests and those of the other side, then develop potential solutions that are likely to be mutually satisfactory.
Opening Negotiations	Take opening positions that are high/low enough so that you will have room to move; emphasize forces that make it difficult for you to move from the opening position.	Avoid taking initial positions; clarify your core interests and your understanding of the other side's core interests; emphasize flexibility and creativity in addressing these interests.
Movement on Issues During Bargaining	Gradual movement on the basis of reciprocity and delay tactics; occasional rapid movement as a result of logrolling[20] and power tactics.	Gradual building of shared understandings on the basis of logic, research, analysis and persuasion; occasional rapid movement as a result of brainstorming.
Interpersonal Communication	Take careful notes on everything that is said; only restate points where you agree with what the other side said; use confrontation to press key points and destabilize the other side.	Use paraphrasing and active listening skills to ensure that you have accurately heard what was said; use confrontation to surface underlying feelings and interests
Coming to Agreement	Either increased openness or problem solving at the eleventh hour when final offers are made and the full agreement is assembled or the parties come to impasse, followed by a strike, lockout, or implemented agreement.	Either the problem-solving tone continues until all issues are resolved (possibly extending past contract expiration deadlines) or the problem-solving tone is set aside for any distributive offers necessary to reach agreement.

---

20 Logrolling: the parties establish or find more than one negotiating issue and then agree to trade off among these issues so that one party achieves a highly preferred outcome on the first issue and the other party achieves a highly preferred outcome on the second issue.

| Ratifying the Agreement | The union must persuade the membership that this is the best possible agreement under the circumstances; ratification is a measure of which side "won." | Both sides must persuade all of their constituents that the agreement is mutually beneficial; ratification is a vote of confidence for both sides and meets the satisfaction of interests test. |

Figure 14: In Practical Terms

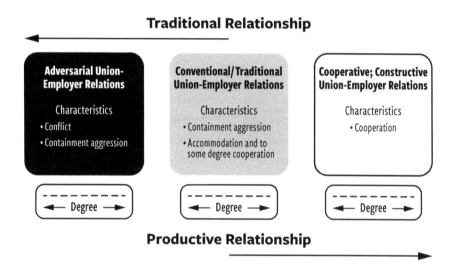

In practical terms, approaches to bargaining vary by degree. A traditional, conventional bargainer may be a maximalist to start being more adversarial, adopting all of the tenets of distributive bargaining and evolve to a variant of an equitable positioner that over time demonstrates a more cooperative approach.

So, to answer the question: why do union-employer negotiations look like they do?

Put not so simply, it is a mix of:

> *People and personalities, education and experience, collective bargaining experiences, union-employer relations experiences, frames of reference, environment and context, invocations of history, posture and intent, what I believe negotiations/bargaining and collective bargaining to be about, impressions and beliefs about the other side, bargaining here and the stories I've been told, the emergent relationship and how it came to be, expectations and pressures from my side.*

Without a Full Appreciation: A Word of Caution

All too often, employers and sometimes unions become enamored with the notion of finding a better way to negotiate terms and conditions of employment. They latch on to concepts such as interest-based bargaining only to realize that they are not yet prepared for an actual change in their approach to bargaining or their day-to-day union-employer interactions beyond good intentions. Goodwill is necessary but hardly sufficient.

In his article, "Bargaining Over How to Bargain in Labor-Management Negotiations," J.E. Cutcher-Gershenfeld, a leading scholar in negotiation theory and practice, made instructive comments concerning attempts at interest-based negotiations:

> A close look at the interest-based experiments in labor relations reveals that adversarial institutional patterns have often been rejected in favor of more collaborative, problem solving techniques *without a full appreciation of the underlying reasons for the establishment of the original institutional patterns*.

A departure from traditional union-employer negotiations requires essentially years of preparation and cultivation of a higher level of trust and candid communication between the parties.

Parties should avoid setting unrealistic targets and raising expectations unduly. In the absence of a crisis or other circumstance that necessitates change, it is unlikely that parties will immediately depart from entrenched practices and beliefs about each other.

There is a very real danger of the workforce and the union becoming cynical over nice-sounding statements and principles when they do not see those same principles being put into daily practice. Moreover, some naively believe that this newfound method of bargaining is a panacea for all previous ills. By inflating the expectations of employees, bargaining team members, unions, managers, executives, board members, and others, the parties may be setting themselves up for failure.

It may be tempting to set lofty goals and stake the organization's reputation on implementing a new bargaining approach only to find that the times are not right, the current circumstances don't provide the necessary impetus for change, or the key decision-makers/influencers are not yet ready. A change on this scale and of this nature requires serious investments in time, money, and personal reputation.

Collective Bargaining and Continuous Improvement

Those responsible for collective bargaining should adopt a continuous improvement philosophy if they wish to move from a traditional labour relations approach to a problem-solving orientation typified by successful integrative bargaining approaches. Attempt to engage in traditional bargaining in a more effective manner, as a first step that does not risk credibility, and allow the parties to thereafter continue to work toward a more productive, open, and trusting relationship.

> The approach during bargaining should mirror the nature of the ongoing day-to-day relationship.

The best time to start this change is during the term of the agreement—*the time in between*—not during collective bargaining when the employer may be seeking, for example, an unpopular change. The approach during bargaining should mirror the nature of the ongoing day-to-day relationship. Do not expect collaborative dialogue at the bargaining table if you choose not to engage in meaningful consultation during the life of the collective agreement.

> The character of union-employer relationships is a product of actions and reactions to problems, organizational change and a host of workplace events. Antagonistic relationships or high levels of suspicion are not created overnight, they emerge over time.
>
> Similarly, they do not disappear simply because of words on paper or commitments made during joint training initiatives. If it is self-evident that relationships evolve over time, then it holds true that any desired changes to the union-employer relationship will take time to affect.

Employers should always consider more constructive approaches to bargaining but not expect to achieve an immediate relationship or operating culture change. One must be prepared to commit time and resources over an extended period—and not simply those at the worksite level but also the management group as a whole.

A Place to Start

- Recognize that while all negotiations **have a value claiming stage**, where parties decide who gets what, how much of what, when, and in what form, many negotiations, including union-employer collective bargaining, **also have a value creation** stage. The stage where parties work together to clarify issues/circumstances, explore ideas, concepts, and options to identify reconciliation alternatives. When bargaining collectively maximalists and equitable positioners focus on claiming the **value that emerges from back-and-forth concession making** and that is resident in the parties' positions. Typically, they adopt the tenets of distributive bargaining from the outset. The integrative approach seeks to identify and create value before entering into the distributive aspects of negotiation to claim it.

- Processes to **create value should precede those to claim value**. The skills and strategies appropriate to each stage are quite different. Distributive skills are called for in the value claiming stage and problem-solving skills using integration techniques in value creation. Processes to create value are effective when done collaboratively and without a focus on who gets what. Claiming value involves distributive bargaining. These processes **must be introduced carefully** so as not to harm the relationship and derail any progress made to that point. The challenge is to place the emphasis on the right stage at the right time and effectively transition from creating to claiming value.

- Make **best use of *the time in between*** negotiations. While the necessities of implementing the newly negotiated agreement and the general *urgency of now* tend to consume the parties' energies and time, use post-bargaining efforts to build a foundation for next time.

- In an evidenced-based and informed way seek to better understand contentious or potentially contentious matters and technical/complex matters that typically are the subject of bargaining. The development of a common knowledge base builds relationships and furthers understanding. This understanding can put the parties in a constructive frame to address matters that may be the subject of collective bargaining. The **analytic frame is a useful tool**—what is/are the issue(s); what do I/we know, what do I/we need to know, and what could be potentially contentious?

- Understand **how we got here**. Relationships, both individual and institutional, are not chosen, they emerge. Using the work of Walton and McKersie as an organizer, develop a collective understanding of how we got here and what we need to do to move forward. Do you understand frames of reference and how they influence choices, actions, and reactions?

- Understand and build **understanding within** your constituent group about the three negotiation orientations—maximalist positioning, equitable positioning, and the integrative approach—the concept of integrative potential and how they relate to the choice of a constructive approach to collective bargaining (if a constructive non-adversarial approach is what you desire).

- Adopt an **unconditionally constructive orientation**. Fisher and Brown, in *Getting Together: Building Relationships as We Negotiate*, set out the imperatives for developing a constructive working relationship through being unconditionally constructive. The guidelines have as a foundation the notion of good faith.[21]

- **Be realistic** about changing relationships and approaches to bargaining. Adopt an approach that focuses **not just on the positions of each party, but on the underlying reasons** and needs of each party, as an invitation to find better and more creative solutions. Recognize that context is important. When the economy is seen as strong, **positional bargaining seems to** end with solutions everyone can live with (even if it does nothing for building the union-management relationship). When it is not so, however, **positional bargaining tends to** entrench parties in a far more emotional way, often ending in bitter fights over very small issues.

- **Take note of the path** to institutionalizing intractability and the differences in stated positions, thought processes, attitudes, understandings, and sometimes even perceptions that animate it. The status quo and acceptance of it, waiting for something to change, and two failures help to institutionalize intractability or measures of it and the discord that flows from it.

    - **Acceptance**, being resigned to, or general observance of the **status quo**: That's the way it is, always like this, tried something—didn't work, likely won't work now, others tell us that...

    - **Waiting**—me, them, and us: Until *they* change. *It's not me, it's them, can't be an us without them first.*

    - **Failure** to use the **time in between**: As we will discuss later in this section the phrase *time in between* implies the presence of at least two events of note, before and after. Given who we are, where we are, what we do, anticipating contentious or potentially contentious situations is essential. Making the best use of the time in between these occurrences is required if you are to identify process and practice improvements and raise collective knowledge on topics of potential contention.

    - **Failure** of **imagination**: With all *we knew* and/or *should have known*—a circumstance when something that is undesirable yet seemingly predictable is not planned for.

---

21 Excerpt from *When Things Happen at Work*, H.J. Finlayson, (Victoria, BC: FriesenPress, 2020), 138.

Imagination, use of the **time in between**, and a motivation to positively influence the future through change to the **status quo** is the path forward to a constructive future. And not **waiting**.

Each round of bargaining will have its own twists and nuances, but there a few **principles** that negotiators should keep in mind that can serve as a backdrop to their preparation and frame their approaches at the bargaining table.

By asking yourself the following questions, you can illuminate the boundaries between the appropriate and the *not so* during the first two phases of collective bargaining (preparation, negotiation) and in the process discover your own ethical standards:[22]

> **Principle 1. Reciprocity**: Would I (we) want others to treat me (us) or someone close to me (us) this way? Am I (are we) responding to a constructive gesture or action with a corresponding one?
>
> **Principle 2. Publicity**: Would I (we) be comfortable if my (our) actions were fully and fairly described in the media?
>
> **Principle 3. Trusted friend**: Would I (we) be comfortable telling my best friend, spouse, or children what I am (we are) doing?
>
> **Principle 4. Universality**: Would I (we) advise anyone else in my (our) situation to act this way?
>
> **Principle 5. Legacy**: Does this action reflect how I (we) want to be known and remembered?

As a central feature of a path forward and a place to start be constructive, keep **each other honest, focussed**. Make each party rationalize their positions, bring good data to support their views (ideally co-create an analytic frame as a *common knowledge base*), and most importantly challenge each other to find solutions beyond the starting positions that each party brings forward at the beginning of the process.

---

22 Adapted from Michael Wheeler. Program on Negotiation https://www.pon.harvard.edu/daily/negotiation-training-daily/questions-of-ethics-in-negotiation/ February 28, 2019

Table 5: Advantages of Unconditionally Constructive Behaviour

Unconditionally Constructive Elements	Advantages for the Relationship	Advantages for Me
1. **Rationality**: Observe, suspend judgement, and balance emotion with reason.	An irrational response and contention are less likely.	I model a reasoned posture and make fewer mistakes.
2. **Understanding**: Even if the other party appears not to understand you, try to understand them. Understand the history and appreciate the context.	The better I understand you, the fewer collisions we will have, and the fewer ill-conceived conclusions I will make.	The better informed I am, the better solutions I can invent and the better able I am to influence you.
3. **Communication**: Inquire, consult, and listen. Seek to understand before seeking to be understood. Use neutral language; provocative language is a positional trigger.	We both participate in making decisions; better communication improves them.	I reduce the risk of making a mistake without giving up the ability to decide.
4. **Reliability**: Even if the other party is trying to deceive you, neither trust nor deceive them. Practice **alert watchfulness**.	It tends to build trust and confidence.	My words will have more impact.
5. **Non-coercive** approaches to influence: Be open to persuasion; try to persuade.	If people are persuaded rather than coerced, both the outcome and compliance are better.	By being open, I keep learning; it is easier to resist coercion if one is open to persuasion.
6. **Acceptance**: Accept and respect the other party's legitimacy. Accept the other party as worth dealing with and be open to learning from them.	To deal will with our differences, I have to be prepared to learn from you.	By dealing with you and your circumstance, I remove obstacles to learning the facts and to persuading you on the merits.

Interests and a *Good* Agreement or Settlement?[23]

What are you trying to achieve? What you're seeking informs your strategy. How you view power, authority, and collective bargaining informs your approach. If you seek to satisfy solely your own interests you will adopt a positional, distributive approach. It is a question of winning or losing. If you seek to satisfy your interests and those of others, you will adopt a more integrative approach. It is a question of what constitutes a good agreement.

---

23 Excerpt from H. Finlayson, *When Things Happen at Work: A Practitioner's Guide to People, Circumstances and What to Do Now*. Victoria, BC: FriesenPress, 2020 page 203.

Win-Win = Good?

Approaches to negotiation has been the subject of many popular books. Challenging readers to find a better way, many of these books extol the virtues of what they characterize as win-win bargaining. A good agreement is a win for me and a win for you, or so the story goes.

In *Conflict Resolved? A Critical Assessment of Conflict Resolution,* Alan Tidwell takes issue with such simplified prescriptions. He finds that these publications tend to:

- trivialize or generalize conflict and provide simplistic solutions.
- routinize methods of handling it.
- undervalue the role that situations, circumstances, and context play in handling matters at issue.

At page 27, Tidwell comments on what he describes as the win-win discourse:

> Generalized across all conflict contexts, the win-win discourse is not genuine conflict resolution, but rather a mechanism for persuading others that they have what they want, without giving anything away. It is clever, but not very productive towards long-term conflict resolution.

Professor Lawrence Susskind[24] of MIT made instructive comments in his 2011 blog report about the oft-used, little understood expression:

> I hear the phrase "win-win" all the time. I'm not sure that very many people who use it know what they are talking about. I have a hunch they mistakenly assume that if everyone would just cooperate, then all parties would get what they want. That, of course, is ridiculous. There are almost no negotiations in which everyone can get everything they want. And cooperation or even compromise isn't the issue.

Susskind went on to encourage thinking clearly about win-win:

> No one should agree to anything in a negotiation that is worse for them than what they are likely to get if no deal is reached. Roger Fisher and Bill Ury made this point thirty years ago in *Getting to Yes.*

---

24 Lawrence Susskind, Ford Professor of Urban and Environmental Planning at MIT and Vice-Chair of the Program on Negotiation at Harvard Law School, *The Consensus Building Approach* blog post August 8, 2011. Accessed June 24, 2109. http://theconsensusbuildingapproach.blogspot.

First, figure out what no agreement is most likely going to leave you with, try to generate something (a walk-away) that's better than that, but when you are in an actual negotiation don't reject something that's better than your realistic walk-away, even if it won't get you everything you'd like to have. Fisher and Ury called this point of comparison, your Best Alternative to the Negotiated Agreement (BATNA).[25]

A win-win negotiation is something that gets all sides an outcome better than their BATNA. It doesn't necessarily get anyone everything that they might want.

Tidwell and Susskind's observations are instructive. The back-and-forth communication designed to reach an agreement is better described as making the optimal decisions to maximize your interests. The parties involved—their roles, motivations, and interests—present an added level of complexity to this form of negotiation that doesn't lend itself to simplistic prescriptions or approaches.

Elements of Good

Something is considered good when it is ". . . suitable to a purpose, effective, efficient."[26]

In their book, *Breaking the Impasse: Consensual Approaches to Resolving Public Disputes*, dispute resolution experts Lawrence Susskind and Jeffrey Cruikshank identify four characteristics of what can be termed a good negotiated settlement or agreement: fairness, efficiency, wisdom, and stability.

Fairness

Fairness is a general concept that implies treating both sides alike, without reference to one's own feelings or interests.

---

25 BATNA is an acronym that stands for *Best Alternative To a Negotiated Agreement*. It is defined as the best course of action for satisfying your interests without the other party's agreement. In other words, a party's BATNA is what a party's alternative is if negotiations are unsuccessful and an agreement cannot be achieved.

Most BATNA formulations direct your attention to what you can achieve outside the current negotiation and independent of your counterpart. Employment relationships however are interdependent ones. More often than not, parties to problems, contentious matters, workplace negotiations cannot achieve what they need to achieve independent of one another. As a practical matter parties to an employment relationship will remain together and must continue to interact. Recognizing the party's interdependence, the BATNA takes a different form.

26 *Webster's New World Dictionary,* 2nd ed. (1982), 602.

Susskind and Cruikshank say that the perceptions of the participants are most important in evaluating the fairness of a negotiated outcome. The key question is: "Were the people who managed the process responsive to the concerns of those affected by the final decision or outcome?" Unfortunately, the issue of fairness is situational and subjective. What one party perceives as a fair settlement may be seen quite differently by the other.

On page 25 of their book, Susskind and Cruikshank observe, "In our view, it is more important that an agreement be perceived as fair by the parties involved than by an independent analyst who applies an abstract decision rule. If the involved parties think a given process has been fair, they are more likely to abide by its outcome; if they do not, they will seek to undermine it."

Efficiency

The second way to judge an agreement is by testing its efficiency. Something is efficient if it directly produces the desired result with a minimum of effort, expense, or waste. Efficiency is established by asking two questions:

- Could one or all of the parties to the agreement be made better off without making the others worse off? If the answer is "Yes," then the agreement is efficient.

- Did it take an inordinately long time and a great deal of effort to reach the agreement? If so, do the benefits of the agreement outweigh the costs associated with achieving the agreement? If the answer to this subsequent question is "No," the agreement cannot be considered a good one.

Wisdom

Something is considered wise if it is informed, sound, and prompted by a considered judgement of the relevant aspects and circumstances concerning the matter or matters at issue. In a sense, wisdom is only obvious in hindsight. Negotiations involve forecasts or predictions on areas of settlement and potential consequences of particular courses of action.

> We only realize that what we have done was an incorrect approach when it is too late.

It is virtually impossible to have complete confidence in a forecast and have that forecast come to pass or stand up to the test of time. Agreements are concluded at a particular time and under particular circumstances, and they govern the relations between the parties over a considerable period. During this time, substantial changes may take place—changes not contemplated when the agreement was reached. It may also take an indeterminate amount of time for the forecast to be tested. We only realize that what we have done was an incorrect approach when it is too late.

Key to a wise agreement is what Susskind and Cruikshank term "prospective hindsight"—an assessment and forecast based on past experiences and knowledge. Unfortunately, in some areas even our past experiences tell us very little, because the result of previous actions has not yet been realized. It is also extremely difficult to remain constantly objective when assessing a problem.

A wise agreement contains all the relevant information to minimize the risk of being wrong. The search for a wise solution requires a collaborative inquiry into the problem. This inquiry breaks down a complex problem into a series of mutually agreed upon pieces that can be examined individually.

By looking at the smaller pieces, we can reach a wise solution that satisfies all the underlying interests, without having to rely solely on our predictions of future consequences. Remember, we are free to choose a course of action, the interests we seek to satisfy, and strategies to employ, but we are not free to choose the results or consequences, intended or otherwise, of our choices.

The concept of wisdom and the consequences of our choices are closely linked to the fourth characteristic—stability.

Stability

Stability is the final element of a good agreement. Something is stable if it cannot be easily moved or thrown off balance, or is not likely to break down, fall apart, or give way. A settlement that is perceived by all parties as fair, that was reached efficiently, and that seems technically wise is unsatisfactory if it does not endure.

A good agreement will endure over time and remain unchallenged by the parties and/or their respective constituents. That is, none of the parties to the agreement will have any motivation to break the agreement before it expires naturally.

Instability can be caused in several ways:

> **Is the overall agreement feasible?** A negotiator may reach an agreement in a labour dispute, but if it cannot be sold to the negotiator's constituents, the efficiency, wisdom, and fairness of the agreement become irrelevant.

Can the agreement be implemented by both parties? If the agreement contains provisions that are not realistic, the agreement will not be stable. It is not helpful to extract unrealistic commitments that cannot be relied on, even if such promises seem like victories at the time they are achieved.

Is the agreement based on mistaken assumptions? In framing the agreement, negotiators should make a commitment that if the agreement has been based on a mistaken assumption, the parties will reconvene and correct that mistake. Remember that one side may grant a large concession, not realizing the potential impact. Once that impact is known, however, it may be used in an attempt to destroy the entire agreement, or used as a weapon in future negotiations. As a result, the agreement, as well as the relationship, is now unstable.

Is the agreement legal? It is of little use to enter an agreement that is not enforceable. Knowledge of the limitations on all parties is necessary. Further, you must know to what both you and the other party are legally able to commit.

The authors conclude that outcomes—whether substantive or relationship—generated by positional bargaining, coercion, and situational compromise often fail to meet these four tests and as a consequence set the stage for further conflict.

The following table summarizes the characteristics of a good negotiation or settlement.

Table 6: Characteristics of a Good Negotiation or Settlement

A good negotiation →	Fair	Efficient	Wise	Stable
Produces better technical solutions		✓	✓	
Increases the likelihood of compliance by constituents			✓	✓
Improves the relationship between the parties	✓			✓
Is most efficient (less costly—time, money, stress)		✓		

CHAPTER 3

In Support of Informed Decisions

The Importance of Information

Collective bargaining involves the communication of information between two parties. Communication and the sharing of information take many forms. Information may be disguised or be subtly presented but is required for the negotiation to be conducted. As a result, each party must accumulate information, both to formulate its objectives and positions and to prepare responses to the positions advanced by the other negotiating team.

As the practice of collective bargaining has evolved, negotiators have found that they need support from extensive research and analysis. Both union and management collect and analyze many types of data. Research data can include the following forms:

- Grievances arising out of the existing collective agreement provisions;

- Information about the actual worksite application of provisions of the current agreement;

- Results of collective bargaining in similar industries or jurisdictions;

- Internal economic data and economic data from other jurisdictions;

- The state of the economy, locally or nationally.

Sources for this information vary from public or private information services, to internal employer or union files, to other media readily available to the general public including on-line. Depending on the nature of the negotiation, the research and analysis may be complex, in part because issues considered in any negotiation are varied and may arise with little warning during the bargaining sessions.

Information generated through research and analysis has two uses in collective bargaining:

- The **first and most important function** of this information is to determine the objectives to pursue and the position a party should take in negotiations. It also

- **helps you to better define your interests**, why are you pursuing this matter in the first place? What concerns are you trying to address?

  The information typically supports initial proposals, as well as the final positions either side may take. To be valuable, the information you gather should support your reasons for advancing a specific proposal. You should conduct this same analysis when assessing the other negotiating team's proposals.

- The **second** function of the information **is to help predict** the other negotiating team's strategy. Proper preparation can give you insights into the issues likely to be raised, how the bargaining may proceed, and where the other party is likely to settle.

In the initial stages of preparation and negotiation, the parties will not necessarily know the settlement positions. An adequate database enables you to respond appropriately to proposals and counter proposals made as the settlement phase nears.

During negotiations, the information can help you maintain momentum. When the other negotiating team puts forward proposals, well-researched replies may demonstrate openness on your part, indicating that you have considered the proposals and made an honest effort to assess them. During the discussion, the information that the other negotiating team presents, and their reaction may help you identify that team's priorities and the real interests underlying their proposals.

When negotiations have concluded, information generated during the negotiation can help convince both negotiating teams' constituents that the agreement the parties have achieved is consistent with their bargaining objectives.

Foundations and the Importance of Understanding

Informed, thoughtful, and thorough preparation for bargaining requires an understanding of six foundational aspects:

- The organization, the **one spoken of** (aspiration statements, senior leadership characterization) and the **one in evidence** through documents, practices and the like (what employees say);
- The **existing** collective agreement;
- Benchmark settlements;
- The organization's **objectives** and limits;

- The **other** negotiating team;
- Why we bargain **the way we** bargain (Chapter 2).

The Organization

Organizations exist to succeed, however that may be defined. To negotiate effectively, the parties involved must be knowledgeable about the objectives, resources, strengths, and weaknesses of the organization concerned. More specifically, negotiators should know the organization's history and its physical and technical characteristics. This requirement applies as much to understanding how the employer is structured as it does to how the union is structured.

With respect to the employer, for example, the most important characteristics that can influence collective bargaining include the following:

- Characteristics of the employer's products or services;
- Nature of the production process or service delivery methods;
- Labour market: Type of employees presently needed and anticipated for the future;
- State of available facilities;
- Product market and/or service area;
- Quality and quantity of management;
- Organizational goals and objectives;
- What is perceived by employees as the employment value proposition (EVP)—the set of attributes that the labour market and employees perceive as the value they gain through employment in an organization. Answers the simple question *why do I work here*?

Knowledge of the history of employee-employer relations is necessary. The historical pattern of negotiations between the union and the employer influences existing relationships considerably. This information can give you useful insights into the current environment.

Understanding the "culture" of the union as an organization and that of the employer is also essential. Organizations have philosophies—fundamental values that define how they operate and do business. The organization's philosophy is the foundation for the operation and the measure against which the organization's actions should be tested. The beliefs, perceptions, attitudes, and values of all the people in an organization form a culture that makes it unique. As mentioned previously in Chapter 1, organizational culture is "the way we do things around here."

As a result, understanding how the union and the employer approach negotiations is another necessary step.

- How does the organization view collective bargaining as a process?

- What is the philosophy with respect to managing employees and, in the union's case, representing employees?

- What is the underlying belief with respect to the role of the union in the workplace, and the way that managers manage?

Understanding the culture of the union and the employer can give you great insight into how negotiations will proceed and how the parties' relationship will continue to evolve.

The Existing Collective Agreement

Collective agreements are periodically negotiated to define and redefine the rewards employees receive for their services, and the conditions under which these services are rendered. Negotiators often find it difficult to draft precise language on all matters. In an attempt to address all the concerns raised when negotiating a complex issue, a measure of imprecise language can emerge.

Vague and ambiguous language may, by bargaining necessity, leave the real question unsettled, creating room for potential misunderstandings and disagreement on the application and interpretation of some provisions during the term of the agreement. Further, the working environment is not static. What was negotiated two or three years ago may be insufficient or inconsistent with today's realities.

Analyzing the strengths and weaknesses of the existing agreement helps you prepare for negotiations. You can organize your analysis of a collective agreement in a number of ways. An analysis should contain cross-referenced descriptions of various clauses that enable you to assess the impact of proposed changes on other sections of the collective agreement. Depending on the complexity of the agreement, you may also wish to have the following information available:

- Historical information from previous rounds of negotiations

- Comparisons of certain clauses in effect in other workplaces
- Experiences with the operation of a clause
- Grievances and the related clauses
    - Interpretation grievance: *we don't agree on what the words mean or how they have been interpreted in making your decision.*
    - Application grievance: *we agree on what the words mean, but we disagree on how they have been applied.*
- Legal issues that pertain to certain clauses.

Benchmark Settlements

Benchmark settlements are precedents or settlement patterns established by other unions, union locals, organizations, and industries or sectors, and about which all negotiators should be well informed.

The Organization's Objectives and Limits

Before entering into negotiations, you need to have a clear understanding of the objectives of your team for the round of bargaining and the reasons for each of your proposals. Further, you need to analyze the other negotiating team's proposals within that context.

When you exchange proposals, they should be analyzed and categorized. One way of initially categorizing the proposals is to code them as follows:

- May result in impasse—**interests in conflict**—a key issue
- Serious issue—**interests potentially** in conflict—a key issue
- Workable issue—apparent **common ground**
- No substantial disagreement—apparent **common ground**—slight wording change
- Rollover of existing language—**parties satisfied** with existing language.

You need to classify each proposal by its relative importance and support it with detailed information. These preliminary classifications may change as the other team's positions are clarified and interests identified. You should also analyze the reasons for the proposal from the other negotiating team's perspective.

As negotiations proceed, you will gain insight into potential areas of agreement. This analysis helps you establish bargaining parameters and limits.

The Other Negotiating Team

To negotiate effectively, you need an understanding of the personal characteristics and attitudes of the other negotiating team's members. This information can give your insight into what they are willing to accept, what their motivation is for various proposals, and what pressures they are operating under. This type of information will also help ensure that members of your team are not surprised or caught off guard by the actions or reactions of the other negotiating team's members or the constituents they represent.

In *Collective Bargaining: How It Works and Why*, Thomas Colosi and Arthur Berkeley observe that on the surface, collective bargaining appears to involve negotiating between two teams—union and employer. There are also internal negotiations. In describing the dynamics within each team, the authors theorize that each team member can be characterized as stabilizers, destabilizers, or quasi-mediators.

- **Stabilizers**—Team members committed to the bargaining table processes and oriented to reaching an agreement. Stabilizers may often be prepared to agree too quickly, in some cases merely to avoid confrontation. While committed to bargaining processes, stabilizers may not be entirely comfortable with them and go along to get along through accommodation, compromise conflict styles, and other like approaches.

- **Destabilizers**—Team members who lack commitment to the bargaining table processes and who may feel more comfortable with self-help techniques (such as meeting with others without the authority of the bargaining team), may engage in disruptive behaviour, and may be unwilling to settle on any terms. They may also feel it necessary to take a hard line, because "that's just the way you negotiate." Destabilizers with this characteristic may become distracted with side issues instead of focussing on the interests the team is there to represent. They typically do not take a long-term view. Destabilizers can however, in some instances, serve a useful purpose by challenging participants to consider other ideas and approaches. It becomes the role of the quasi-mediators to make best use of the destabilizer's interventions and limit any distraction from the matters at hand.

- **Quasi-mediators**—Usually the team leaders who are charged with the responsibility for the success of the negotiation, in terms of both process and substance, and who see their role as harmonizing the interests of the stabilizers (who may too readily concede) and the destabilizers (who may take impractical positions). Although clearly advocates for their side, quasi-mediators are interested in achieving a workable settlement, one that meets the test of a good agreement—one that both sides can live with.

  Quasi-mediators understand that negotiation is communication for the purpose of persuasion and is the pre-eminent mode of dispute settlement. Further, they recognize that negotiation is integral to the ongoing relationship between the union and its members (the employer's employees) and the employer (and its management representatives).

When analyzing the other negotiating team, your understanding of the individual members' backgrounds, beliefs, and particular constituents they represent will help you characterize their participation style on their team. And recognizing that negotiations are conducted both internally and across the table, you can also consider your bargaining team.

> **Remember!** What you say of them is also true of you! Who are the stabilizers, destabilizers, and quasi-mediators on your team? How will they affect your internal negotiations and your negotiations with the other team?

Summarizing the Last Negotiations

Preparation for the next round of negotiations begins as soon as the last round is completed—it is a continuous process. As soon as any round of negotiations has been completed, the following information should be summarized:

- Proposals made by the union:
    - Substantially agreed to by the employer
    - Dropped by the union
    - Resolved through accommodation, compromise (detail the process and substance)
- Proposals made by the employer:

- Substantially agreed to by the union
- Dropped by the employer
- Resolved through accommodation, compromise (detail the process and substance)

- A brief statement of the final settlement and its costs
- A brief statement of the major unresolved issues that remained in the "final round" of negotiations
- Additional comments about the effect the last settlement may have on the next negotiations, including issues certain to reappear
- A determination of how you will collect information during the life of the new agreement as part of your ongoing preparation for the next round

This information can be taken from a variety of sources including the bargaining status worksheets, minutes of the negotiating sessions, and personal notes.

A post mortem after the collective agreement is signed is valuable for future planning. If you seek to continually improve how you negotiate, including your preparation for negotiations, the result will be an improved agreement. With respect to your preparation, determine the following:

- Were we really prepared?
- What worked and what did not?
- What additional information would have helped?
- Were the information-gathering and analysis models accurate and flexible?
- Were constituents informed and engaged at each step in the process?

Conduct a similar analysis of your bargaining team and bargaining table processes. The key is to learn each time you negotiate and use what you learn to improve your results.

Outreach to Inform

Collective bargaining is a representative process. There are a variety of ways unions and employers inform themselves about the matters at issue as the foundation to develop bargaining objectives, proposals and determine their relative priority. These include on-line resources, meetings, focus groups and questionnaires like the following. It is important to remember, however, that *asking* can raise expectations. A representative, transparent outreach process is required.

Figure 15: Union Bargaining Questionnaire

The Bargaining Committee will use this questionnaire to determine bargaining priorities for the negotiations with our Employer. All individual responses will remain confidential within the Bargaining Committee. (Source: BC Government & Service Employees' Union (BCGEU) Bargaining Questionnaire, 2019)

Classification: _____ ☐ **Regular Full-time** ☐ **Regular Part-time** ☐ **Casual**
Work Location _____ **Number of dependents** _____

Please identify your top 5 bargaining priorities and rate in order of importance (choose one option only):

1. **Please Specify:** _____ **Must Have** _____
   Should Have _____
   Like to Have _____

2. **Please Specify:** _____ **Must Have** _____
   Should Have _____
   Like to Have _____

3. **Please Specify:** _____ **Must Have** _____
   Should Have _____
   Like to Have _____

4. **Please Specify:** _____ **Must Have** _____
   Should Have _____
   Like to Have _____

5. **Please Specify:** _____ **Must Have** _____
   Should Have _____
   Like to Have _____

Identify your most important issue and include any additional comments regarding your bargaining priorities:
_____
_____
_____

> **Is there any language in the current collective agreement that has been a problem or that you would like to see changed? Why?**
>
> _____
>
> _____
>
> _____
>
> **Are there any other issues that you would like the bargaining committee to be aware of? Please be specific.**
>
> _____
>
> _____
>
> _____

Understand the Issues, Understand Your Audience

It is important to remember that the negotiation or renegotiation of a collective agreement is not top of mind for most people. Many are unfamiliar with bargaining generally, the history and progression of bargaining in their place of work, and the bargaining environment of the current round. Some only become interested and to varying degrees active when there seems to be a crisis at hand—strike, lockout, or debate over a matter considered central to an agreement. Social media increasingly becomes the source for information and the *truth* about bargaining and the *other side*.

You can never over communicate. Make a purposeful effort to put the current round of bargaining in context and describe what your objectives are and how they came to be your area of focus. Use this foundation resource as the background for your communications efforts as bargaining progresses, in some cases for months. Because we all learn and absorb information differently use a variety of communication vehicles and media.

Ultimately you will be judged on the agreement achieved and the process used to achieve it. Make sure you *bring you side along with you* on the journey to an agreement through effective, concise, accurate and timely information.

Considering Probable Demands and Costs

From a strategic perspective, the identification of potential demands of the other party assists in planning. You may be able to identify probable demands by analyzing the following aspects:

- Issues **dropped by either party** or that remained unresolved from previous rounds of collective bargaining.

- **Trends** in collective bargaining nationally, provincially, locally or in the industry or sector.

- Issues raised, and **remarks made frequently** during union-management interactions or the grievance process during the year.

    - Reasons for the other party asking that a particular item be raised in collective bargaining. Using your analysis of the relationship between the parties and the activities during the term of the collective agreement, consider what has happened in the external environment, as well as in the organization, to create issues that, from the union's perspective, require provisions in a collective agreement.

- "Position papers," which some employers/employer associations and/or larger unions issue, highlighting what to expect. You can secure these documents directly from the union, industry/sectoral associations of employers, or labour information services; union newsletters or information bulletins may also **help in identifying** potential issues.

When you have considered the points listed above, you can begin to assess the potential cost of having to address these items in a collective agreement.

- What are the direct costs?

- What are the indirect costs, and how might they change management's current ability to organize and direct the workforce?

- In addition, how might they change management's ability to organize and direct the workforce based on expectations of future circumstances?

Developing Bargaining Objectives

When developing bargaining objectives and proposals, the General Negotiation Framework (GNF) is a helpful organizer. It illustrates the difference between the two types of objectives and bargaining proposals. The GNF is the foundation for the negotiation and is developed against a particular backdrop. This backdrop establishes the general parameters for bargaining. The parameters include a statutory component—the rules under which bargaining will occur—and a contextual component—relevant background, environment, and conditions.

Figure 16: General Negotiation Framework

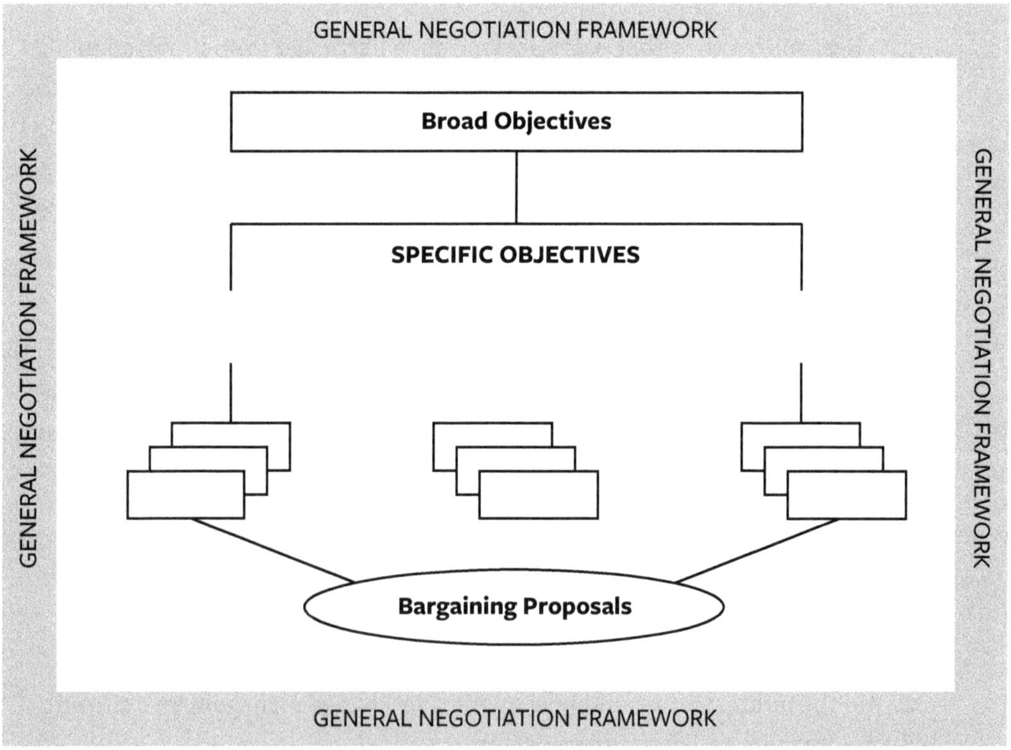

Bargaining teams establish objectives concerning what they seek to accomplish. Interests (why they seek to accomplish that objective) are embedded in the objectives. An objective is a statement of desired outcomes, or a statement of what your settlement will contain. An objective is not a position but is rather the rationale for your position.

To develop bargaining objectives, follow these steps:

1. Understand the *business* you are in. Review the organization's business plan and strategic objectives. Through your input and advice-gathering process, determine how the terms and conditions of employment affect the organization's current and future direction.

2. Seek input from those in the organization affected by or responsible for administering the collective agreement. The collective agreement needs to support and not inhibit the organization's strategic direction.

   When you are seeking input during this initial stage, you should include all conceivable objectives, even those that appear to have questionable merit. At this stage, focus on developing a list, not on evaluating each item. It is better to eliminate trivial or improper items from the final list than to overlook important items during your initial discussions. When discussed, seemingly trivial issues may lead to the development of significant and constructive objectives.

   Preparation for collective bargaining is a continuous process. As a result, and in order to keep current on collective agreement issues, those who work most closely with the collective agreement should keep notes during the life of the agreement. Make note of clauses or situations that demonstrate the following characteristics:

   - Interfere with efficient operations
   - Are costly
   - Unduly limit the ability to act
   - Result in unproductive conflict, excessive grievances
   - Are unclear or ambiguous in meaning
   - Violate current statutes governing employment
   - Are incompatible with the strategic direction of a specific group, department or the organization as a whole

   Clauses such as those described above should never be bargained in an initial agreement. Where they exist, make consistent attempts to modify or eliminate them.

3. Compile a list of possible clauses that are not contained or are inadequate in the present agreement—from an employer perspective for example, clauses that:

   - Unduly limit the exercise of discretion

- Address skill, ability, and provisions related to selection and assignment
- Impact your ability to organize and direct the workforce

4. Analyze all of the grievances during the life of the present agreement by:
    - Department or service area
    - Type of grievance (interpretation or application)
    - Contract clause or clauses involved
    - Final disposition

    If the matter was resolved through arbitration, analyze what the result was and how the result has impacted the collective agreement.

    Also review arbitration awards that have resulted from disputes involving other collective agreements and that have been published during the term of your agreement. These awards may impact the interpretation or application of provisions in your current agreement.

5. Prepare a list of contract violations, if any, on the part of the union or any of its members during the life of the present agreement.

6. Focus on the future. When preparing for negotiations, some negotiators simply take a retrospective approach. They fashion their proposals in response to what has happened and seek to modify the collective agreement to deal only with these past issues. However, taking a prospective view is recommended.

    > Consider the future—how does your organization intend to positively influence the future? How do you align the organization's objectives and goals with the collective agreement as it is currently written? How will it have to be amended to deal with future challenges, changes, and business opportunities? Note the degree and if at all.

7. Establish a set of overall broad objectives based on your discussions and research. These broad objectives are general statements that commit you to specific purposes. As the specific objectives and proposals are developed, the meaning of these statements will become clear. These statements are consistent with and support the organization's mission (why the organization exists) and its strategic direction or initiatives.

8. Establish specific objectives by article or section of the current collective agreement that are necessary to achieve your broad objectives. These specific objectives

should support the overall broad objectives described in the previous step, since they will be the basis of your proposals. Consider these objectives as concrete illustrations of the types of outcomes that would satisfy your overall broad objectives. Table 4 lists examples of specific objectives.

9. Revisit the objectives you have developed and reflect. What are they in aid of? What are the interests you are trying to satisfy? What interests are your priorities?

Table 7: Example of Broad Objectives

1. Recognize changing technology and the need for continuous upgrading skills in the workplace.
2. Achieve a balance between the rights of employees and the responsibility of the employer, such that the employer has the flexibility to meet changing market demands.
3. Ensure that compensation conforms to industry practices.
4. Establish mechanisms to facilitate the ongoing improvement of union-management relations, including a mechanism for the expeditious settlement of disputes.
5. Establish uniform language throughout the agreement and better organize the clauses to ensure clarity of application.

Table 8: Example of Specific Objectives

Article	Objective
Articles 14 and 15, Hours of Work	Establish processes that permit the alteration of shifts based on established criteria related to the production schedule and business cycle.
Article 19, Grievance Procedure	Employ procedures that reduce employees' downtime resulting from the time needed to process disputes.
Article 25, Overtime Pay	Overtime assignments/work based on skills required and the availability of employees; expedite process for assignment of overtime shifts.
Article 65, Recall Procedure	Reduce the number of moves necessary to accomplish the recall procedure. Be able to predict, in advance of call-back, employees able and qualified to fill a position.
Article 12, Vacation Pay	Define the time allowable and the period in which vacation will be taken, with consideration given to production schedules.
Article 77, Lead Hands	Select lead hands by supervisory potential, technical skills required in the work area, and related post-secondary coursework.

Note: Your objectives are not the proposals that you will exchange at the bargaining table. Your overall broad objectives delineate how you will measure your success at the bargaining table. The specific objectives detail how you will measure your success with respect to a particular section or clause. Underlying each of your proposals are the desired outcomes you are seeking to achieve by advancing a specific proposition—your specific objectives in the context of your overall broad objectives.

Developing Bargaining Proposals: For what problem is this the solution?

> *It isn't that they can't see the solution.*
> *It is that they can't see the problem.*[27]
>
> —G. K. Chesterton

Once you have developed your overall broad objectives and your specific objectives, you can then prepare your bargaining proposals. Hold meetings with your constituents to review the final list of matters to be advanced at the bargaining table as proposals (in the form consistent with your approach to bargaining).

Proposals will have varying degrees of importance. Some will be considered essential and important enough to become serious issues. Under certain circumstances, you may present proposals calculated to offset the demands of the other side based on your analysis of probable demands. However, no proposal should be ridiculous or without merit. All proposals should make sense to those who are required to administer and manage the collective agreement, even if some proposals are of lesser weight than others. Your opening proposals are where you start. Where you finish is not likely going to be where you started! The concessions, compromises, and general back and forth of bargaining finally produce an agreement. In the process, each party usually drops some issues entirely, concedes some issues, and modifies its views on other issues to produce a certain division of the objective each anticipates. Proposals need to be crafted in such a way so as to recognize this dynamic.

Your proposals should incorporate into the collective agreement all written supplementary agreements reached since the last round of negotiations—unless, of course, such agreements are considered undesirable. Informal understandings of past practice may also be incorporated if desired. Identify all proposals you intend to make by article, section, and clause. Some will be written out in full; some may indicate only words to be changed, and some may simply indicate "clarification needed." In this latter case, you are indicating that these provisions will be the subject of discussion and possible wording changes in later negotiating sessions.

Negotiating teams use a variety of ways to present their proposals, for example:

1. Actual language—presentation of a specific provision or clause as that provision or clause would appear in the new collective agreement.[28]

---

27 G. K. Chesterton (29 May 1874–14 June 1936), was an English writer, poet, philosopher, dramatist, journalist, orator, lay theologian, biographer, and literary and art critic.

28 Note the *As Written Dilemma*: When you write proposals as contract language the more invested you become in the exact wording. You can create an anchor of sorts. You know what

2. List of elements—a list of specific ideas, concepts, provisions that the negotiating team wants included in a newly negotiated provision.

3. General statement—broad general statement identifying an issue of concern on which negotiations will be conducted.

The method chosen will be consistent with the orientation you adopt. As noted earlier, *we are influenced by our frames of reference and how we see the world, our view of power, authority, and what we believe specific interactions to be about. Taken together, a general orientation emerges that informs our approach to potentially contentious discourse, as well as the approach we adopt to reconcile matters at issue. Orientations can be placed in one of three general frames—maximalist positioning, equitable positioning or the integrative approach.*

The three orientations give rise to one of two approaches to reconciling matters at issue: distributive—dividing up a resource or array of resources that parties have identified—or integrative, integrating across multiple issues to create new sources of value. Often, what looks distributive is in fact integrative, as there may be additional issues that can be added to the discussion.

No matter what method is chosen, negotiating teams must ensure they choose the presentation method that provides them with the best strategic advantage and that most clearly identifies the item to be negotiated and the issues of importance to their team.

It is also important to remember that the form and substance of what you propose has implications for how you engage your constituents and the consequences that flow from that engagement. What does bargaining success look like concerning progress at the table? Why were certain proposals dropped and others amended? What will be the subject of ratification and how does that relate to what we were seeking to achieve in the first place?

Do You Really Need to Make a Proposal?

Sometimes, the most difficult task is deciding whether or not to introduce certain proposals. Suppose your agreement contains no clause covering "contracting out work" or "hiring and assigning seasonal replacement employees." Ordinarily, the absence of such clauses would mean that managers or administrators have reasonable freedom of action in these areas. If the absence of these clauses has not caused problems in the past, it might be a serious mistake to propose them. Their inclusion along with other proposals might open a discussion that leads to serious negotiation difficulties.

---

you intend, why you chose the words, the nuances, the subtleties and the like.

The introduction of such a clause may also be taken as a recognition that you do not have the right to act and therefore are seeking it through negotiation. Also, remember that in general, each time management and union bargain a new provision in an agreement, management discretion in directing the functions of the operation is further limited.

Some members of management misunderstand the concept of management rights.[29] Some erroneously consider that they cannot manage unless what they want to do is spelled out in the collective agreement. A management rights clause by itself is not an accurate guide as to the areas in which the employer can act unilaterally and those in which his actions are abridged by the terms of the agreement. For this, one must consider the agreement in its entirety.

For example, a management rights clause which states that the employer shall have the "right to promote" may be circumscribed by job posting and seniority provisions and, more significantly, by an arbitration procedure which extends to any and all disputes between the employer and the union.

The management rights clause is probably of greatest significance in disputes over issues on which the agreement is otherwise silent. In such cases, this clause serves as tangible evidence to the arbitrator that the issue was meant to remain the prerogative of the employer. It is also believed to be of educational value for those who are concerned with the daily administration of the collective agreement.

Generally, you should follow the principle that you have all rights to manage that are not restricted by the collective agreement or by a longstanding practice.

Assessing the Bargaining Climate

Collective agreements are not negotiated in isolation. Collective bargaining is one of the integral activities in the ongoing union-management relationship. Participants in collective bargaining should monitor the environment to find clues about likely concerns. For example:

- Does the culture of the organization, and the way that people work within that culture, give you an insight into how the negotiations will proceed?

- What is the employer's philosophy with respect to managing employees, and in the union's case, what is the philosophy with respect to representing employees?

---

29 Referred to as *management rights, inherent rights,* and *residual rights*. A shorthand expression for the principle, applied in the interpretation of collective agreements, is that any rights that the employer has not expressly bargained away in the agreement are retained by management.

- What is the underlying belief of the parties with respect to the role of the union in the workplace and to the way that managers manage?

- How do the parties view collective bargaining as a process?

- Are specific issues emerging as questions or areas of concern?

- Is a "message" being sent by an increase in workplace conflict and formal grievances?

- Are certain workplace issues more difficult to resolve or remain largely unresolved?

To help you confirm that you have gathered the information you will need in preparing for negotiations, see Resource Two: Collective Bargaining Process (CBP) Checklist: Sample Checklist.

CHAPTER 4

Choosing a Negotiating Team

Consider your organization's reason for being, its mission and its vision of the future. A team that understands the organization and is representative of it is essential. Individual skill sets, roles they have and where should be considered as well as their standing among their management colleagues. As negotiations proceed, more likely than not these individuals will be called upon to explain the negotiation process and progress. A negotiating team may be selected at different times during the preparation phase, depending on the needs of the parties. Notwithstanding other specific considerations, you will have to make decisions about the following:

- Number of members required

- Personal attributes that are most desirable

- Individual who would best serve as the spokesperson at negotiations

- Role of individual team members

Number of Team Members

The number of members you choose depends on the size and resources of the organization being represented. The size of the negotiating team can contribute to determining the final outcome of negotiations. In general, many who have been involved in collective bargaining find that bargaining teams composed of more than five members tend to be difficult to control and not conducive to promoting an effective and timely agreement. Since negotiations are also conducted within the bargaining team itself, a larger team is likely to result in more areas of dispute, requiring extended internal negotiation.

Personal Attributes of Team Members

The size of a negotiating team is not nearly as critical as the quality of the members selected. The personalities and skill set of the members may influence the number of members actually needed.

The process of negotiating a collective agreement depends on the values, judgement, and skills of the individual negotiators. The ideal negotiator has the following attributes:

- A **value system** that includes personal integrity, credibility, courage, and a genuine belief in collective bargaining as an effective method of jointly making decisions and reconciling conflicting interests.

- A sound **sense of judgement** derived from thorough knowledge of the essential facts relevant to the interests of the parties, and of the pressures influencing both parties, including an understanding of each party's constituents.

- Specific skills, including the ability to speak and write clearly, to be a patient listener, to be creative, to inspire confidence by making **sound and reasoned** decisions, and to differentiate interests from stated positions, seeking opportunities for mutual gain.

- An **understanding** of the underlying reasons for each proposal, and of how those proposals relate to other proposals and to the organization's overall strategic direction.

- **Foresight** in thinking of all possible contingencies; ability to recognize possible consequences of decisions when choosing a course of action; ability to anticipate problems; effectiveness in taking preventive action.

- An understanding of the **union-employer relationship**. Does the relationship provide a foundation for productive bargaining through constructive dialogue and exchange of views? Do bargaining norms, experiences and expectations lead the parties to bargain positionally (maximalist, equitable positioners) or in a more integrative manner?

- Appreciation of the existence of **varied constituent groups** on both sides and the variety of interests and motivations resident in them.

While few individuals possess all of these attributes, you can frequently choose a team whose members demonstrate many of them.

Qualities of the Spokesperson

After selecting the negotiating team, you need to select a spokesperson. A spokesperson must have the attributes of a "quasi-mediator." A spokesperson must be capable of coordinating the team's presentation, dealing effectively and decisively with the other negotiating team, and providing control and direction of his or her team at all times.

Spokespersons must be just as effective in negotiating at the bargaining table as they are in negotiating internally with their bargaining team and constituents. To be effective, spokespersons should know how far they can go and have the authority to deal informally with members of the other negotiating team if the opportunity arises.

Bargaining Roles

Your negotiating team must agree on the internal bargaining protocol and the role each team member will play during bargaining meetings. The team must also establish ground rules for how it will function so that it operates as a team.

In determining each member's strengths/role, consider who best fulfills the following:

- Subject matter expert(s)
- Bargaining procedure expert(s)
- Spokesperson(s)
- Constituent liaison responsible for progress reports and information sharing
- Leader/facilitator
- Lead record keeper; each team member should keep their own notes and be alive to body language and other non-verbal cues
- Keeper of CB Resource 4: Working Resource—editor/language expert
- Financial and related numbers expert

Experienced members of union and employer negotiating teams have their own "language," their own set of cues and signals, to let their fellow members know when a caucus is needed or when the person talking is heading into a potentially contentious area. Similarly, a team should agree in advance whether the spokesperson will do all the talking at the bargaining table, or whether specific team members will answer questions directed to them. The degree of team member's interaction with the other team's members while at the table will be largely dependent on which one of the three bargaining orientations is in evidence. Position-based approaches are more restrictive and controlled than integrative ones.

As a general rule, the fewer who speak at the bargaining table, the less the likelihood of conflict and contradiction. Negotiating has its own vocabulary and code words, and the wrong message can easily be sent inadvertently. Not only should your negotiating team function smoothly but also, more importantly, the other team should see it as operating in a coherent, coordinated, and focused manner. Smooth functioning can only happen if your team members define their roles, discuss and agree on an internal communication protocol, and work together in a common direction.

CHAPTER 5

Organizing Information During Bargaining

Proper organization of data and effective use of information during negotiations will prevent unnecessary delays, confusion, and mistakes, and will help to successfully conclude negotiations. Negotiators use a variety of methods to organize the data they believe to be most useful during negotiations. The following systems for organizing data have proven effective:

- CB Resource 1: Contextual Data/Information Resource
- CB Resource 2: Historical Clause Development
- CB Resource 3: Proposal—Counter Proposal—Agreed in Principle Resource
- CB Resource 4: Working Resource
- CB Resource 5: Bargaining Status Worksheet
- CB Resource 6: Bargaining Notes or Minutes

For the purpose of this section, we are discussing the organization of information in terms of hard copy. The information can be organized in hard copy, soft copy, or a combination of both. Searchable resources and databases are preferable to written, printed documents.

CB Resource 1: Contextual Data/Information Resource

CB Resource 1: Contextual Data/Information Resource is a compendium of information relevant to employment and in particular collective bargaining. Separated in an easy to access, searchable format it contains all of the back-up data needed in negotiations including:

- Pay and benefit surveys in the following categories:
    - National, territorial, provincial, and local
    - Industry or sector

- Competition
- Other settlements
- Cost of living data
- Workforce distribution by the following categories:
    - Seniority
    - Age and gender
    - Pay grades or wage scale
    - Job classification
    - Length of service
    - Shifts, work location
- Internal economic data
    - Average straight-time hourly rate, or where applicable, annual salary
    - Cost of benefits in cents per hour
    - Participation in benefits plans
    - Average gross earnings
    - Average overtime earnings
    - Sick leave usage; absence statistics

Detail human resource practices and processes, for example:

- Promotion procedure
- Leave practices
- Evaluations, achievement and growth plans
- Professional development, skills currency and development; maintenance/achievement of designations
- Scheduling procedure

In certain jurisdictions and typically in the public sector, codified public policy requirements may alter:

- Pay:
    - Maximum increase permitted
    - Minimum pay required
- Benefits:
    - Maximum increase permitted
    - Minimum benefits required with respect to health and welfare, statutory and related holidays, vacations, life insurance, sick pay, and termination pay

You may wish to include supporting documents relating to each subject in CB Resource 1. This resource is used constantly during negotiations to support the employer's positions.

CB Resource 2: Historical Clause Development

CB Resource 2 consists of the sections of the existing and previous collective agreements, side by side. Some section or article numbers are likely to change with each negotiation, so identifying the agreement by the year in which each section appears is recommended. Each page of this resource contains a clause from the present agreement and similar clauses from preceding agreements, as shown in the following table:

Table 9: CB Resource 2

Most Recent	Previous Negotiation	Previous Negotiation
Article 10	Article 10	Article 10
An employee's name shall be removed from the seniority list and the payroll of the Employer in the event he or she is: (a) terminated, or (b) laid off for a period that exceeds the amount of seniority he/she has acquired at the time of layoff, or five (5) years, whichever is the lesser; but in no case shall an employee lose his/her seniority due to layoff of less than one (1) year.	An employee's name shall be removed from the seniority list and the Active Payroll Schedule of the Employer in the event he or she is: (a) terminated, or (b) laid off for a period longer than one (1) year, except that employees actively employed on or after the effective date of this Agreement will retain their seniority, if laid off after such effective date, for a period of two (2) years or for a period equal to their length of service at the time of layoff, whichever is lesser.	An employee's name shall be removed from the seniority list and the Active Payroll Schedule of the Employer in the event he or she is: (a) terminated, or (b) laid off for a period longer than one (1) year.

CB Resource 3: Proposal-Counter Proposal-Agreed in Principle Resource (P-CP-AiP)

CB Resource 3: P-CP-AiP Resource includes proposals and articles agreed to in principle, is a storage system with tabs by article or section for each clause being negotiated. This system may be provided at the start of negotiations to the principal employer and union negotiators.

Each employer- and union-written proposal, as presented or modified, is dated and inserted in chronological order in the appropriate section. As the parties reach agreement, each party initials and dates two copies (one for each team) of the final agreed-on clause. These final copies become the new agreement.

CB Resource 4: Working Resource

This working resource comprises initial proposals and current collective agreement language and is prepared as soon as proposals have been exchanged. Both management and union proposals are arranged in the order of the current agreement. Four types of information are arranged from left to right as follows:

- Identification of clause or section
- Current language in the collective agreement
- Union proposal
- Employer proposal

Arranging the proposals in this way allows you to easily and readily examine proposed changes to the agreement, as shown in the following table.

Table 10: CB Resource 4

Clause	Current Language	Union Proposal	Employer Proposal
Article 1:12, Access to Work Site	Representatives of the Union will report to the site office prior to conducting Union business.	Representatives of the Union shall have access to **each work site during working hours**.	Roll over.

As the negotiation progresses, counterproposals will be made. File these counterproposals chronologically in CB Resource 3. CB Resource 4 and 5 will become the two key documents during bargaining. To be effective tools, they must be organized and current.

CB Resource 5: Bargaining Status Worksheet

Collective bargaining can be a long process. The Bargaining Status Worksheet can help to summarize the progress to date, as shown in the following table:

Table 11: CB Resource 5

Clause	Name	U/M	Proposal	Status	Comment
1:3	Membership Requirement	U	Mandatory union membership	To be discussed next week	
1:7A	Right to Representation	U		Agreed (date)	New language
1:11	Bulletin Boards	U/M	Roll over	Agreed (date)	
7:3	Parental Leave	U	One day (paid) as counter- proposal	To be discussed with monetary package	Subject to costing

Leave sufficient space for brief notes. All references to proposals should be in informal language, since these are simply worksheets. Issue copies to each person at the bargaining table. As negotiations progress, negotiators make their own notes. As unsettled items are reduced, new sets of worksheets may be issued from time to time. These sheets provide quick reference to remaining unresolved items at any time.

Many negotiators think that copies of worksheets should not be provided to the other team's negotiators, because many proposals will be lost in the back and forth of negotiations toward the end of the process. They contend that worksheets will serve as a constant reminder to the other team of unresolved items.

Each negotiating team is responsible for managing its bargaining agenda and for ensuring that each of its initiatives is dealt with in one of three ways:

- Negotiating and reaching agreement
- Withdrawing the item
- Negotiating the item to impasse and then taking the necessary actions

Ensure that each subject or article advanced by your team is dealt with and conclusion is brought to each article or subject.

As noted earlier, the following categorization is a handy way to classify both employer and union proposals:

a) May result in impasse—conflict of interests—a key issue

b) Serious issue—potential conflict of interests—a key issue

c) Workable issue—apparent common ground

d) No substantial disagreement—apparent common ground—slight wording change

e) Rollover of existing language—parties satisfied with existing provisions

CB Resource 6: Bargaining Notes or Minutes

A member of your negotiating team should be responsible for keeping the bargaining notes or minutes of each meeting. Keeping verbatim minutes using tape recordings or stenographers is not common and not necessary.

Nevertheless, a brief but accurate (and dated) record of what transpired and who attended should be kept for each session. These chronological notes should include:

- Subjects discussed, and who discussed them
- Articulated positions and understandings
- The parties' expressed intentions
- Chance remarks that indicate the interests underlying a party's positions
- Verbal commitments
- All other relevant information
- Are interests emerging or becoming clarified?

The individual designated to keep minutes must be a keen listener and observer of people's actions and reactions. He or she must be able to grasp the subtleties and implications of negotiating, as well as be familiar with the bargaining process and with the proposals that his or her team puts forward.

Not only are these minutes valuable as a reference during bargaining, but also, during the term of the agreement, they may assist in settling subsequent disputes over the meaning or intent of a provision. Bargaining notes are often used in arbitration cases as evidence of the meaning of a provision.

It is neither necessary nor desirable to provide the other team with copies of your minutes or to obtain their approval of the minutes.

Points to Remember When Taking Notes

- During each meeting record the:
    - Purpose (meeting with the union, employer preparation meeting, mediation etc.)
    - Date
    - Meeting number
    - Place the meeting held
    - Employer's committee members in attendance and absent
    - Union's committee members in attendance and absent
    - Time the meeting starts and ends
- Identify every speaker and ensure that the notes clearly identify the topic (e.g., on page 8 under 7.3) and the ensuing conversation
- Identify the title of the language or proposal and the time it is exchanged. Record whether the document was given/received by the union. Write this information on the proposal/documents exchanged as well as in the notes
- Identify when a caucus occurs and when bargaining resumes
- Identify when a committee member leaves and returns
- Identify the name and title of resource people brought into negotiations, the purpose of their involvement, and the time in and out
- Use something to differentiate employer and union documents when exchanging documents; different coloured paper for example (e.g., employer always uses blue)
- While at least one person should be designated as the note taker, it is helpful if others take notes as well since it can be difficult to capture all of the detail.

CHAPTER 6
Costing Proposals and Determining Wage Criteria

Costing the Proposals

No standard methodology is used to cost collective agreement proposals. However, you should ensure that you are costing proposals on the basis of total compensation, which refers to remuneration including salary and benefits received by an employee from an employer. The costs fall typically into two categories:

- **Direct costs**—costs directly attributable to a negotiated item. For example, the direct cost of a wage increase is the increase in wage payments

- **Impact or "roll-up" costs**—costs that result from a negotiated increase in direct costs—for example, the increase in vacation costs resulting from a wage increase

Although more difficult to quantify, some costs that result from new provisions in the collective agreement require management to adjust policies, procedures, and certain management practices. These adjustments may impact efficiency or productivity or entail additional supervisory resources.

The objective of costing is to provide factual information conducive to meaningful negotiations. Consider the following guidelines:

- Keep the costing method as simple as possible. Whenever assumptions you make, you should clearly identify them

- Present a fully costed position statement early in the negotiations. Doing so helps to achieve some consistency between the two parties on terminology and methodology

- Although you can estimate many of the initial costs, use greater precision as negotiations progress

Both parties should have a clear understanding of the language and costing methodology. They will then be able to concentrate on substantive bargaining issues, as opposed to procedural issues.

Views differ on the value or type of costing procedures. Many employers are reluctant to make relevant data available to unions, while some unions contend that the costing of contract proposals is simply a sophisticated bargaining device and view the costing with skepticism. Depending on the nature of the relationship and in an effort to be constructive, there is an advantage for the parties to operate from a *common knowledge base* when it comes to compensation and related matters. Ideally this resource or Analytic Frame can be developed before negotiations and used as required during them.

Determining Wage Criteria

Wages constitute one of the basic issues in any round of negotiations. Both the union and the employer use a variety of criteria to justify a particular wage increase, though neither party uses a single criterion for this purpose.

Consider the following four issues when examining wages:

1. Comparability of wage rates
2. Productivity
3. Ability to pay
4. Cost of living

Comparability of Wage Rates

Wage comparisons require the parties to look at what is being paid elsewhere to ensure "equal pay for equal work." Unfortunately, the problems associated with securing agreement from the parties about which particular comparisons are valid are by no means easy to resolve, for a number of reasons:

- The content of job classifications designated by the same job title varies widely among employers
- Comparability of wage rates is impaired by variations in the method of wage payment
- The effects of regularity of employment must be assessed in defining comparable wage rates

- The terms and conditions of employment typically include a variety of benefits in addition to the stated wage rate

- Geographic implications must be considered, e.g., working in Vancouver is more expensive than Prince George

Productivity

As is the case with wage comparisons, discussions about productivity (output per person-hour) frequently stir up emotions during wage negotiations. In fact, some advocate that productivity alone should provide the basis for establishing wage or salary increases. Attempts to use a change in productivity to justify a particular change in wage rates generally involve the following complications:

- The rate of change in productivity in the economic system varies widely among the component segments

- The measurement of productivity presents one of the more difficult problems of economic analysis, econometrics, and statistical measurements

- Between any two periods, output per person-hour may vary as a result of many factors, some of which are quite distinct from the services that employees provide

Ability to Pay

Both parties have frequently found it useful to justify their positions on the basis of the employer's ability or inability to pay. The application of this criterion is highly subjective, raising many questions, for example:

- Which period should apply with respect to ability to pay?

- How should the effect of wage-rate changes on costs be estimated?

- How does the character of competition in the markets in which the products must be sold affect the ability to pay wage increases? What constitutes a reasonable rate of return on investment for a particular organization?

- Is it appropriate to use income before or after-tax deductions in defining ability to pay?

- What do interest arbitration awards indicate with respect to ability to pay (particularly in the public sector)?

Some argue that the ability to pay for some things and not others is a choice. The negotiated outcomes will determine which choice is made.

Cost of Living

Union negotiators frequently argue that compensation for the other two criteria described above should come after wages have been adjusted to reflect changes in the purchasing power of the dollar. In practice, the cost-of-living criterion presents the following difficulties:

- Accurate measurement of changes in the cost of living is difficult

- The selection of an appropriate base period or starting point for adjusting wages is a controversial subject. Disagreement will likely arise over the issue of whether former wages were properly adjusted.

- Automatic adjustment of certain wage rates to allow for changes in the cost of living may be inappropriate where former wages were "over-adjusted," productivity has been falling, or a particular company no longer has the ability to pay for such an adjustment.

How do you cost proposals or an agreement? An approach to consider:

Have a Standard Set of Definitions

1. *Total Labour Cost:* All wage or salary payments, plus wage-impacted and non-wage-impacted benefits, for a given bargaining unit. Total Labour Costs include basic pay, incentive payments, paid time off, allowances, premiums, and employer contributions to pensions and health and welfare benefits for regular, auxiliary, or casual work. Total Labour Costs also encompass "backfill" wages and benefit costs for absent employees as well as non-negotiable statutory payments such as CPP/QPP, EI, and Worker's Compensation.

2. *End Cost:* The "annualized" cost of all changes to the collective agreement over the term of that agreement. For example, a 2% benefit decrease and a 2% wage increase have an end cost of 0%.

3. *Actual Cost:* The cost of a change to the collective agreement from the effective date through to the end of the collective agreement year in which it came into effect.

For example, a 2% wage increase effective in the middle of the first year of an agreement would have an actual cost of 1%.

4. *Incremental Cost:* The additional or incremental cost that arises as a result of a change to a collective agreement. Costs in each collective agreement year are determined on the basis of change to the total labour cost compensation base at the beginning of that collective agreement year relative to the end of that year.

Develop Costing Principles

Consistency—be able to demonstrate:

- End costs;
- Actual costs; and,
- Incremental costs in each year of the proposed settlement.

Transparency—costing must capture all changes to total labour cost that arise out of a settlement (on an end and actual cost basis):

- Identify any changes to a collective agreement that may have cost impacts following the expiry of the agreement and estimate and include those costs in its costing
- All settlement changes that may have cost implications but are not included in a formal costing should be noted with a brief explanation.

Comparability—Compensation base and related assumptions must be clear:

- Cost changes should be calculated assuming constant service volume and employee seniority (i.e., incremental costs assumed to be constant) unless specific changes in agreement language related to these issues will have cost impacts. Where the changes will have cost impacts, these impacts must be explained and included in the costing.
- Where staffing levels are seasonal, the average wage calculation should be based on expected average staff levels throughout the year rather than the staff level at a particular point in time.
- Changes in the compensation base resulting from demographic changes should not be included in collective agreement costing, unless required as a result of negotiated changes to salary grids, etc.

Standard Methodology for Identified Cost-Related Matters

1. Compensation Trade-offs—costing of proposed savings must use realistic and conservative assumptions. Costing should clearly identify these assumptions, the base data on which the savings are calculated, and an adequate explanation of how the savings will be generated, including proposed collective agreement language changes.

2. Wage-impacted Costs—the settlement costs for each year of a proposed agreement include the impact of all wage and benefit changes on total labour costs. The effect of wage increases on statutory and non-statutory wage impacted benefits must also be included in costing. Examples of wage-impacted benefits include long-term disability benefits, pension plan premiums, and statutory benefit costs such as EI, CPP/QPP and Worker's Compensation coverage.

3. Lump-sum Payments—Lump sum or other one-time payments must be included in employer bargaining agent costing but are not included in the compensation base as they do not increase ongoing compensation costs.

4. Non-wage Impacted Benefits—Benefits that are not affected by changes to wages (e.g., medical services plans, dental, extended health benefit plan premiums) are assumed to remain constant for the purposes of costing, unless the language in the agreement changes the cost of the benefits.

5. Business Reimbursement—Exclude proposed changes to business reimbursement allowances (e.g., meal and mileage allowances, safety equipment reimbursement) in costing, provided that the treatment of the changes is consistent with applicable provincial, territorial or federal legislation and standards, uses defensible assumptions (e.g., estimates of cost of living increases), and are likely to be of limited consequence.

6. Targeted Adjustments—Wage or benefit adjustments that are targeted at a particular group or subset of a bargaining unit (e.g., labour market adjustments targeted at particular occupations) must be identified and distinguished from general adjustments and costed separately.

7. Training Allowances, Professional Development—Training and the like that are considered compensatory should be included in costing where:

   - There is a fixed dollar allocation per employee
   - The allowance is not provided on the basis of reimbursement

Allowances are generally not considered compensatory and need not be included in costing where the allowance is not allocated on a per employee basis and employers approve the purpose of the development activity and where the allowance is provided on a reimbursement basis.

CHAPTER 7

Crafting Collective Agreement Language

Subjects of Collective Bargaining

Thousands of collective agreements are in effect in Canada at any time. Although they relate to specific groups of employees and workplaces, they have the following basic similarities:

- Layout—Like most legal contracts, collective agreements are divided into articles (sections or clauses) and sub clauses

- Purpose—Most agreements begin with a statement of purpose

- Definitions—A complex agreement includes a list of definitions used in the agreement

- Groups of clauses—The body of the agreement comprises groups of clauses or articles

Groups of clauses or articles can be grouped as follows:

Group 1: These clauses set out the **definition of the bargaining unit**, outlining management rights and union security, establishing a grievance arbitration procedure, and covering related topics.

Group 2: These clauses **specify hours of work and details of pay**—what is termed the "wage-effort bargain." They define the length of the workday, overtime provisions, rights to time off with or without pay, wage schedules covering different classifications of employees, and similar topics.

Group 3: These clauses define how the internal labour market and production, services provision **systems will be operated**. They include, for example, rules governing how promotions are made, how technological change is instituted, and how layoff provisions are implemented.

Group 4: These clauses set out the conditions **governing the work environment** (health and safety) and conduct, work behaviour (discipline).

The collective agreement usually concludes with a clause that specifies the duration of the agreement, followed by the signatures of the union representatives and the employer representatives. Many agreements also include appendices containing details of specific articles that are either too detailed or too lengthy for the main part of the agreement (for example, wage schedules). Finally, attached to some agreements are letters of understanding that, depending on their wording, may be considered part of the agreement.

Mandatory Provisions

The following provisions are considered mandatory in any collective agreement in most jurisdictions:

Recognition—Identifies the group of employees bound by the terms of the collective agreement, and for whom the union has bargained a particular agreement. Typically, the recognition clause describes the bargaining unit in the same terms as in the certification order issued by the appropriate labour relations board.

Grievance and arbitration provisions—Labour relations statutes usually require the parties to agree on the methods for final and binding settlement by arbitration of any differences between the parties arising from interpreting, applying, or administering a collective agreement.

No strikes/no lockouts—Labour relations statutes normally require that every collective agreement contain a provision to prohibit strikes and lockouts while the collective agreement is in force.

Term—This provision sets out the duration of the agreement. Most statutory jurisdictions dictate that an agreement cannot be in force for less than one year.

Other mandatory articles—Labour relations statutes in certain provinces/territories require other mandatory provisions in collective agreements. Some jurisdictions reduce the scope of bargaining by establishing a minimum below which the parties cannot bargain

Other Articles

Collective agreements contain provisions covering all manner of subjects that are not mandatory. Other negotiating subjects include the following:

- Hours of work

- Job posting and assignment of positions

- Leaves of absence

- Management rights

- Overtime

- Purpose

- Relationship

- Seniority

- Shop stewards, staff representatives

- Union security

- Vacation with pay

- Wages

Drafting Collective Agreement Language

The terms and provisions of a collective agreement are typically obtained by a process in which each party first establishes bargaining positions on matters, then gradually modifies and changes its views, until the parties' find common ground on which they can reach a settlement.

However, drafting precise provisions on all matters covering all situations is difficult. Collective agreements are negotiated at a particular time and in a particular context. They are also negotiated at a specific time in an organization's business life. Consequently, the collective agreement that emerges represents an understanding of the essential matters set within the environment and the operating context at the time the agreement was negotiated.

Finally, while the parties negotiate and conclude an agreement at a particular time and under specific circumstances, its terms govern the relations between the parties over a considerable period. During this time, methods of operation, equipment, technology, and workforce organization may change substantially. As a result, an agreement may contain provisions that cannot be satisfactorily applied to an unforeseen situation, or the agreement may be silent on matters that have emerged since it was negotiated.

The characteristics described above often cause disputes over the operation, interpretation, and application and administration of the agreement's provisions, notwithstanding the varying nature of the provisions. Some are overly concise, while others are purposely vague, even those that seemed at the time of drafting to be perfectly clear. Further, much of the content of a collective agreement describes how things will be done—procedures to be followed—rather than sets out agreement on what precisely will be done. The process of fitting procedures to situations that are often unforeseen when the procedures were set up causes controversy during the term of the agreement.

Given the context in which an agreement is reached, negotiators must ensure that the clauses and articles have been carefully worded and fully thought out so that they will apply in a variety of situations during the life of the agreement. Failure to draft the agreement in this way may lead to situations such as the following:

- Unproductive conflict and ongoing disputes in the workplace

- A strained working relationship between the union and management, and between individual employees and supervisors

- Unwarranted time and resources devoted to resolving grievances, including preparing for and presenting arbitration cases

General Guidelines

When drafting a collective agreement, consider the following general guidelines, which will improve both readability and ease of interpretation:

- **Use plain language**. Carefully draft provisions with the reader's needs in mind.

- **Organize the provisions** in each clause and the collective agreement as a whole for the reader. When drafting provisions, **follow the reader's logic**—ask yourself what information the reader needs first.

- Shorten and **simplify sentences**. In general, keep to sentences of no more than 20 words. An average of 15 words is preferable.

- Use the **active voice**. The active voice states directly "who does what to whom" to help the reader keep the distinction clear. Passive voice sentences put the "who" (the actor) at the end of the sentence, or leave the "who" out altogether, making the clause ambiguous, as the following example shows.

> **Example**
>
> *Within three working days the union will be notified in writing (by the company).*
>
> To change the passive voice to the active voice, identify the action, ask by whom or by what, and put the answer at the front of the sentence, before the action verb, as follows:
>
> *The company will notify the union in writing within three working days.*

- Avoid the use of terms that are **common in legal documents**. Words and phrases such as "in lieu of," "whereas," and "at their discretion" are not part of the vocabulary of many employees or workplaces.

- **Avoid using terms** that are common in legal documents when speaking of the contracting parties. Wherever possible, avoid calling them "employer" and "employee" (telling them apart is hard on the eyes). Instead, refer to the parties as the company and the union (without capitals).

- **Analyze all procedures** that are part of the agreement (for example, the settlement of grievances), and describe them step by step. Use subheadings, e.g., Step 1, Step 2, and so on. Ask yourself, does the procedure work? Is it practical?

- If you state rules in abstract terms (seniority rules, for example), provide two or more **examples to show** their practical application. A single example might be misinterpreted. Be sure to indicate that all examples are illustrations only and nothing more.

- Strive to **eliminate ambiguity**. Clauses should be clear, concise, and understandable.

- Use the **singular form**, not the plural, to be precise—for example, the employee, he, she, instead of them, their, they, employees.

- Before agreeing to a particular clause or article, **reread the article and clarify** the meaning of the words and, more importantly, the intent of the parties. Each side should keep clear notes of these discussions.

- Discuss issues directly and fully, and **draft provisions fairly**. Avoid the temptation to gain an advantage or improve the deal by cleverly drafting the provisions. This tactic leads to unnecessary friction at the table and erodes credibility and trust. When you have settled an issue in principle, draft language that reflects the settlement.

- Consider: Which example is more **likely to be misinterpreted**?

> **Example A**
>
> 1: If employees are discharged or suspended, the union shall be informed.
>
> If the parties consider the issue has been unjustly dealt with, they may refer those issues to the grievance procedure to have this dispute conclusively settled.

> **Example B**
>
> 1: Union to Be Advised of Discharge and Suspension
>
> 1:1 In the event an employee is discharged or suspended, the Business Agent of the union shall be advised in writing within one working day of the suspension or discharge.
>
> 1:2 Where the employee or the union believes the employee has been suspended or discharged in violation of this agreement, this dispute shall constitute a grievance. This dispute shall be settled in accordance with Article 8 (Grievance Procedure) of this agreement.

Negotiators should be aware of statutes that regulate or affect the collective agreement. Clauses that contravene applicable statutes are normally unenforceable. Such statutes include those that regulate the following:

- Labour relations
- Minimum or basic employment standards
- Human rights
- Workplace health and safety
- A particular industry, sector, or profession

Negotiators must constantly resist pressure from the other negotiating team to accept quick settlements that contain imprecise wording, clauses that conflict with other sections of the collective agreement, and clauses that contravene prevailing statutes.

> **Drafting Test:** *Is there any way this provision could be interpreted apart from the meaning I wish it to have?*
>
> Ask someone who doesn't know the intent of the clause or provision you are intending to propose how many ways they can interpret it.
>
> If they can come up with more than one—the one you intended— redraft it.

While parties sometimes purposely draft ambiguous language in order to avoid a problem at bargaining they otherwise can't solve it is a practice to be avoided. The ambiguity *sows the seeds* for disputes during the term of the agreement.

This Doesn't Need to be in the Collective Agreement, Does It?

Not every term and condition of employment or workplace policy needs to be codified in the collective agreement. Based on an analysis of your objectives, what are you trying to achieve with collective agreement language (or to not achieve by including language) related to a matter or matters at issue? Before deciding to address such matters with provisions in your collective agreement, review and determine the following considerations:

- What are the implications for the organization of including collective agreement language?

- Is it in your interest to address the issues and/or include provisions addressing the issues in the collective agreement?

- Does the inclusion of contract language impose limits or restrict your actions or discretion when your objective is to create or maintain flexibility?

- Will the inclusion of the language introduce terms that could lead to ongoing disputes owing to the interpretative nature of the provisions(s)—for example, any vague or general expressions or statements?

- Is there another way of dealing with the matter or matters at issue that would not require collective agreement provisions?

- What is the potential *reach* of such a provision? What are the implications for decision making (process and authority) regarding the provision of services central to the organization's mandate? Certain collective agreement provisions can have direct implications for the way work is done and the nature, type and kind of services that are provided. Those that set staffing levels or specific case/work levels for example. The subject of some controversy, they can be characterized as:

    - conditions of work;

    - conditions of service: the manner in which they are preformed and the consequences that flow from their provision in that manner, and

    - conditions of spending.[30]

---

30 Provisions that set out working conditions in the form class size and composition in education, patient or client ratios in health/community care are examples: conditions of work. conditions of learning or conditions of care; conditions of spending.

Interpretation of Language

> **"Rules or canons of construction:** General rules or maxims used to assist in the interpretation of statutes or collective agreements—e.g., where a conflict exists between provisions in a collective agreement or statute, specific clauses override general clauses."
>
> —J. Sack and E. Poskanzer. *Labour Law Terms: A Dictionary of Canadian Labour Law.* (Toronto: Lancaster House, 1984), 35.

Generally, arbitrators interpret the provisions of the collective agreement in light of the plain meaning of the language and the purpose or intent of the parties as evidenced in the overall context of the collective agreement.

Further, arbitrators rely on their knowledge of labour relations practices and refer to previous arbitration awards, dictionaries, and labour relations texts, and use of similar words in statutes.

If the collective agreement is ambiguous or an argument of fairness or estoppel is raised, the arbitrator will consider the parties' past practice and negotiation history. In such situations, notes of negotiating sessions are particularly valuable.

Arbitrators frequently rely on "the rules of construction" to help determine the negotiators' intent. They generally follow certain rules on meaning and related aspects, as outlined in the following sections.

The Meaning of the Provisions

Ordinary Meaning

As one rule of construction, the parties drafting the collective agreement should give the words of a collective agreement their ordinary and plain meaning. The parties should ensure that the meaning of each clause is the meaning that both parties intended. If a clause seems logical and clear, the language will be applied in the sense in which it is used, even if the result is offensive to either party. A clause may not be applied except as its language dictates, and words may not be added to accomplish a different result.

This basic rule is qualified by the following rules of construction:

> **Ordinary meaning leading to an absurd result**—Arbitrators will modify the literal meaning of words if this meaning leads to an absurd result. However, irregular or unanticipated results are not sufficient to justify altering the plain meaning of words. Similarly, an interpretation of the collective agreement that causes hardship

to one party is no reason to change a decision, although arbitrators have ruled that the result of a particular interpretation on the reasonable operation of the organization may be relevant.

De minimis rule—If the basic clear-meaning rule is applied and the result provides only minimal or trivial relief, the relief is denied. This rule has been applied in arbitrations but is likely to be strictly used to help consenting parties determine the value of a decision.

> "**De minimis (non curat lex):** Literally, the law does not concern itself with trifles; a claim may be dismissed as *de minimis* if it is too trivial or insignificant to warrant the attention of the court or tribunal."
>
> —Sack, *Labour Law Terms*, 51.

Trade use and words used in a special sense—Arbitrators must consider a word's meaning in the trade, especially if the term is ambiguous. The context may also show that the parties have not used words in their ordinary grammatical sense. However, if this intention can be established only by extrinsic evidence—evidence external to the collective agreement such as past practice or negotiating history—the ordinary meaning will still be applied.

Two Possible Meanings

Although hardship to a party is not a reason to alter a clear meaning, it is a reason to choose one of two equally plausible meanings. A presumption in law states that when language may be interpreted in more than one way, and when one interpretation would lead to obvious injustice, that interpretation should not be used.

If one of the two equally plausible meanings would strip a clause of any real effectiveness, that meaning should be avoided. When two interpretations of a provision are possible, the one that best suits the meaning of the document as a whole should be chosen.

Similar Terms and Similar Meanings

Similar terms used in different parts of a collective agreement should be given similar meanings. However, also recognize that terms used more than once in a document must be taken in context.

Dissimilar Terms and Different Meanings

If dissimilar words or phrases are used in different places in the collective agreement, they should not be given the same meaning.

Redundancy

When interpreting collective agreements, the meaning of each word should be considered, and a word should not be disregarded if some reasonable meaning can be given to it. Words in legal documents—public or private—should not be considered redundant without sound reason.

The rationale for this rule is that a subsection cannot be meaningless, since the parties who drafted the subsection obviously intended it to have a meaning or they would not have bothered to insert it.

Pyramiding Benefits
The term pyramiding means providing two or more monetary benefits. In interpreting collective agreements, arbitrators avoid the pyramiding of benefits or penalties. In the absence of specific wording in the contract, if a contract is open to two interpretations and one interpretation involves the pyramiding of overtime while the other interpretation does not, an arbitrator should accept the interpretation that does not provide for the additional penalty payments.

Many arbitrators require clear evidence before they allow payment of two benefits for the same period.

The Meaning of 'Shall' and 'May'
The words "shall" and "may" are often the subject of interpretation. Ordinarily, "shall" is imperative (meaning that a party must do something), while "may" is permissive (meaning that a party can do something at its discretion). Sometimes, however, the word "shall" is interpreted to mean "may," and vice versa. Determining the context in which the words appear is important. Case law helps in this determination.

Headings as a Guide to Meaning
Headings may be used to help interpret an agreement's provisions.

Other Interpretive Issues

- **Reading the Whole Collective Agreement**
  Arbitrators widely accept that the collective agreement is to be construed as a whole. Words and provisions must be interpreted in light of the entire agreement. All terms of the agreement must be read together, and an arbitrator will likely be highly skeptical of an interpretation of one article that would nullify or render absurd the effect of another article.

- **Earlier Provisions Override Later Provisions**
  When two parts of an agreement conflict, the part of the agreement that appears first overrides the part that is written later, unless the latter clause clearly indicates that it overrides the former. When the appendix to a collective agreement is inconsistent with the collective agreement, the collective agreement governs.

- **Specific Provisions Override General Provisions**
  The general principle that earlier provisions govern later provisions is balanced by the principle that a specific provision takes precedence over a general provision. Similarly, a specific description qualifies a general description. This principle, of course, affects the general-purpose clause and its value.

- **No Retroactive Effect**
  Unless specifically stated, provisions of a collective agreement should not be applied retroactively. This rule is derived from general contractual law.

- **Clauses Not to Be Implied into an Agreement**
  As a matter of law, the implication of a clause into a collective agreement should be restricted. Clauses should only be implied under the clearest circumstances, because the role of an arbitrator is to construe the agreement as it stands, not to create a new one for the parties.

Summary

Consider the following guidelines when drafting collective agreement language:

☐ Give words their ordinary meaning.

☐ Where two meanings of agreement language are possible, consider the efficacy of an interpretation in practice in determining the proper meaning.

☐ Give similar meanings to similar terms used in different parts of the agreement.

☐ Give different meanings to dissimilar terms.

☐ Ensure the collective agreement has no redundancy. All words have meaning.

☐ Use headings as a guide to a provision's meaning.

☐ Read the collective agreement as a whole.

☐ Remember that what comes first overrides what comes later and that specific provisions override general provisions.

☐ Unless specifically stated, provision of a collective agreement should not be applied retroactively.

☐ Provisions should not be implied into a collective agreement.

CHAPTER 8

Establishing a Bargaining Protocol

The procedure to follow in negotiations does not conform to any particular prescription. The parties in successive rounds of negotiations tend to develop their own particular approach to collective bargaining. Some negotiating parties prepare a written Bargaining Protocol. Other parties have only general agreement on how they will conduct the bargaining, since they have an established bargaining relationship and practice, and see no need to commit the agreement to writing.

Bargaining protocols are negotiable. Neither party, however, may negotiate protocol matters to impasse (refer to Chapter 10: Good Faith in Collective Bargaining).

Bargaining Protocol: Considerations

Before starting negotiations, the parties should meet to address such bargaining protocol matters as the following:

- Time and place of meetings
- Length of meetings
- Rules concerning conduct of meetings
- Order of presentation of the bargaining items
- Procedures for dealing with each item
- Method of approval of items

At this stage in the bargaining, the parties must reach an understanding about whether they can introduce additional bargaining items during negotiations. As a matter of practical necessity (not of law), the parties usually agree not to introduce new items during the negotiations, to avoid chaos and disruption to the process.

As a rule, you should advise the other negotiating team that you will only negotiate the items that both parties have tabled in the initial package. The one exception to this rule is when both parties agree to table a new item as a result of events (for example, legislative change) after the negotiations have started. However, this exception is not liberally applied.

Location, Timing, and Length of Meetings

When the parties are developing bargaining protocol, they may have to decide whether to hold negotiating meetings on the employer's premises or at some neutral location, such as a hotel meeting room. Usually, both parties want to hold the meetings away from the workplace or other operation and on neutral ground.

If the meetings are held on the employer's premises, they will undoubtedly be interrupted, breaking the concentration of both negotiating teams. In practice, when negotiations are held at the workplace, discussions where some members do not participate in the negotiations are difficult to avoid because of breaks and other interruptions. Further, the workplace may not offer a suitable place for the parties to hold a caucus in private. Such a caucus is an important element of any negotiation session.

The only difficulty with holding the meetings at an outside location is the cost of the facilities. Of course, the parties may make cost-sharing arrangements, but most parties simply rotate the cost of the meeting room, or the employer pays for the meeting room and the union, if it wishes, provides its own caucus room.

When determining the location, timing, and length of the meetings, consider the following:

- Whether to hold meetings at the employer's facility, if it offers a satisfactory and adequate meeting room, or away from the employer's location at a hotel or elsewhere

- Whether to hold early meetings in one location and final sessions in another

- Whether to hold the meetings during regular working hours, outside working hours, or through a combination of the two

- Whether to hold the meetings in the morning, in the afternoon, or at night, and what days are most desirable

- How long the sessions should be

Wages for Employee Members

The collective agreement may obligate the employer to pay the wages of employee members of a union bargaining committee for time spent in negotiation. If a particular collective agreement does not contain such a provision, however, the employer is not legally obligated to pay employee members.

While nothing prevents an employer from agreeing to pay wages to employees serving on a union bargaining committee, this kind of arrangement is more common when an employer and a union have a longstanding collective agreement relationship, and when attitudes on the union's role have stabilized. Even then, the arrangement the parties reach will often cover negotiations up to but not including dispute resolution processes, such as mediation and interest arbitration that are employed to assist negotiations or resolve a dispute.

In other words, the employer will pay the employees only while negotiations are under way. The rationale for this position is that if a union chooses to escalate the process (work stoppage, slowdowns, or protracted bargaining sessions), the employer may respond by expecting the union to bear at least part of the cost.

The parties must settle the issue of payment of wages initially, so that this controversy does not sidetrack them in the latter stages of negotiations.

When determining whether committee members will be paid, consider the following questions:

- What are the relevant provisions of the collective agreement?
- What is the past practice and total cost?
- Should pay cover working hours only?
- If over eight hours, should pay be straight time or at the overtime rate?
- What should be the limit on total negotiation hours paid?

Negotiation Proceedings

After determining when and where to hold the meetings, and whether employees will be paid, the parties need to decide how the negotiations will proceed by considering the following:

- Bargaining history, experiences, and negotiator orientations. Is this what has been characterized as traditional bargaining or more constructively oriented? The answer to this question will inform how the first meeting of the two negotiating teams will be structured.

- How both parties will exchange proposals and whether they will exchange all of their proposals when negotiations begin.

- How the parties will signify agreement on a particular item—for example, the union and the employer will sign each change as "agreed in principle," and all items "agreed in principle" will form the new agreement, subject to ratification by both sides.

- Where the parties will start, and who will go first.

- Will committees and sub-committees be used to address and be a resource on complex and/or potentially contentious issues?

Other Protocol Considerations

The parties also need to consider the following:

Confirm Authority

- That the negotiating committee has the authority to bargain.

- If negotiating committee will recommend the resulting "agreement in principle" to its constituents.

- Whether the parties have any preconditions to this recommendation (for example, "We will recommend this provided you . . .").

- Whether the parties will commit the bargaining protocol to writing. It is not required but it does demonstrate the parties' ability to reach basic process agreements and have *a meeting of the minds* on how negotiations will proceed.

Roles and Responsibilities

- Who will be at the bargaining table and who will speak for the committee?

- If the parties will permit anyone other than committee members to attend negotiation sessions.

- Whether the parties have any considerations relating to communicating with their respective constituents (such as public statements, bulletins, and contact with the media).

Draft Collective Bargaining Protocol

Negotiators are encouraged to explicitly address protocol matters before collective bargaining begins. Whether the parties choose to commit protocol matters to writing will be the subject of discussions between the bargaining committees. Any protocol agreement should be consistent with the collective agreement and local bargaining practices. Following is an example of a formal written bargaining protocol.

Example: Collective Bargaining Protocol Agreement

1. Pursuant to Article X, the bargaining committees shall consist of (number) members that the employer appoints and (number) members that the union appoints. The bargaining committees have the authority to bargain on behalf of their respective principals. Bargaining committees have the authority to sign a memorandum of agreement, which is subject only to final ratification by their respective principals.

2. In addition to the bargaining committee members, each bargaining committee will declare a chief spokesperson. Spokespersons may call upon a member of the other bargaining committee to speak.

3. All proposals will be clearly dated and numbered, and if necessary, have the time noted.

4. All agreements will be in writing, and the chief spokesperson of each party will initial and date each article or clause at the time at which the parties reach agreement.

5. During negotiations, either party may bring forward proposals and counter-proposals that are related to the original proposal but are not new items. Either party may introduce new items by mutual consent of the parties or in the event of new enacted legislation affecting the bargaining between the parties.

6. Both parties are free to caucus at any time. A party that requires a caucus of more than 30 minutes is obliged to give the other party an estimate of how much time it needs.

7. Either party may cancel a scheduled meeting and will make every reasonable effort to give 48 hours' advance cancellation notice.

8. The site of negotiations shall be a mutually agreed-on location, which will include a room for one of the parties to hold a caucus separately from the negotiations. The cost shall be divided equally between the parties.

9. At the conclusion of each session, as a final item of business, the parties will agree on an agenda for the next session.

10. Resource persons may attend negotiating sessions and may speak only by mutual agreement of the parties.

11. Others may attend negotiating sessions as observers only.

12. The number of resource persons and observers combined will not exceed three for each party during any one bargaining session.

13. Public communications during bargaining will be by mutual agreement or with advance notice to the other party.

14. All bargaining committee members are aware of the need for security and confidentiality of information that they provide and discuss during the bargaining sessions.

15. Any resource person or observer who attends a bargaining session is required to provide a commitment to observe confidentiality of information discussed during bargaining sessions.

16. Where either party intends to have resource persons and/or observers present during a bargaining session, the party shall provide the other party with a minimum of 48 hours' notice, in writing, of the name and reason for the attendance of the resource person or observer.

17. Either party reserves the right to restrict the attendance of any resource person or observer during bargaining sessions where the need for confidentiality indicates that the attendance of only the bargaining committees would further the best interests of bargaining.

Agreed to this .... day of ...., year

Signed   Signed

For the employer   For the union

Exchanging Initial Proposals

Following preparatory work and the development of a bargaining protocol, the parties should exchange initial bargaining proposals. The parties may make the exchange at a pre-negotiation session or as a part of the first stage of the negotiation process. Some collective agreements require that the parties exchange their respective proposal packages in advance. More often, however, the exchange is a matter of agreement in the bargaining protocol.

The parties' presentation or exchange of proposals brings into focus the items that they will negotiate. The union usually takes the initiative by presenting to the employer its proposals for changes in the collective agreement. However, this is not a legal requirement—nothing prevents an employer from taking the initiative and making the first move. Whether an employer should make the first move depends on its strategy.

The union presentation may be formal or informal or be in detailed language or by bargaining items only. The employer then provides a general response to the union or presents its own proposals.

Before negotiations begin, the negotiating teams must decide whether the parties will exchange their proposals simultaneously as described above, or the party requesting changes will present its package first and the other party (usually the employer) will respond with its proposals at a subsequent meeting.

Some argue that a simultaneous exchange stimulates the development of issues that are not serious or real—a "shopping list." Although it is preferable to examine the other team's proposals before submitting your response, the parties' negotiating experience and relationship will determine whether this approach is appropriate. Proponents of this method of exchange readily admit that it will not prevent the shopping list; however, in their experience, it tends to make the list much shorter.

At this point, the parties must be sure that the bargaining priorities and objectives on each negotiation item are fully understood before actual negotiations begin.

CHAPTER 9

To the Table: Considerations

Chapter 9 assumes that a constructive approach, whether it be position-based or observes the concept of integrative potential, will be adopted. *Collective Bargaining Preparation Essentials: The Handbook* is based on the simple proposition that while there are a variety of bargaining techniques that lead to a successfully negotiated agreement, nothing replaces effective planning and thorough preparation.

How can you improve the collective bargaining process and resulting bargaining outcomes? As participants in the bargaining process prepare to negotiate a collective agreement, they can consider the following observations, ideas, and strategies that experienced negotiators and writers have identified.

To Start: Is this a First Collective Agreement?

While the concepts in Chapter 9 apply to first collective agreement negotiations as well as the renegotiation/renewal of an existing one it is important to note the unique aspects of first agreements. First collective agreements between employers and a newly certified unions can prove difficult to conclude. This may result from

- the inexperience of the parties,
- a difficult certification dispute, including unfair labour practices,
- a negotiation that is in fact a continuation of a recognition dispute, or from
- a bitter and protracted strike or lock-out.

Canadian jurisdictions have adopted distinct approaches to assist with the negotiation of first agreements. In BC for example, the LRB sets out the principles[31] governing the mediation/arbitration of a first collective agreement under Section 55 of the Code.

---

31 *Yarrow Lodge Limited,* 1993, 21 C.L.R.B.R. (2d)

The LRB adopts two overriding principles that interest arbitrators are to employ. The first being the replication principle and the second, what is fair and reasonable in the circumstances.

- Replication principle: Attempt to construct a collective agreement that would replicate as nearly as possible an agreement that conventional bargaining would have produced.

- Fair and reasonable: Avoid imposing any agreement that would reflect an undue imbalance of power between the parties. In the application of these two principles an interest arbitrator will rely on one primary objective factor—the terms and conditions of employment of other employees performing similar work. This is known as the "comparator principle."

In determining the actual terms and conditions of a first collective agreement the LRB in the seminal case[32] set out the following factors that are to guide an interest arbitrator:

> *Our objective is to provide arbitrators with both guidance and flexibility in determining the actual terms and conditions of employment. These factors are as follows:*
>
> 1. *A first collective agreement should not contain breakthrough or innovative clauses; nor as a general rule shall such agreements be either status quo or an industry standard agreement.*
>
> 2. *Arbitrators should employ objective criteria, such as the comparable terms and conditions paid to similar employees performing similar work.*
>
> 3. *There must be internal consistency and equity amongst employees.*
>
> 4. *The financial state of the employer, if sufficient evidence is placed before the arbitrator, is a critical factor.*
>
> 5. *The economic and market conditions of the sector or industry in which the employer competes must be considered.*

As a general rule, the LRB will not impose either the status quo (the employer's current terms and conditions) or a union's master agreement. Rather, the focus is on basic collective agreement rights, such as seniority, layoff and recall rights, promotion clauses, a grievance/arbitration process, and union security provisions.

With these observations in mind negotiators, their teams and those they represent should approach first collective agreement negotiations based on the assumption that

---

32   Ibid page 48

the decisions they make may be adjudicated by a third party to ensure that your decision and its associated reasoning can withstand third-party scrutiny.

Putting Collective Bargaining in Context: Reflections on the Alternatives Chosen

Are You Ready? Reflections on Process

- Be sure that you have set **clear objectives on every bargaining item** and that you understand on what basis the objectives were established. Link you objectives to you interests and their relative priority.

- While the past isn't necessarily a predictor of the future, it does play a role. **Understand** how your union-employer relationship came to be and how that journey may influence the process of bargaining and what is eventually achieved in this round. Be historically alert and contextually grounded!

- Understand the **four sub-processes** of collective bargaining—distributive, integrative, intra-organizational bargaining, and attitudinal structuring. Given your union-management relationship and the key individuals involved in bargaining how does this understanding inform you? Are there planning and process implications for you, your team, and your constituents?

- Resources, roles, plans, and contingencies: **success results from effective planning** and thorough preparation.

Make a Considered Assessment: Options and *Best Alternatives*

In most negotiations, parties are influenced consciously or unconsciously by their assessment of the *no deal* alternatives, the alternatives to a negotiated agreement. The better their alternatives, the more they may push for a more favorable settlement. The worse their alternatives, the more accommodating they may be in the settlement terms.[33]

Unfortunately, parties frequently fail to undertake an accurate and comprehensive analysis of their alternatives and, therefore, negotiate based on unrealistic and uninformed ideas of what they might obtain in the absence of a negotiated agreement, the *no deal* reality.[34]

---

33 An alternative is a proposition or situation offering a choice between two or more things only one of which may be chosen.

34 This section draws on the work of Sebenius, James K., BATNAs in Negotiation: Common Errors and Three Kinds of 'No' (March 9, 2017). Negotiation Journal, April 2017 Harvard

BATNA is an acronym that stands for *Best Alternative To a Negotiated Agreement*. It is defined as the best course of action for satisfying your interests without the other party's agreement. In other words, a party's BATNA is what a party's alternative is if negotiations are unsuccessful and an agreement cannot be achieved. A WATNA, the worst alternative to a negotiated agreement is the least beneficial of those alternatives.

Most BATNA formulations direct your attention to what you can achieve outside the current negotiation and independent of your counterpart. It is characterized as your walkaway alternative–your best course of action or *no deal option* for satisfying your interests without the other party's agreement.[35]

Employment relationships, however, are **interdependent ones**. More often than not, parties to problems, contentious matters and workplace negotiations cannot achieve what they need to achieve independent of one another. As a practical matter parties to an employment relationship and a collective agreement will remain together and must continue to interact long after negotiations have concluded and a new or revised agreement is in force. As a result, the BATNA takes a different form.

Instead of thinking of your BATNA in terms of your outside options that are independent of the other party, consider options in an interdependent frame:

- The ***Artful Use of No***. The consequences to the negotiation process of saying "no" to the other party's proposals, propositions and positions including the possibly of continuing to negotiate, with or without a pause. Make a considered *No* choice whether tactical, to re-set, or final:

    - "**tactical no**" Simply turning down a proposition or proposal in hopes of generating a better offer later in the process.

    - "**no to re-set**." This "no" may occur at any stage of the process. It can involve moves "away from the table" to improve your own no-agreement option and/or worsen that of the other side. This can involve private conversations with influencers and/or members of the *back tables* to *take the temperature* of the current state and to informally test process/substance options. You often employ the "no to re-set" with the intention of continuing to negotiate or returning to active negotiation with your original counterpart, but in a setup that that you have more actively modified to be more conducive to reaching your preferred agreement.

Business School NOM Unit Working Paper No. 17-055; Harvard PON Working Paper.

35 William Ury in Getting Past No (1991: 21- 22)

- ○ "**final no**" Bringing the process in the present form to an end. Given your interdependence remember the relationship will continue. Assess the implications of this final no. If no, now what?

    What does this mean for your minimum conditions for going forward? Theirs? The prospects for a more favorable agreement, associated processes? What now? Be realistic. Is this final no just your final act masquerading as a tactical no or no to re-set? Have you telegraphed your intentions by using this tactic before?

- How you can most accurately estimate and perhaps most effectively influence how these consequences will affect each party's interests (preferably positively for you and negatively for them).

- The spillover effect and the implications for working relationships, employee engagement, productivity and the like.

As negotiation scholar James Sebenius notes in *BATNAs in Negotiation: Common Errors and Three Kinds of 'No'*:

> *In short, a great virtue of a focus on one's BATNA is the discipline of systematically asking of any possible deal: "as compared to what?" The acronym has proved irresistible but common descriptions can be problematic or worse. It would enhance clarity to emphasize that, typically, one's BATNA is only meaningful with respect to a specific counterpart and class of possible deals with that counterpart.*
>
> *And some tweaks that distinguish among the three types of "no" could enhance the value of "BATNA" even further.*

In determining and developing your BATNA:

1. Analyze the **current state**. Who are the negotiating parties and their constituents? To date, what has been proposed, discussed, agreed upon or set aside? Given that there is likely a myriad of issues how are the issues interrelated? What has been the bargaining history generally and, in this circumstance, specifically?

    - What do you know, need to know and what might be contentious or potentially contentious? The answers to these questions form an Analytic Frame. If one was not contemplated or developed prior to negotiations, one can be developed now to form a *common knowledge base*. If one was developed it may be helpful to review the contents and revise it as necessary given new information that has been learned through the negotiation.

2. Confirm the matter **central to the point of contention**, the problem you are seeking to solve and/or opportunity you are seeking to take advantage of. How does this matter relate to other matters that are, will be or can be part of these negotiations? With respect to #2 differentiate your positions from your interests.

3. Generate your **options**–go for quantity, not quality at this stage: options are ideas that you may generate within the context of a negotiation for possible reconciliation. You analyze these options, formally or informally, to see how well they satisfy your interests.

Options may include relationship and substance components as well as process matters; parties may have more than one process path they can follow that does not involve negotiation with the other party.

A common path taken in contentious or protracted negotiations is bargaining assistance in the form of mediation. Even though mediators are just assistance, mediation is undertaken with the hope that interests can be satisfied better than anything the parties might be able to obtain in direct negotiations. In this instance, when analyzing process options, focus on the outcomes should the mediation process fail to convince the other party to adjust their position. Other alternative paths that may be chosen could include:

Unilateral Paths

- Seeking **intervention** from a higher authority within the other party's organization.

- Going to the **media** (broadcast, print, social) to make the case.

- As applicable, **accessing other** suppliers, service providers or contractors. Seeking other employees, reassigning duties and responsibilities.

- Accessing statutory authorities with the responsibility to regulate the aspects of your endeavor that can **influence or otherwise direct** the reconciliation process and/or determine the outcome.

- Seeking a **strike or lockout mandate**; exercising same.

- **Abandoning** your efforts in the hope that the situation will improve.

Paths Requiring a Measure of Agreement

- Agreeing with the other party to a form of **third-party assistance** such as arbitration to determine the terms of agreement. The authority to decide the matters at issue and in turn the control over the process and the resulting outcome is transferred from the parties to a third party.

- Proposing a **cooling off** period to allow the parties to refocus their efforts.

- Proposing a **contingent agreement** if the parties disagree about how future events may play out. "If this happens, then we do this or that" commitments.[36] A contingent agreement:

  - **eliminates** the need to come to agreement on the specific issue in contention. By allowing parties to bet on their predictions, a contingent agreement enables parties to "live with" their differences.

  - makes **commitments self-enforcing** by eliminating the need to reconvene or renegotiate when something unforeseen occurs.

  - **eliminates** the need for arbitration/litigation by reducing the likelihood that conflict will arise over surprising events and by spelling out exactly what will happen if a conflict emerges.

  Each of these process paths has its' own best and worst outcomes, risks and costs. It is important to analyze the possible outcomes along more than one path, depending on which strategies might realistically be pursued separate from negotiation with the other party.

4. Consider #2 and #3 relative to all the options available and assess:

   ☐ your ability to act unilaterally to implement each option, and

   ☐ the degree to which the options would reconcile the matters at issue.

   Categorize them from best to worst.

5. Complete #2, #3, and #4 from the perspective of the other party. This exercise provides you with a more complete picture of what the other party may think they can achieve on their own and how that may influence their approach to negotiations.

---

36 Process to develop a contingent agreement.
- Outline the scenario that each party imagines will happen in the future.
- Negotiate expectations and requirements for each of these visions of the future.
- Codify the scenarios in the agreement.

Craft with care, practice a*lert watchfulness*. Before negotiating a contingent agreement, be sure to consider that the other party may have access to information that you lack.

6. Of the options identified from best to worst, identify the best alternative (or combination of alternatives) you can achieve on your own versus through a negotiated agreement with the other party.

In developing your BATNA, you will have generated a more informed understanding of the options available to you and the other party to either walk away or resolve the matter at issue which should assist you in finding a negotiated resolution.

Where you choose to enter into a negotiation, use your BATNA and consider the following when analyzing the other party's proposals, propositions and positions:

- **Cost:** Identify and consider how much it will cost to accept the proposal as presented relative to the cost of your no deal option/best alternative. Cost estimation may include both short-term and long-term considerations.

- **Feasibility:** Of the two, the proposal as presented, and the best alternative which option is the most feasible? Which one can you realistically initiate within the necessary time frame?

- **Implications and Consequences:** From the perspective of a negotiator's universal concerns of substance, process and relationship identify the implications of pursing what you have concluded is your best alternative to a negotiated agreement. Determine the outcomes associated with the proposal as presented and your best alternative.

- **Constituents:** Do you need support from specific constituents or constituent groups before being able to adopt your BATNA?

- **Now What:** If you choose a BATNA alternative and pursue it, given your degree of interdependence what happens after?

Do You Have a Contingency Plan?

Work stoppages are generally an unpleasant topic for any employer to consider. However, it is important for an employer prepare a comprehensive plan in the event that the threat of a work stoppage becomes a reality during bargaining. Preparing a contingency plan does not mean that the employer is "looking for a strike." Rather, it is a component of bargaining preparation undertaken by all responsible employers. Ensure the following topics are addressed in the contingency plan.

Strikes and Lockouts: Rules and Regulations

Review the applicable labour relations statute concerning the processes, limitations, and obligations regarding strikes and lockouts. Do essential service provisions (if any) of the labour relations statute play a role? If yes, timing of an application will be critical.

Plan Manager

Designate a senior employer official as the Plan Manager. That individual should be responsible for implementing and overseeing the operational aspects of the Plan. The ability to access organization resources is required if the Plan Manager is to be successful.

Continuation of Operations

Determine whether operations will continue in any fashion during a strike/lockout.

Assess your ability to provide regular programs and services, and to continue to allow the use of facilities by external users in the event of a work stoppage.

Communications Plan

During a work stoppage, it is critical that the organization ensure frequent, regular communications with key clients, users of your services, and, as applicable, the media.

An official spokesperson should be designated as the point of contact for media inquiries. This person should be readily available to respond to media questions.

Security Implications

During a work stoppage, the security of staff, buildings, and equipment is a major consideration.

If you use a contracted security firm to monitor, for example, facilities outside of normal operating hours, ensure that the security firm is well informed and properly advised of their role in the event of a work stoppage.

Approaches to Interactions at the Table

Clarifying Interests and Concerns

- Constantly be **alert to the real interests** of the other party, with respect not only to goals, but also to priorities

- Do not concern yourself with only what the other party says and does—**find out why**. Look for the interests (underlying reasons) behind each position. Ask "Why?" or "For what purpose?" Remember that economic motivation is not the only explanation for the other party's conduct and actions.

- Understand your interests. Test their **importance in relation to one another** as the bargaining process continues. Constantly ask:

    - As a result of this round of negotiations, what do we want to achieve?
    - Why is this achievement important to us?
    - What will achieving this outcome help us do?
    - What will happen if we do not achieve what we want to achieve?

- Remember that every participant in a negotiation has **two universal concerns**: the outcome, or substance, of the negotiation, and the relationship with the other party. People have varying degrees of interest in these two concerns.

Listening and Checking Assumptions

- Be a good listener. **Seek first to understand**, then to be understood.

- Learn to **understand people and their personalities**; this understanding will assist during negotiations.

- Put yourself temporarily in the **other's shoes**.

- Check and **recheck the assumptions** you and the other party are making. Never assume knowledge on the part of others.

- Avoid spending time in your caucuses **debating what you think** the other party is saying or thinking. If you do not know, ask them. Check your assumptions!

Managing the Process

- Be sure that you have set **clear objectives** on every bargaining item and that you understand the basis on which the objectives were established.

- Measure **each move** against your objectives.

- As you make each bargaining move, be sure that you know its **relationship to all other moves**.

- Be well prepared, with firm data supporting **clearly identified** objectives.

- Conduct negotiations in a **methodical manner**, supported by a documented plan to achieve your objectives.

Deciding When a Caucus is Needed

- When **in doubt**, hold a caucus.

- Hold a caucus or team meeting before you agree to anything important.

- Talk things over with your team, but if you formally call for a caucus, be sure to **give the other team something to work on**; otherwise, they may expect a concession or may just talk about you and raise the temperature! Hold a caucus for targeted and specific reasons only.

Taking Care of the Relationship

- Do not lose sight of collective bargaining's role in the **ongoing employer-employee relationship**. What you do during negotiations will affect what you do together and how you work together in general.

- Respect the **importance of face saving** for the other party, the reputational interest.

- Maintain **your integrity**. Remember that putting one over on the other party for a short-term gain could sour the relationship later on.

Working Effectively, Ethically and Constructively

- Build a reputation for being fair but firm.

- Maintain your integrity.

- Do not hurry.
- Do not try to short-circuit the process—be patient.
- Learn to control your emotions; *savour* your reputation.

Ensuring the Desired Outcomes

- Pay close **attention to the wording** of every clause negotiated. Words and phrases are often the source of grievances. Be alert to the assumptions you and others are making.
- Ultimately, you will **be judged not on your debating skills** but on the settlement reached.
- Consider the impact of present negotiations on negotiations **in future years**. And finally,
- **Learn** each time you negotiate.

At the Table: Guidelines for Bargaining

Preparing for the Initial Negotiating Session

When preparing for negotiations, do the following as often and thoroughly as possible:

1. What is the purpose of the negotiation and what do you want to achieve (substance, process, relationship)?
2. Identify the real issue(s) in conflict. Is there common ground on some issue(s)?
    - Differentiate your objectives and positions from your interests. Why do we seek what we seek?
3. Review your basic and underlying concerns and interests. Consider:
    - What are the criteria by which we will judge whether the negotiation has been a success or a failure?
    - If we fail to achieve our objectives, what then?
4. Review your no agreement or walk-away alternative.

5. Assess your relative strengths and weaknesses. consider:
    - What sources of power, leverage do you possess?
    - What sources of power does the other party possess?
    - How can I increase my relative power position?
6. Learn sufficiently about the organizational culture of the people you are going to negotiate with: their customs, norms, values, and practices. Beware of making assumptions. This is an evidence-informed exercise. Test your assumptions.
7. Determine your approach and associated strategy for the first meeting.

Developing Your Initial Meeting Strategy

1. How will we frame the negotiations? How will we open the first meeting?

    Frames are the conceptions that parties have of the situation and the matters at issue. They allow the parties to begin to develop a shared definition of the issues involved, and the process needed to resolve them.

    When the frames of both parties generally align, they are more likely to focus on common issues and have a common definition of the situation. However, when the frames do not, communication between the parties is likely to be more difficult. Unless the different outlooks on the problem begin to overlap, it is unlikely that negotiations will be successful.

    If negotiators understand what frame they are operating from and what frame the other is operating from, they may be able to shift the conversation and develop common definitions. The way in which parties define the problem can shape the rest of the process.

2. Are we clear on our objectives and how our proposals relate to those objectives? Do we understand our interests and their relative priority? What form will our proposals take and in what order will they be presented?

3. Do we have enough factual data and information to support our objectives and the associated positions?

4. If not, what extra information could be available?

5. Does every member of the team understand what is important and agree with the team objectives?

6. What are the different team roles? Consider who will:

    - Lead the discussion?
    - Check the understanding (test assumptions; verify facts)?
    - Ask the questions? What is the questioning strategy?
    - Respond to the other side's questions?
    - Summarize to confirm understanding?
    - Call for team caucuses and the adjournments?
    - Record proceedings and keep track of any documents exchanged?

7. How will the spokesperson communicate with the other team members during the negotiations?

8. What are the specific roles of each team member?

Questions and Questioning

Questions **are not neutral**. Questions that are really statements of assumptions put in the form of a question can be aggressive, which often leads to hostility.

Asking leading questions when you are seeking information closes off options, whereas asking open questions when you are intending to move a person towards the conclusion you want them to reach can be counterproductive. Hypothetical, reflective, and leading questions help generate ideas, motivate people, and develop insights. Other question sets are designed to gather information.

To be effective, you need to know the objectives of the questions you are asking and then design the questions to support the objective, which could be information gathering or trying to solve problems and create alignment.

To develop your strategy consider:

1. In general, how do we intend to approach this negotiation? Based on what we know so far, what questions do we have concerning both process (how negotiations will proceed) and substance (what the other party appears to be seeking)?

2. What questions should we ask the other party at this point?

3. What questions are they likely to ask us?

4. How and who will we answer these questions?

Opening the Negotiations

The opening stance in a negotiation is critical, as it:

- Conveys information about your attitude and aspirations.
- Shapes the bargaining climate.

There are a number of process matters that can be dealt with before the first meeting. For example:

- Confirm meeting and attendance logistics.
- What do we want to accomplish in the first meeting?
- How long do we intend to meet?
- Who is going to be involved?
- Who is going to lead discussions, about what matters?
- When will you or the other side respond?

When opening the negotiations, be prepared to:

1. Introduce yourself and your team members.
2. From the outset, emphasize the importance of getting agreement together.
3. Give your general views of the issues to be covered.
4. Mention your underlying concerns.
5. Obtain a briefing on the other side's view. Ask questions for clarification.
6. Keep the first meeting short and exploratory.
7. Adjourn after each side has expressed its views on the broad field to be covered.
8. Summarize before you leave the meeting.
9. Agree what you and the other party will do when you resume the negotiations.

Note: This opening meeting must be consistent with your specific *Bargaining Protocol* as it applies to the exchange of proposals and the manner in which negotiating sessions will be conducted.

Building Understanding

We often assume that others think the way we think or instantly understand what we expect from them. Our natural way of thinking and acting is so innate that we often don't notice we're doing it or that it's different from anyone else's perspective. It's natural for all of us to not realize how unique each person's assumptions and expectations are.

In negotiations seek to build understanding:

1. **Suspend judgement** and assume positive intent. Recognize that individuals are probably doing the best they can with what they have or what they know. Engagement and considered inquiry will help to identify relevant considerations and apparent motives.

2. **Do not interrupt** the other party. Talk less and listen actively. Presentations are narratives or stories. [37]You want to deconstruct the narrative for understanding and shift from narration to conversation.

3. Ask **open** questions. For example, "Tell me about . . .", "Could you describe what you think are . . .?"

4. Ask **probing** questions. For example, "Could you tell me more about . . .?", "What do you mean by . . .?"

5. Ask **closed** questions to receive simple yes and no responses.

6. Use caucuses to keep control over your team and discussions. Remember to **"leave the other party something to work on" when you caucus**.

7. Set yourself a **clear, specific, and realistic** goals before entering a meeting.

8. Summarize **regularly** to list the points of explanation, interpretation, and understanding.

9. Avoid **weak language**, such as "We hope," "We like," "We prefer."

10. Don't always **criticize** the other party. Look for common ground.

---

37 A narrative or story is coloured by one's background, experiences, and frame of reference. This narrative has implications for how the matters at issue are identified, understood, and reconciled.

11. Avoid irritators. Value-loaded words like "unfair" or "unreasonable" tend to provoke a defensive or aggressive response.

12. Avoid **emotional** outbursts, blaming, personal attacks or sarcasm, cheap point-scoring, interrupting and being "too clever." Practice signaling, questioning, paraphrasing, using humour, building rapport, and remaining silent.

13. Be **careful** about your body language and the meaning attached to the other party's gestures, tone of voice, silences, and facial expressions.

Improved Problem Solving

1. Define and frame the issues in terms of **interests not positions**: Reasons why you take a particular stance on an issue or propose something; your needs, concerns.

2. For technical issues, ones that are contentious or potentially contentious co-create an **analytic frame** (preferably in advance of formal negotiations). As the analytic frame is developed, factual foundations, areas of agreement, and areas of difference become clarified.

1. Define the **criteria** for evaluating potential solutions. Prioritize the criteria.

2. Decide what will happen if **no viable** solution is found.

3. Brainstorm **possible solutions** that satisfy the needs of all the parties.

4. Select a solution in **terms of the criteria** established earlier.

5. **Plan who** will do what, where, and when.

6. **Evaluate how** you handled the problem-solving process.

To Facilitate Movement Toward Agreement

A variety of tactics can be used. Remember: You are your behaviour. Some of the most effective tactics include:

1. **Advice and suggestions**—promises to indicate that compliance with what you want will benefit the other party.

2. Indication that failure to comply with your approach will have **adverse consequences** as far as the other party is concerned.

3. **Explanations** to tell the other party exactly why you want him or her to take certain actions.

4. Praise to let the other party know what kinds of things you value and therefore are likely to appreciate in future.

5. **Criticism** to let the other party know that you are highly dissatisfied with his or her behaviour.

6. **Leading questions** to gain compliance or acceptance.

7. **Apologies to stop** a "perceived" emotion inhibiting rational discussion.

8. **Reflecting** back the emotional content of what the other person is saying, in a concerned and non-evaluative way.

9. Adjournments as a means of **handling high emotion**.

10. Humour to **reduce tension** and help create a bond between the parties.

11. Summaries of **progress** to prevent reversion to earlier arguments.

Closing the Negotiations

Because we tend to interpret things differently, to avoid unpleasant surprises, before adjourning the last round of discussions:

1. **Clarify** the terms of agreement.

2. List the points of **agreement**, interpretation, and clarification as you see them

3. **How** will the agreement be recorded (memorandum of agreement, MoA)?

4. Confirm the **ratification process**: when, where, and how will it be reported out and to whom?

5. What are the **next steps after** the meeting? Who will do what, when?

6. **How** will the parties' constituents be informed of the agreement and next steps?

Learning from Results: Checklist for Reviewing Your Negotiation

When negotiations have concluded, you should review your experience. Review your objectives (broad and specific) and the approach you adopted to the negotiation. Consider the following questions:

- ☐ How satisfied are you with the **outcome** of the negotiations?

- ☐ Were you satisfied with the negotiation **process**? Was it efficient? Did it serve to enhance working relationships (individual and institutional), was it neutral or did it set the relationships back?

- ☐ Do you have a ***good* agreement**? Examine your agreement for a discussion of what constitutes a good agreement. Does what you have negotiated meet this test (fair, efficient, wise, stable)?

- ☐ Who was the more **effective** negotiator?

- ☐ Who conceded most? Why? Consider how matters were framed, the nature of the agenda and/or the degree to which the parties were in command of the issues.

- ☐ What **strategies** and actions helped the discussions most?

- ☐ What actions **hindered** the discussions?

- ☐ Did you **trust** the other party? What affected this feeling most?

- ☐ How well was **time** used? Could it be used better?

- ☐ How well did people **listen to each** other? Who talked most?

- ☐ Were **creative solutions** suggested? What happened to them?

- ☐ What were the **strongest arguments** put forward by the other party? How receptive was the other party to your arguments and ideas?

- ☐ Did you have a good understanding of the **underlying** issues and concerns of the other party? Did the other party understand yours? Did you **understand your own interests** and their relative priority? Did you satisfy your interests well? Why, why not?

- ☐ Conduct a process analysis of all phases of the negotiation from the preparation phase to the conclusion of the negotiations. What **improvements** could we make and how do we implement these process improvements?

☐ How adequate was your preparation? How did this affect the negotiation?

☐ What are your **main learning** points from this negotiation? What would you do differently next time?

☐ Did you move to the implementation phase thoroughly understanding the changes made to the agreement and the practical implications of those changes? How were those changes to be communicated to the workforce and ultimately implemented?

CHAPTER 10
Good Faith in Collective Bargaining

Duty to bargain: Obligation under labour relations statutes to bargain in good faith with a view to reaching a collective agreement; the duty to bargain in good faith includes the obligation to recognize the other party, to meet and engage in a rational discussion of the matters in issue, and to bargain with an intention to enter into a collective agreement.

Collective bargaining statutes in federal, provincial, and territorial jurisdictions require both employers and unions to bargain in good faith and make every reasonable effort to reach a collective agreement. Labour relations boards have the statutory authority to administer these good-faith provisions. They place the greatest emphasis on the 'how' of bargaining (the manner in which negotiations are conducted), as opposed to the 'what' (the bargaining proposals themselves).

Labour relations boards are reluctant to become involved in negotiations or to interfere with the economic forces that are key components in any negotiation. While these boards have typically not sought to address an imbalance of economic power, they have established other limits on the legality of proposals, communication between the parties' constituents, and attempts by one party to arbitrarily limit the scope of bargaining.

During heated bargaining sessions, it is not uncommon for one side to accuse the other side of bargaining in bad faith. However, the accusations far outnumber the actual violations.

Determination by a labour relations board as to whether a party has breached the duty to bargain in good faith has both a subjective element and an objective one. The intent of a party to frustrate negotiations and therefore hinder the conclusion of a collective agreement can be inferred from the party's actions and through the application of two tests:

- **Subjective Test**—Relates to the assessment of a party's motivation. This assessment is based on the labour relations board's perception of the negotiating process. For example, is one party simply going through the motions of negotiation? This assessment leads to an objective test.

- **Objective Test**—An objective analysis of the specific actions and reactions of the parties. This analysis allows a labour relations board to determine whether a party is making every reasonable effort to conclude a collective agreement.

Hard bargaining is not in itself a breach of the duty to bargain in good faith, provided there is no evidence that the employer or union is attempting to avoid reaching a collective agreement through the use of hard bargaining tactics. While a labour relations board will not usually examine the reasonableness of bargaining proposals, it will assess a party's conduct, to ensure that the party has not employed tactics that unreasonably inhibit the process of achieving an agreement.

Guidelines: The Duty to Bargain in Good Faith

Failure to meet certain general conditions can cause a claim of failure to bargain in good faith. The determination by a labour relations board as to whether bad faith bargaining has occurred will depend on the particulars of the situation. There are three general conditions that must be met, arising from labour relations board decisions throughout the country:

1. The parties must meet, and the employer **must recognize** the union as the exclusive bargaining agent for employees.

2. The parties must engage in **rational, informed** discussion.

3. The parties must **intend to enter** into a collective agreement.

The Parties Must Meet

When the parties meet, the employer must recognize the union as the exclusive bargaining agent for the employees. The implications for the employer are as follows:

- Direct bargaining with another union, or with the employees themselves, is prohibited.

- Tactics such as disparagement of the union, discrimination against union negotiators or unionized employees, and spying or infiltration are forbidden.

- The employer must send to the bargaining table negotiators who have authority to make bargaining decisions, or who are close to those who do.

- While the employer may communicate its bargaining position directly to its employees, it must do so accurately and without disparaging the union.

- The employer may not implement its wage proposals, even though the statutory "freeze" on changes in working conditions may have expired, before it negotiates them with the unions and reaches an impasse.

- The employer may not bypass union negotiators by granting a wage increase, even after the right to strike or lockout accrues, before a bargaining impasse is reached with the union.

- The employer may not insist on ratification by the employees (except in jurisdictions where legislation requires ratification).

- The employer may not demand that bargaining await the outcome of negotiations with other parties.

Implications for both parties are that:

- Neither party can object to the composition of the other party's bargaining committee, nor can the union include employees of another employer.

- While the parties can discuss the matter at the bargaining table, they may not take to impasse (a strike or lockout) a demand that the scope of the bargaining unit in the bargaining certificate be narrowed or widened.

The Parties Must Engage in Rational, Informed Discussion

Meeting and concluding a collective agreement requires discussion. The parties must be ready to meet with reasonable diligence and should be prepared to commit reasonable time and preparation to the collective bargaining process. The parties may not:

- Refuse to meet and may not engage in perfunctory attendances or take inflexible positions at meetings.

- Insist on discussion of one matter to the exclusion of others, or on settlement of one matter before other matters are discussed.

- Refuse to negotiate simply because a termination application has been made or a judicial review proceeding is pending, but a sale of a business may justify delay pending clarification of the union's bargaining rights.

- Break off negotiations arbitrarily.

The discussions between the parties must be rational and informed. While tactless and intemperate remarks may be tolerated, the parties must be honest and avoid deliberate misrepresentations. The parties should be prepared to justify particular negotiating positions and, if requested, the employer must provide relevant information to the union, including information regarding existing wages and working conditions, and—if inability to pay is asserted by the employer—financial information.

The employer may need to provide economic justification for any proposal that requires financial concessions such as wage reductions, changes to benefits, and the like. The employer must advise the union of firm plans or decisions that will affect the employees during the term of the contract, and if asked, must disclose plans that have a real likelihood of significantly affecting the bargaining unit.

The Parties Must Intend to Enter into a Collective Agreement

Labour relations boards have provided guidelines for the negotiating parties, for example that a party may not:

- Demand that negotiations be conducted in public, that members of management be included in the bargaining unit, or that the parties waive the protection of labour relations legislation.

- Make sudden and unjustified changes in position—for example, change its position on monetary issues without evidence of changed economic circumstances.

- Seek agreement to an illegal condition.

- Fail to seek ratification when it is a term of the settlement.

- Unduly delay execution of a negotiated settlement in order to reduce financial obligations.

While a party can put forward a position that would predictably fail to receive acceptance, it may not make a demand that is deliberately inflammatory or is tailor-made for rejection

The employer has particular guidelines to observe, including that the employer may not:

- Foster dissension among employees, favour anti-union employees, or suggest economic suffering if union representation continues.

- Threaten to close part or all of the employer's organization unless closure is in fact an economic reality.

- Refuse to accept an offer until the union holds a ratification vote.

- Refuse to execute the terms of a negotiated settlement on the ground that its governing body has rejected the settlement, when the settlement was not made subject to ratification.
- At the last minute, refuse to enter into a collective agreement when all terms have been agreed on.

Some labour relations boards guidelines address the specifics of strikes and lockouts such as a party may not:

- Strike or lockout in order to secure agreement that the bargaining unit be altered, or that work jurisdiction be reorganized where jurisdictional dispute procedures exist.
- Respond to acknowledgement by the union that its strike is lost by insisting on outrageous conditions.
- Threaten an illegal strike or lockout.
- Strike or lockout after agreeing to interest arbitration.

Other considerations include:

- An employer may not refuse to agree to arbitration respecting the discharge of employees for strike-related activities and demand that employers returning to work following a strike be deemed probationary employees.
- By refusing to negotiate, a union may not force the employer to rescind lawful discipline of strikers who engaged in illegal conduct.

Remedies for Failure to Bargain in Good Faith

Depending on the jurisdiction, labour relations boards can impose many remedies for breaches of the duty to bargain in good faith. Boards attempt to tailor remedies to each case. In general, boards follow these principles:

- A remedy is not considered a penalty
- Monetary relief is compensatory
- A collective agreement may not be imposed unless permitted by statute.

Where statutory authority permits, a labour relations board may:

- Impose the terms of a collective agreement on the parties
- Direct one party or the other to put forward or withdraw a particular proposal
- Issue a directive that further negotiations be conducted in good faith
- Order the parties to resume bargaining with the assistance of a mediator.

In addition, where it is determined that a strike has been caused or prolonged by bad-faith bargaining and the union's position has been eroded as a result, the labour relation board may reinstate the employees and direct that lost wages be paid.

Although a labour relations board needs to safeguard the substantive rights it administers, compliance with labour legislation ultimately depends on the negotiating parties respecting the statutory framework, the labour relations board, and the board's directives.

"Every now and then, I find myself in a room filled with people who are wrong."

Used with permission, The New Yorker Collection/The Cartoon Bank, 2020 by Frank Cotham (2018)

CHAPTER 11
At an Impasse: Strikes and Lockouts

Labour statutes grant broad discretion to unions and employers and their pursuit of collective bargaining objects. Public policy suggests that bargaining statutes must balance two objectives:

- Allow the parties the freedom to pursue their goals while,

- Reducing the costs of union-employer conflict and the costs resulting from decisions to resolve this conflict.

The following is an overview of strikes, lockouts, and bargaining assistance.

Strikes, Lockouts, and Picketing

Strikes and lockouts are tools that can be employed to pressure one side or the other to accept their bargaining demands. A strike is the withholding of labour by employees in order to obtain better compensation or working conditions. A lockout is the opposite, being the temporary shutdown of an organization by an employer to compel employees to accept certain conditions.

Labour relations codes regulate strikes, lockouts, and picketing. A "strike" includes a cessation of work, a refusal to work or to continue to work by employees in combination or in concert or in accordance with a common understanding, or a slowdown or other concerted activity on the part of employees that is designed to or does restrict or limit production or services.

- Generally speaking, a strike is a refusal to work by employees acting with a common purpose. The usual purpose of a strike is to compel an employer to agree to terms and conditions of employment proposed by the union. A strike need not be a complete stoppage of work; for example, overtime bans and work slowdowns can constitute a strike. A withdrawal of services by employees, which arises from a legitimate concern for their own safety or health, or to enforce a non-affiliation clause, is not a strike.

- Similarly, a lockout is a restriction by the employer of work that normally would be available for employees, generally by suspending work or closing the place of employment. It is generally intended to compel those employees, or to aid another employer to compel employees, to agree to terms and conditions of employment proposed by the employer.

Strikes and lockouts during the life of a collective agreement, and every agreement *must* contain a provision prohibiting "wildcat" strikes or lockouts. Any differences arising during the term of a collective agreement must be settled through the grievance and arbitration procedures set out in the agreement.

Preconditions to a Strike or Lockout

Certain legal preconditions must be satisfied before a strike or lockout can begin. The pre-conditions can include:

- ☐ The union and employer must have engaged in collective bargaining.

- ☐ A vote must have been held to determine if the majority of employees favour a strike or, in the case of an accredited employers' association, if the majority of the employers of the association favour a lockout.

- ☐ Strike or lockout notice of a specified number of hours must have been given to both the other party and to the LRB, and the specified number of hours must have expired; or

- ☐ In some jurisdictions, if a mediation officer has been appointed by the LRB or by the Minister of Labour, that appointment must have come to an end, and a specified number of hours must have passed.

These preconditions are intended to ensure that bargaining takes place before strikes and lockouts begin. They also ensure that strikes and lockouts are supported by the majority of those who will be taking the action and that the potential disruption caused by a strike or lockout is reduced by providing notice that it is about to occur.

A strike vote does not necessarily mean there will be a strike right away. There are limits to when however. In British Columbia for example, strike can be called within three months after the date of a favourable strike vote. If a strike is not called during that time, another vote must be held in order to renew the union's strike mandate. The same restriction applies to lockout votes.

A union must give 72 hours written notice of its intention to strike to both the employer and the LRB, and the full 72 hours must elapse before engaging in strike activity. Similarly, an employer must give 72 hours written notice of a lockout.

In certain instances, as when perishable property is involved, the LRB may lengthen the normal 72-hour period of strike or lockout notice. If services designated as essential are involved, the union or employer must provide a new 72-hour notice if one notice period ends without any strike or lockout.

What are the Consequences of an Unlawful Strike or Lockout?

If any of the preconditions mentioned above are not met, either the employer, or the union may make an application to the LRB alleging an unlawful strike or lockout. Generally, upon receipt of such an application, the LRB will, on short notice, hold a hearing. If the LRB finds that the strike or lockout is unlawful, a variety of remedies, including cease and desist orders, is available to it. The LRB may also make other remedial orders. These orders, like any LRB orders, may be filed in court and are enforceable as court orders.

Continuation of Benefits

Most existing health and welfare benefits normally provided by the employer must continue to be available to legally striking or locked out employees, provided the union pays the total costs or premiums of such benefits (both the employer and employee's portion).[38] This means that striking employees do not have their benefits coverage interrupted as long as the union is willing to pay for them.

Picketing

Striking or locked out employees are entitled to picket where they normally perform work that is an integral and substantial part of the employer's operation and under the control and direction of the employer. Other operations of the employer may not be picketed. For example, if the employer operates at more than one location, the striking or locked out employees can picket only the location(s) for which their union is certified and at which they perform their work.

---

38 In British Columbia, for example, pursuant to LR Code section 62 Continuation of benefits.

With the permission of the LRB, picketing may also be conducted at other sites; for example, where an employer attempts to have "struck work" performed away from its premises. Striking or locked out employees may also picket the place of business of an "ally" of their employer. An ally is a person who assists an employer in a lockout or in resisting a lawful strike. Ally picketing is restricted to the site at which the ally performs work for the benefit of the employer who is directly involved.

Where more than one employer—a college or independent daycare within school district boundaries, for example—carries on business at the same site (referred to as a "common site"), the LRB generally restricts picketing so that it affects only the employer involved in the labour dispute or the ally of that employer. The LRB does have the discretion to regulate picketing at a common site to ensure that the union does have a way to picket in pursuit of legitimate objectives. This means that the LRB, in some circumstances, may allow regulated picketing at a common site that does affect third parties. Such circumstances occur when the union has no other way of picketing at the workplace of the striking employees. As a result, a college class or day care centre operating on school district property may find itself behind a picket line.

Strikes, Lockouts, and Essential Services

Federal and provincial/territorial labour relations statutes and certain sector specific statutes address strikes, lockouts, and the designation of essential services. The designation of certain facilities, productions, and services as essential does not remove the right to strike from a union. A strike under an essential service regime is what has been termed a "controlled strike." Paul Weiler, former chair of the BC Labour Relations Board, commented on the controlled strike concept in his seminal book, *Reconcilable Differences*:

> This legal device performs not only its manifest function of protecting public safety in the community, but also the latent function of protecting the collective bargaining process as well. The absolute and unrestricted right of hospital workers to shut down the hospitals in a community (or of police officers to cut off police protection) is actually incompatible with the logic of free collective bargaining. When there is no police force in a large urban area, or the hospitals are shut down, panic spreads in the community. Irresistible pressure mounts for the government to do something immediately: either to settle the dispute at any cost or at least to legislate an end to the strike and force the parties before a third party for a binding decision. Since everyone knows this will happen, and then whatever may appear in the face of the statute, the legal prospect of a strike cannot play its intended role in real-life negotiations. Knowing full

well that any strike would be allowed to last only a few hours, why should the police board and the police union make economically painful and politically touchy compromises at the bargaining table in order to avoid the even more unpleasant consequences of a protracted work stoppage?

The essential services designation process contemplates that the bargaining agents involved generally work together with the assistance of a LRB mediator to determine what services are necessary and essential to prevent serious and immediate danger to the health, safety, or welfare to a jurisdiction's residents. The statute defines the nature and scope of essentiality. If agreement cannot be reached, the LRB makes the designation.

Causes of Strikes and Lockouts

Strikes and lockouts—tools, tactics and strategies to pressure one side or the other to accept their bargaining demands—often seem to be grounded in sound strategic decisions. Unfortunately, a considered analysis suggests otherwise. There are a number of factors that contribute to strikes and lockouts that need to be addressed well before one is contemplated. These include:

- **Lack of clarity to begin with**: Collective bargaining is one of the most complex areas of negotiation. There are rarely clear cut or mutually agreed upon notions of what a fair salary and benefits package would be, so employers and unions, either individually or collectively, often find themselves at odds. Further, bargaining is rarely limited to questions of compensation. Working conditions, safety concerns or questions about employee rights, regularly surface and must be reconciled.

  Clarity of purpose and process or lack thereof is often at the root of a strike or lockout pursuit. While you may believe that those you represent have the necessary degree of familiarity and understanding of the objectives of the negotiations, the reality is that the specifics are lost on them. Even though the issues and options are set out clearly and you have the documents to prove it, people tend to hear, see and internalize generalities and generalizations. This is their interpretive lens focused on "getting and not getting", "concessions", "legitimate and illegitimate demands", and "them and us". The decision to strike or lockout is viewed through the lens of generality.

- **Stance, orientations and the status quo**: Extensive, well publicized agendas, in some cases with item by item membership approval, sets the stage for difficult days ahead. Couple the agenda creation with maximalist or equitable positioning bargaining norms, now you are collectively challenged to reach a collective agreement. To some this represents the status quo, this is how negotiations are done. Strike votes, strikes, and lockouts are just additional features. Many are invested in this status quo, whether they be consultants, influencers, purported labour relations/legal experts, commentators and others have convinced themselves that *things will never change.*

- **Failure of imagination**: With *all we knew* and/or *should have known*—a circumstance when something that is undesirable (impasse) yet seemingly predictable is not planned for—animated by differences in stated positions, thought processes, attitudes, understandings, and sometimes even perceptions. Made increasingly intractable by positioning and position taking.

- **Overconfidence and the rightness of *our* case**: The case that is made in pursuit of bargaining objectives often lead negotiators to believe that their case is stronger than it really is, while underestimating the other side's willingness to stand firm. When one side doubts the other side's claims, a strike or lockout becomes even more tempting.

- **Rightness and the fairness pursuit**: People tend to view the world in a self-serving manner and define the rational thing to do or a fair outcome or process in a way that benefits them. Combined with the *rightness of our case* can blind negotiators to elements, packages and deals that would leave both sides better off. It is sometimes taken a step further: to make a point or send a message by punishing those believed to have treated your group unfairly in the process so that *this never happen again. This will teach them for next time.*

- **Misinterpreting your dual concerns:** Viewing negotiation as a competition to be "won" keeps us focused on position based negotiation employing all the tenets of distributive bargaining at the expense of the integrative potential that is resident in employment matters. This stands in the way of an agreement that will satisfy, to a degree, everyone's interests. Further, representatives at the bargaining table can have incentives that are misaligned with the interests of those they represent. At times they may be more concerned about appearing to positionally "stand firm" than with working out an agreement.

- **Investment and commitment**: Incremental commitment to a strike or lockout can make it difficult to end one. When the decision to "hold out for a few more days" is repeated, a strike or lockout can last for months, even years. The notion of "sunk costs" weigh heavily on us. The decision to cut our losses can be extremely difficult to make.

Consider: If these are the causes of strikes and lockouts what are the remedies?

CHAPTER 12

Bargaining Assistance: Conciliation, Mediation, Arbitration and Inquiry

There are a variety of forms of bargaining assistance that can be accessed by the parties in the event of a bargaining impasse. As Figure 17 illustrates, they range from consensual process assistance to determination of the matters through adjudication such as interest arbitration.

It is important to remember that consensual processes are the most advantageous and help build understanding and working relationships. If you and the other party opt to have a third party adjudicate the matters at issue and resolve them for you, it means that the parties are agreeing to give up control over the outcome. The third party has control of the process and any decision that flows from that process.

Figure 17: Bargaining Assistance Alternatives Continuum

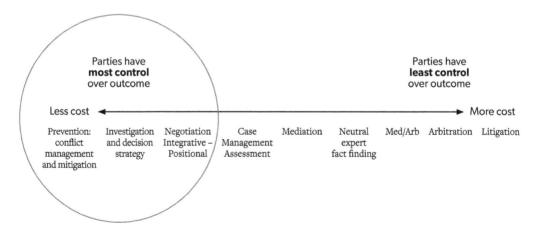

Conciliation and Mediation

Conciliation and mediation are forms of bargaining assistance. They can be initiated by the parties, on application to the administrative agency responsible for the labour relations statute or in certain cases by the government. Conciliation and mediation are terms used in federal and selected provincial/territorial statutes and mediation in most Canadian jurisdictions.

Parties engaged collective bargaining are often unable to reconcile their differences alone, or fail to reach outcomes that are adequate for both parties. Mediators can add a great deal of value by helping parties to efficiently and effectively examine the issues at hand, take the interests and perspectives of all the stakeholders into account, and identify creative solutions that leave the parties better off than they would be in the absence of agreement. Mediators offer a suite of techniques to support effective problem-solving.

> Mediation is the intervention into a dispute or negotiation by an acceptable, impartial, and neutral third party . . .
> It is an extension of the collective bargaining process.
> It is essentially a continuation of negotiations under the control and supervision of a third party.

Mediation is the intervention into a dispute or negotiation by an acceptable, impartial, and neutral third party to assist the parties in voluntarily reaching their own mutually acceptable settlement. It is an extension of the collective bargaining process. It is essentially a continuation of negotiations under the control and supervision of a third party.

Mediators do not make judgements or determine outcomes—they ask questions that help to uncover underlying problems, assist the parties to understand the issues, and help them clarify the options for resolving their difference or dispute. The mediator has no authority to make the final decisions. The prime responsibility for reaching agreement rests solely with the parties themselves, as the employer and the union must live with the result of the deal.

Why Mediate?

Mediation is most effective when used as early as possible, before a conflict becomes too entrenched. The reasons bargaining parties request mediation include when:

- The parties are encountering **difficulties in communicating**, let alone negotiating (e.g., personality conflicts).

- One or both of the parties may have maneuvered themselves into positions from which they **cannot be extricated without loss of face**. The intervention of the mediator provides an opportunity for each to move, in response to the suggestion of an outsider who is not a party to the dispute, without appearing to yield to the other.

- The parties have **reached a deadlock**, know that further movement might be possible, but need the impetus of a neutral third party to propose ways in which a compromise can be reached. The mediator can assist the parties in exploring "avenues of accommodation"—he/she can gauge the receptiveness of an approach to resolving a particular matter in dispute without either party formalizing the approach into an offer, thus jeopardizing their bargaining postures.

- The parties have reached an impasse over somewhat **complex issues** and are unable to reach agreement on **an accommodation or even a compromise** solution. In such cases, the mediator can act as a "new voice," suggesting novel solutions to the issues at hand.

- It is obvious that the **mandates of the parties are well apart**, and little is being served by continuing in direct negotiations; at the same time, neither party is ready for strike or lockout action.

Mediation Process Guidelines and Suggestions

The decision to seek mediation is an important one for negotiators, and having made such a decision, it is important to get the most value possible from the intervention. The following is a handy checklist when preparing to participate in a mediation exercise:

- ☐ Understand the matters that will be the subject of the mediation and your interests. Don't **confuse your interests with the positions** you have taken.

- ☐ Focus the mediator on the **first-order issues** (i.e., the primary topics or problems of the dispute); don't assume the mediator will "just know."

- ☐ Don't **over-inform the mediator** by filling in the second-order issues (i.e., underlying or subordinate concerns that, while important, don't address the immediate focus of the dispute); a good mediator will be able to discover such underlying problems independently.

- ☐ Don't tell the mediator **your overall agenda or long-range plan** with regard to the dispute or your relationship with the other party; this may distract the mediator or taint the mediator's approach to the dispute.

- Be **specific and realistic** about the benefits to be gained through mediation and realize that it is necessary to surrender some process control to salvage and secure a better outcome; you do not surrender control over the outcome.

- If you are unsure about the nature or extent of the mediator's role, say so; your degree of benefit from the process is **directly proportionate** to your support for, and understanding of, the mediation process.

- Don't be afraid to **express your concerns or objections** (the mediator has specific skills in addressing and clarifying positions and issues)—be prepared, though, to commit to the clarification once it is made.

- Understand that a good mediator often functions as an "**agent of reality**," helping both parties manage their expectations, as well as clarifying the likely consequences of no agreement.

- A thoughtful mediator **may help you test** a tentative agreement by asking probing or "what if" questions to assist in identifying all potentially involved parties (whether present at the mediation or not).

- Expect assistance, but **don't expect miracles**; mediators are process "mechanics."

- Recognize that mediation **often involves** resolution development by a process of elimination; when parties specify what they don't want, what is left is usually the only viable resolution.

When all else is said and done, the problem is still between you and the union; it is not the mediator's. Mediation **reinforces your ultimate responsibility** to identify, choose, and implement your own outcome.

Other Alternatives

Inquiries and Statutory Commissions

- **Fact Finding**
  In some jurisdictions labour relations statutes provide for the appointment of a fact finder in any collective bargaining dispute. The role of the fact finder is to confer with the parties to determine which matters they have agreed to and which matters remain in dispute.

The fact finder's report may include any matter that is considered relevant to the settlement of a collective agreement, but the report is not binding on the parties. Both parties receive a copy of the fact finder's report, and it may also be made public.

- **Commissions of Inquiry**
  In Canada, federal, provincial, and territorial jurisdictions have the power, where deemed in the public interest, to appoint commissions of inquiry into union-employer disputes. In BC for example, the minister responsible for labour relations may appoint an Industrial Inquiry Commission to *maintain or secure labour relations stability and to promote conditions leading to the settlement of disputes*. Such commissions work with a specific mandate from the minister. The union and employer may agree to be bound by the report of an Industrial Inquiry Commission. Such inquiries are infrequent.

Mediation-Arbitration (Med-Arb)

Med-Arb is a process whereby the parties engage in mediation first. Failing resolution of the dispute through mediation, interest arbitration would be invoked. This method was developed by recognizing the advantages and disadvantages of mediation. This model allows the parties to develop and craft their own settlement, while providing for a full and decisive resolution to the bargaining impasse.

Final Offer Selection (FOS)

FOS is a method of dispute resolution that requires the arbitrator to choose between the final offers proposed by the union or the employer. This method is designed to encourage the parties to take reasonable and realistic positions during collective bargaining.

There are numerous variations on the basic FOS model. The goal of FOS is to refashion interest arbitration, so it is comparable to a strike. Both parties put their final offers on the table, and if they cannot agree, the arbitrator selects one of the two offers. In this case, the arbitrator is not allowed to put together a new package; one of the two proposals must be selected.

This method is believed to force both parties to make reasonable demands and to empathize with the needs and demands of the other party. If one party chooses to make unreasonable demands, that party faces the risk of losing it all. This is believed to make the negotiations and the bargaining atmosphere more conducive to reaching a voluntary settlement.

Although FOS increases the likelihood of a settlement, it does not guarantee it. This is because the arbitrator is locked into an either/or choice. For whatever reasons, both parties may not be able to put forward a proposal that goes against what they see as their principles. Or, one of the parties may attempt to slip something into a contract that may appear moderate in monetary terms or in terms that reduce management rights or union security, but that never would have been agreed to under normal collective bargaining.

In arbitration, normally the arbitrator does not make any major changes to the collective agreement, whereas this method allows major changes to be slipped into the agreement. In addition, the parties often cannot agree on issues that are not truly commensurable—that is, when the common denominator is not money. FOS is not a common dispute resolution choice in Canadian jurisdictions.

Final Offer Selection Variants

- Dual Total Package
  Under the dual total package procedure, the parties have the option of submitting their final offer plus one alternate final offer.

- By-Issue Selection
  FOS by issue means that the collective agreement results from the party choosing the best final offer on an issue-by-issue basis, so that the final agreement is a mix of items proposed by the union and the employer. The selector may choose items from either party's package but cannot change the item selected.

- Tri-Offer Selection
  Under this model, the selector has three offers to choose from for each issue—the union's, the employer's or the recommendations of the fact finder, which have been made known to the parties before arbitration starts. The fact finder's recommendations may endorse one of the two parties' final offers or may be completely different. Similarly, the parties may endorse the recommendations of the fact finder for any issue.

- Repeated-Offer Selection
  This procedure is the same as total package selection, except that in instances where the arbitrator considers both final offers to be unworkable and unfair, the parties may be ordered to submit better final offers. This procedure must be used sparingly in order that it not affect the negotiating incentive that is the strength of the FOS.

- Modified Final Offer Selection
Modified FOS also functions as regular, total package FOS. However, in the event the arbitrator receives two unacceptable offers, the arbitrator has the option of writing his/her own settlement. The arbitrator's settlement can only become the agreement by consent of both parties. If one party vetoes the arbitrator's proposal, then one of the original two final offers must be selected.

- Multiple-Offer Final Selection
Under Multiple-Offer FOS each party submits multiple offers to the arbitrator. Three would probably be the ideal number. The arbitrator then considers all six of the offers and chooses the best among them. The arbitrator does not reveal which offer she selected; only which party submitted it. The other party is then left to decide which of the three it wants. The advantages of this system are that each party has an incentive to submit three different and reasonable offers with the hope that one of them will be chosen.

Interest Arbitration

Interest arbitration is a form of arbitration used to establish the terms of a collective agreement where the parties are unable to do so through negotiations. This form of arbitration occurs primarily in the public sector where statutes have removed the parties' right to strike. Interest arbitration can be an effective dispute resolution mechanism because it:

- Protects the public interest by preventing strikes.

- Safeguards employee interests by equalizing bargaining power.

- Regulates group conflict, and

- From the union's perspective, can be beneficial because it typically results in higher wage settlements.

Some argue, however, that interest arbitration is not always an ideal solution, and has its own range of disadvantages. They posit that, more often than not, an arbitrator has little or no understanding of:

- Public finance.

- The long-term effects on the employer's budget of small changes to working conditions.

- Substitutability of capital for labour as proposed wage increases make labour more expensive.

- Long-range costs of funding pension increases as the composition of the workforce changes.

And because of the limited background knowledge or understanding, the following tendencies arise:

- Decisions are made conservatively, because arbitrators do not want to make any major changes to the agreement.

- Arbitrators tend to stick to the simple monetary issues where they only need to decide "more or less."

- Decisions tend to fall in the middle of both parties' initial positions. As evidence of this, interest arbitrators seldom write a decision explaining why they chose one wage rate or benefit over another.

- When interest arbitration becomes the norm, the union does not need to consider what the real needs of its membership are. The union simply makes up a long list of demands and allows the arbitrator to decide.

In some provinces, interest arbitration has moved away from being a fail-safe mechanism to replace the strike/lockout threat, towards being a goal of one or the other parties. This phenomenon is referred to as the "narcotic" effect, with the parties having undue reliance on interest arbitration as the mechanism to conclude an agreement. Interest arbitration allows both parties to elude responsibility for the content and the wording of the collective agreement and allows both parties to avoid responsibility for selling, defending, and criticizing it.

This dispute resolution method allows both sides to escape accountability for the terms and conditions of the new collective agreement and allows them to hide behind the defence that it was the arbitrator who decided the exact terms of the agreement. This has what is referred to as a "chilling" effect on the bargaining process leading to a further undue reliance on interest arbitration as the mechanism to conclude an agreement.

CONCLUSION: PREPARING TO Constructively Engage on Things That Matter

Collective bargaining enjoys a unique degree of complexity and a measure of tradition in the field of negotiations. One feature that is typically absent is that of continuous improvement. Relying on past experiences and what we believe collective bargaining to be about, we tend to replicate what we are used to, a variant of Friedman's experiences described in Chapter 2. The belief that bargaining is more than likely a zero-sum proposition—a gain for the other side represents a loss for me, both in terms of process and substance—causing you to behave in ways that creates a competitive atmosphere. Consequently, the approach to reconciling matters at issue leads to a focus on position taking and positioning characterized by zealous advocacy of each party's positions.

As bargaining progresses you tell your constituents about the difficulties and dynamics of this latest contest. When finished you set about to implement an agreement that was "okay" given the circumstances.

Maybe it's not that *we replicate what we're used to* but rather we act as we do and make the process choices we make because of the other side, *them*—the *intractables*. Do you find yourself or members of your constituent groups lamenting on the state of bargaining generally and the other team's approach to bargaining specifically. Do any of these themes or comments sound familiar?

> *They just don't know how to bargain. With impractical, fixed positions they can't make a deal on anything. They seem to always be catering to the radical elements. Their structure leads them to impasse on day one. They ask the membership what it wants, create proposals, ratify the list and present them as written. To make a change they always need to check. Look at our history. We start slow followed by endless meetings. The big issues are always left to the end and then we have a problem.*

While an agreement is eventually reached working relationships are tested and in many cases the stage is set for continuing disputes during the term of the agreement.

But, is this the best we can do? As a preparatory matter it is instructive and helpful to reflect on the following five points at the outset of negotiations and make purposeful choices re the matters at issue, the approaches/processes to reconcile those matters and the desired relationships between the participants in the endeavor rather than simply react to events in the moment.

1. Consider You and *Them*

During what we assume or come to believe as difficult, apparently intractable collective bargaining circumstances, we can often turn our attention to the other team and say *but for them, we could get a deal*.

> Realistically, though, the only person we can truly control or manage in a contentious situation is ourselves. And in managing our own reactions, in seeking more constructive responses from ourselves, we inevitably change the interaction with the other person(s). When we change, and improve the quality of the whole interaction, then we may increase everyone's capacity to act differently or "better."

Consider the power of what people see and hear. It is possible that the one party has prior perceptions and expectations about the other. Find opportunities to act inconsistently with those prior views. When you can act in a way that directly contradicts those preconceptions, it can effectively send a message that you are interested and open to another approach.

Recognize that collective bargaining is a collective effort—between two parties who have multi-facetted, variably motivated constituents and groups. And whether you are the bargaining spokesperson, a team member or a resident in a constituent group, you never think alone and are not a sole actor. Making change requires marshalling the many individuals with their ideas, assumptions and frames of reference in support of the agreed upon direction. Remember Figure 5 *What You See and Hear and What you Don't See and Hear* with what you don't see and hear driving individual's decisions.

2. From Now to Understanding

Since we live and work in context, situate yourself and your organization in context. Taking Friedman's observations and the Walton and McKersie emergent relationship model as organizers how do you characterize union-employer relations and in particular collective bargaining? Take the Emergent Relationship Quick Test (Figure 9). What relationship predominates—conflict, containment aggression, accommodation, cooperation?

Note the influence of frames of reference, the blend of feelings, values, and data related to how people see the world. From a union-employer relationship and in particular a collective bargaining perspective, another way to view these frames is as ideologies of management control. As identified in Chapter 1 the predominance of a particular frame—unitarist, pluralist, radical determines:

- one's perceptions of existing employer-union relations in the workplace;

- one's evaluation of the status quo—the current state of things—in the workplace;

- one's responses to the status quo when (if at all) it is sought to change the balance of power in employer-union relations.

One's perceptions, evaluation, and responses influence how parties develop bargaining objectives, positions, and how they choose to conduct bargaining.

How are you informed?

3. Awareness in preparation: Unconscious Biases, Perceptions, and the Matters at Issue

You probably regularly encounter situations where you are convinced that you know exactly what is going on, only to find out that things are not as you thought.[39] The complexities of preparing to bargain collectively is no exception. Keep the following concepts in mind as you work with the people, circumstances, and thinking of those we are working with to complete this effort.

When it comes to how we view our environment and the people we interact with, there is often a disconnect between what we *think* should be and *what* is.

This disconnect is usually the result of an unconscious perception error or bias. As you make decisions and take action based on your perceptions, there is a risk that these unconscious biases could negatively affect the outcome.

People have general tendencies in how we process information and establish meaning that drive the dissonance between our perceptions and our reality.

There are many types of cognitive biases but there are two basic examples that regularly come into play when we try to make sense of the world.

---

39 Adapted from the *Constructive Deliberations Tool Kit*, the Centre for the Study of Educational Leadership and Policy (CSELP) at Simon Fraser University (SFU), 2019-2021.

Confirmation Bias

As we try to determine meaning in the world around us, we subconsciously give weight to information that confirms our existing perceptions, and we discount information that would force us to re-evaluate these perceptions.

Common examples of confirmation bias are the **recency effect** (our tendency to give more weight to information that we have encountered more recently) or the **primacy effect** (our tendency to seek out information that confirms our first impressions of things).

Confirmation bias might come into play in the workplace, for example, when you determine the course of action to address a contentious or potentially contentious situation. You might be convinced by recent stories you've heard, articles you've read or in what you believe to be lessons from analogous situations even though *this matter at issue* has its own specific set of facts, context, and history.

While it is often helpful to be informed by other like events, confirmation bias can make it harder for us to objectively identify and consider matters at issue and the constructive alternatives available to you.

To reduce confirmation bias, consider what you know, what you need to know and what might be contentious and reflect on the circumstance from an outsider's perspective. If you knew nothing about the situation and were reading about it for the first time, how would you react concerning what you know and what you don't? Your answers might reveal some information needs and challenges that confirmation bias had shrouded.

False Consensus Effect

We overestimate how much other people think and behave like we do. This error in perception may cause us to believe that other people agree with our decisions and actions—even when they don't. Since people tend to associate with other people with similar opinions and views, we also think those people see things the same way we do.

False consensus effect comes to life at work in many scenarios. For example, you might be convinced that your first reaction to an issue and your proposed approach to address it enjoys a consensus. However, when you share your conclusions and approach you find that others question your snap judgement and your ideas built on that foundation.

Inability to anticipate a different point of view or to reconcile two distinct perspectives can lead to a deadlock, which prevents you from moving forward.

There are many other biases that cause complications as we look specifically at individual behavior. Errors often occur when we try to assess our own input and that of others relative to the outcome of implementing decisions. When we attempt to attribute success or failure to various decisions or behaviors, two key biases come into play.

Self-serving Bias

When it comes to evaluating our own decisions and behaviors, we tend to attribute successes to our personal characteristics and to blame failures on external causes.

Fundamental Attribution Error

Conversely, when we evaluate the outcomes of actions taken by other individuals, we place more weight on factors that we relate to their personal characteristics as opposed to external factors that may affect them.

One Way Forward

Whether it's a lack of accuracy in our perception of the world around us or a more specific bias in how we analyze information and behaviors, there are steps that you can take to minimize negative effects.

The first step is acknowledging that these biases exist and can impact our decisions and actions.

The next step is to increase your awareness of specific values, beliefs, and perceptions that you hold. Self-awareness is key in creating an empathetic approach to interacting with other people.

Finally, increased interaction and communication with your colleagues will help you reduce the risk of misinterpreting their intentions and subsequent behaviors.

Working to identify and minimize the effects of perception bias can help you generate a more accurate picture of the world and people around you.

4. Consider Your Approach and the Pursuit of Constructive Alternatives

As a General Proposition

If your approach can be best characterized as positioning, position taking, and predominately distributive in nature, is this approach the best in the circumstance? A plain reading of the concept of integrative potential contrasted with traditional collective bargaining approaches with their positional, distributive features would lead you to answer no. An examination of the Emergent Relationship Model (Figure 8) in your context, maybe the stories you've been told or union-employer experiences you've had, may give you pause. Are we making purposeful choices? Do you (we) adopt positioning approaches—maximalist positioning, equitable positioning—for a reason or just by default? Are there constructive alternatives?

Before the *Intractables* Become Irreconcilable: Preparation Focussed on Potentials

How are you informed by your bargaining history? Does it tell you that *more often than not we are at impasse, stalemate, stuck* or however you characterize the circumstance at some point in negotiations? What if the ideas, facts, statements or positions of the parties are again so different that it seems no common ground can be found?

The time to **consider the potential of intractability is before** negotiations begin. It is a matter of anticipation, preparation, and being unconditionally constructive. Your bargaining history and experiences gives you a sense of the potential for impasse on specific issues, groups of issues or an agreement generally. If so, what now? How do we prepare?

The **first principle** is to **learn** from results, the last rounds of bargaining and to make the best use of the time in between negotiations. If there were items, subjects, or areas that were contentious, subjects of disagreement and have a likelihood of being contentious again identify them.

Invite your negotiating counterpart to identify, review, investigate these matters and co-create an analytic frame, a common knowledge base to inform these issues. Deliberations and decisions are informed and improved by using a jointly developed knowledge base or analytic frame as a resource.

To make an informed decision an **analytic frame helps** answer the questions central to that effort: what do I (we) now, what do I (we) need to know and what might be contentious or potentially contentious? This common knowledge base limits if not eliminates unproductive conflict (what I think vs. what you think debates) that often arises during efforts to reconcile the matters at issue.

The **second principle** is to consider your **bargaining stance**. According to William Ury, co-founder of the Program on Negotiation at the Harvard Law School, in his book, "Getting Past No," people commonly react in one of three ways when they find themselves in intractable situations. They:

- **Respond in kind**, strike back: Fight fire with fire so to speak. This reaction usually involves reacting to the apparent intractability with direct and as deemed necessary inflammatory language. Firmly anchor positions using maximalist positioner strategies. To some degree perform for your audience, your own side.

- **Give in**, concede: When intimidated or exasperated people may give in to unreasonable arguments and demands just to conclude the conflict. A variant of the give in approach is to compromise or make less than optimal accommodations in the hope that we can just move on. There's nothing I can do, they are always this way.

- **Break off**: This involves a total break in discussions/negotiations with the party one views as obstinate, unproductive and unwilling. This ends the problem for the immediate term in hopes that the other party will have come to their senses if and when discussions continue.

Rather than default to one of these common reactions Ury suggests that it is much more productive to simply "go to the balcony." The "balcony" is a metaphor for detaching oneself from the circumstance even though your personal allegiances and objectives may lead you to have strong opinions about the best result. From this perspective, you are dispassionate—detached and unemotional, able to see a clearer picture of the problem, the union and employer as bargaining institutions, and the people (advisors, influencers, central characters, and constituents). As someone involved in or responsible for the collective bargaining effort you must recognize that the alternatives chosen, decisions made, and agreement reached must satisfy the interests of the broader organization as well as those central to the matters at issue.

Taking a time out and going to the balcony can help preserve a working relationship and maintain a constructive posture. It can help you see more creative ways of addressing matters by allowing you to broaden your perspective of the problem. It gives you time and a frame of mind to be able to understand the concerns of the other party and think of possible process and substance alternatives.

"We are not under siege, Your Majesty. You just have a siege mentality."

Used with permission, The New Yorker Collection/The Cartoon Bank, 2020 by Dana Fradon (1984).

In the stress and frustration of an apparently intractable situation you need to find your inner balcony and:

Suspend judgement and hold your reaction

- Consider the three common reactions and the limitations of them.
    - Respond in kind
    - Give in
    - Break off
- Identify your triggers. Something that generates a prolonged emotional reaction in you. These reactions animate any conflict triggered by them. What gets you to react and why?

- You may have strong emotions in the circumstance. Don't be demonstrably emotional: "Have" vs. "be" your emotions.

Stop, reflect and think

- **Pause and say nothing**. While you can't eliminate your feelings you can refuse to react to what the other party is saying. You need to disconnect the automatic link between emotion and action.

- **Rewind** *the tape*: Slow down the conversation by playing it back. You can tell your disputant what you understand from what they said and see if you heard them right. For instance, try saying "Let me make sure I understand your point of view, you think we should… because…"

- Take a **time-out**: Give yourself and the other party a chance to cool off and go to the balcony. Whether it be 5 minutes, or the need to revisit the topic another day, taking the time can let you think through your emotions. Consider for a moment, *"you know, maybe they have a point here"*

- **Don't make** important decisions on the spot: After suspending your initial reaction, you can then consider the problem and your options in a more objective fashion, out on the balcony. As necessary take time to consult with your group.

With this re-orientation return to the matters at issue and review, recast, reframe and proceed. Use this framework to inform your approach to negotiations, circumstances that arise, and the potential of intractability.

- Does the circumstance meet the **good faith test**—a willingness to meet, engage in rational discussions with a mind open to persuasion? Are you:
  - acting honestly, openly, and without hidden or ulterior motives
  - raising issues in a fair and timely way
  - being constructive and cooperative
  - being proactive in providing others with relevant information and consider all information provided
  - responding promptly and thoroughly to reasonable requests and concerns
  - keeping an open mind, listen to others and is prepared to change an opinion about a particular situation or behaviour, and
  - treating others respectfully?

Is process assistance needed? See Figure 17 *Bargaining Assistance Continuum*.

- Consider the **notion of *ripeness*** and whether you are at that point. A matter or matters at issue is said to be "ripe" for settlement when it has reached a stalemate or particular point and the parties have determined that their alternatives to negotiation **will not get them what they want or need**. Are you at that point? If so, the parties are likely ready to negotiate a form of settlement that will attain at least a measure of their interests, more than they are getting otherwise or stand to get if they pursue their current tactics further.

- What's the problem **you're trying** to solve? What's the problem **they're trying** to solve? If you were to describe the circumstance to the other party would they agree with your characterization? If not, how do we get to a meeting of the minds on the fundamentals of this matter?

- Consider your **best alternative** to negotiating described earlier in this chapter. What can you achieve on your own vs. with the other party? Is timing an issue? What are the substance, process, and relationship implications of taking such action? Can you live with the consequences?

- What do we know, need to know, what is or might be contentious? Invite to amend and/or co-create an **analytic frame** as a foundation and common knowledge base on technical or contentious matters. If the other party won't or can't participate, create a draft for discussion.

- If the other party remains reluctant and the matters remain important enough to engage on propose **third party assistance** options considering the cost and control realities. Recommend one (Figure 17 *Bargaining Assistance Continuum*).

- Above all remember you are **not a sole actor**. You have constituents and are an agent not a principal. You **never think alone or bargain alone**. You also live with the results of bargaining together. Consider how you will keep your constituents, your community so to speak, informed.

In all cases remember that every situation is part of an ongoing relationship; that what you are experiencing is the consequence of past experiences; and that what you do today will affect what happens tomorrow. Even if your current experience is frustrating you are wise to remember the "big picture" and do everything you can to maintain or improve relationships to increase the likelihood of more constructive deliberation in the future. Above all, do no harm and remember:

- Instead of avoiding, compromising

- Recognize the **limitations** of a compromising approach.
- Focus on **interests noting the priories**.

* Instead of accommodating
    - Revisit your **Dual Concerns**.
    - Protect your **interests noting the priorities**.

* Instead of attacking (competing)
    - Connect with **their interests**.
    - Take a moment, appreciate the *role of ripeness*.

* Broaden Your Perspective Further: **Consider the Third Side**[40]

We tend to see conflict, bargaining in particular as two-sided, union and employer; them vs. us and we frequently fail to see that there is always a third side. Consider the context within which collective bargaining occurs. It is resident in a community of sorts. Colleagues, neighbors, like professions and professionals, volunteers, support personnel, observers as examples.

The Third Side is a way of looking at the conflicts around us not just from one side or the other but from the larger perspective of the surrounding community. You can have natural sympathies for one side or the other and still choose to be informed by the Third Side. Taking the Third Side means:

- **Seeking** to understand both sides of the conflict
    * Test yourself: Can you persuasively and constructively make the other team's case just as you can your own? How does this inform you?
- **Encouraging** a process of cooperative negotiation
- **Supporting** a wise solution – one that fairly meets the <u>essential needs</u> of both sides and the community. A conclusion on terms that all but the most extreme can live with and accept.
- **Focussed** on the future. This is a continuing relationship. There will be a next time and *we have the time in between* to make the necessary progress on the matters at issue.

---

[40] A concept advanced by William Ury: https://thirdside.williamury.com/what-is-the-third-side/

5. What Stands in the Way

The process and practice of collective bargaining always presents challenges. It is easy to feel like the way we have always done things will be the way things will always be done. The less than optimal process and the resulting outcomes it yields however can also breed the exact kind of action you need.

> A quote attributed to Roman Emperor Marcus Aurelius is instructive: "Our actions may be impeded, but there can be no impeding our intentions or dispositions. Because we can accommodate and adapt. The mind adapts and converts to its own purposes the obstacle to our acting. The impediment to action advances action. What stands in the way becomes the way."

Changing the negotiation dynamic from the traditional to the increasingly constructive is never easy. It can be uncomfortable and even stressful. Sometimes it can feel so overwhelming that you're not sure how to keep going. However, if you can embrace that which stands before you, accept the problem as it is and prepare to challenge it, you can find the way that you didn't know was there. The simple truth is that in any given bargaining situation, the only thing that you and your team truly have control over is yourselves. As difficult as it may seem, you always have the choice to recognize the obstacle for what it is, find something positive, and work for better outcomes.

What stands in the way?

6. Where to Start and When

Collective bargaining and the agreements that result have a *periodic regularity*. As illustrated in Figure 3 there are three distinct phases or stages based on the agreement's term and the statutory requirements. When negotiations conclude, the meetings and related work to implement the negotiated changes begin. The urgency of now consumes one's time and energy. Negotiations become a distant memory not to be revisited again until a few months before the next round.

In reflecting on collective bargaining and its eccentricities I came across the idea of *the time in between* and found it particularly applicable. "The Time In Between," says the author, "may initially strike us as a mundane phrase describing an uneventful period of time."[41] Yet, to even employ such a phrase implies the presence of at least two events of note. And so, as I pondered this theme of the time in between, I began to think of the

---

41   Excerpt from the remarks of Reverend Bryn MacPhail, St Andrew's Kirk, Nassau, Bahamas, December 28, 2003. Reverend MacPhail was born and raised in Niagara Falls, Ontario.

different ways we respond to such an interim period, in our case the time in between negotiations: The author elaborates:

> *One response to the time in between is boredom, or indifference. Many times, people don't care very much about what takes place between two important events. For example, think of the intermissions in a hockey game. The time in between periods is often used to obtain another beverage; it is a time to stretch the legs or make a sandwich. For the hockey fan, what takes place in between periods is of little consequence, and so we approach this time with indifference.*
>
> *Another response to the time in between is anxiety. We see this, for example, when someone is diagnosed with a serious condition that requires surgery. It is often the case that a person has to wait a number of months between the time of diagnosis and the surgery. Because of the uncertainty of what lies ahead, this time in between often produces tremendous anxiety.*
>
> *A third response to the time in between is diligence. We see this in the example of a student who uses the time in between the assigned exam date and the writing of the exam, to study. The student could conceivably respond with indifference, and subsequently fail. The student could respond to the assigned task with anxiety, but this often leads to procrastination. But if the student wants to ensure a positive result, the best response is diligent study.*

If you accept the notion that the best response to the time in between is diligence what does this mean for the time in between negotiations, how do you (we) start?

In Summary: Building a Framework for Thinking, Understanding, and Action

A framework—a system of concepts, ideas, beliefs, or rules—is a useful tool for making better sense of the complexity of collective bargaining and a way forward. A place to start building one is by situating you and your organization in context. Taking Friedman's observations and the Walton and McKersie emergent relationship model as organizers how do you characterize union-employer relations and in particular collective bargaining? Are you satisfied, is this the best we can do?

Next, understand the foundations of what you are trying to achieve through relationships both personal and institutional. What are you trying to achieve? In answering this question, it is helpful to return to what can be characterized as the *conceptual beginning*. What you're seeking (see Figure 1) informs your strategy and approach.

Then, consider the likely matters at issue. Do the matters at issue meet the test of one with integrative potential? Would the parties be assisted by a common knowledge base developed prior to negotiations? If so, develop an Analytic Frame or a series of subject specific ones. The analytic frame is a useful tool—what is/are the issue(s); what do I/we know, what do I/we need to know and what could be potentially contentious

What is the balance of your dual concerns (see Figure 10) that leads you to the choice of one of the five conflict responses (see Table 2)? Given the nature of your response what is your orientation and approach to reconciling the matters at issue (see Figure 11)? Who are my constituents (see Figure 4) and who are the influencers? Who is most invested in the status quo? What are the implications for bargaining? Answer these questions re the other party. The answers to these questions begin to answer, *is this the best we can do*?

And finally, when do we start? Effectively use post bargaining efforts and the time in between to build a foundation for next time. A foundation of familiarity through working together and one of understanding through joint work on matters of collective importance.

In an evidence-informed way seek to better understand contentious or potentially contentious matters that remain in whole or in part from the last round or arise during the term and technical/complex matters that typically are the subject of bargaining. The development of a common knowledge base builds relationships and furthers understanding. This understanding can put the parties in a constructive frame to address matters that may be the subject of collective bargaining.

And remember, continuous improvement is a continuous activity. It takes time and diligence, after all, that's almost always better than the alternative!

Are you prepared?

HJF

IN CLOSING
Credits and Final Observations

Collective Bargaining Preparation Essentials: The Handbook is drawn from a variety of sources and a series of collective bargaining experiences. Following my first rounds of bargaining as a spokesperson, I began teaching labour relations and collective bargaining at the British Columbia Institute of Technology (BCIT), School of Business part-time studies. While I had read much about bargaining, learned from experienced negotiators, had my own experiences, and participated in learning opportunities, in particular those offered by the Program on Negotiation—An Inter-University Consortium at Harvard Law School, with few exceptions I could find few resources that articulated the unique nature of collective bargaining and provided bargaining preparation ideas and perspectives—a resource that could be used with constituent groups, bargaining teams, and as a reference for classroom activities.

A working resource was developed. Bargaining experiences and continued professional development led to revisions to that first effort. Different perspectives and preparation ideas were added and others modified based on experiences at the bargaining table, in the classroom, and through continued studies. I long recognized that every round of collective bargaining is different and no one prescription can be applied to this unique form of negotiations. One fundamental truth was evident, however—while there may be a variety of techniques or approaches that lead to the successful negotiation of a collective agreement, nothing can replace effective planning and thorough preparation.

Collective Bargaining Preparation Essentials: The Handbook assumes that the parties intend to bargain in good faith in an effort to conclude a collective agreement. It is a resource. My hope is that it provides readers with insightful perspectives, practical strategies, and adaptable frameworks to help them prepare for collective agreement negotiations. However, it is only a guide—negotiators are expected to use the systems and strategies that best meet their individual styles and their team's objectives.

Every effort has been made to acknowledge those responsible for the ideas and theories contained in this book. However, we realize that we may have unintentionally neglected to mention some people. If you are aware of any piece of work contained here that has not been properly credited, please do let us know so that we can make amends in future editions of this book.

We are interested in hearing from you if you have enjoyed the book or if you have any suggestions or ideas that would improve it. Please send your thoughts via e-mail to WTHaW.CBPE@gmail.com.

RESOURCE ONE

CB Statutes and Rules Test:
What do I need to confirm?

Each province and territory in Canada—and the federal government, in federally regulated industries —has its own statute to regulate union-employer relations.

In preparation for the next round of collective bargaining test your knowledge: *what do I know, what do I need to confirm*? **Identify the details and cite the source or point of reference** (statute, associated regulations, rules; published resources).

Part One: Statutory Structure[42]

Item/Topic	Description/ Details	Reference/ Source
1. Statute		
2. Associated Regulations		
3. Rules		
4. Resources published by the governing authority		
5. When was the statute last amended? • What were the amendments and what gave rise to them? • What are the implications, if any, for collective bargaining?		
6. Who regulates and otherwise interprets the statute?		

---

42 An **Act** or **Code** is a Bill which has been legislatively passed and received Royal Assent to become **law**. Setting out broad legal/policy principles, generally Acts establish minimum standards while Codes establish a policy framework and are procedural in nature. **Regulations** are commonly known as "subsidiary legislation" and require publishing in the Government Gazette to become legal. These are the guidelines that dictate how the provisions of the Act or Code are applied. **Rules** set out practice processes to implement the provisions of an Act or Code.

Part Two: Collective Bargaining Specifics

Topic	Description/ Details	Reference/ Source
Current Status		
1. Is this round of negotiations for a first collective agreement or the renewal of an existing one?		
2. What are the process differences between first agreements and renewals?		
3. If a renewal, when does the current agreement expire?		
Bargaining Unit		
1. How is the bargaining unit defined?		
2. Who of the employer's employees is included in the bargaining unit and who is excluded?		
3. Of the employees included in the bargaining unit are they all members of the union? What is the effect, if any, of non-membership?		
Commencing Collective Bargaining		
1. When can bargaining commence? When must bargaining commence?		
2. Are there any preconditions to commencing bargaining?		
3. What are the basic statutory obligations concerning: • *good faith*, and • *unfair labour practices*?		
4. Are there any matters that cannot be bargained collectively i.e., not in the scope of bargaining?		

Strikes, Lockouts		
1. What is a strike and what form can it take?		
2. What is a lockout and what form can it take?		
3. What are the preconditions to initiating a strike? • strike votes, form and substance • strike votes, length of time actionable		
4. What are the preconditions to initiating a lockout?		
5. What is considered picketing and are there limitations on picketing?		
Assistance		
1. Pursuant to the prevailing labour relations statute what bargaining assistance can be accessed by the negotiating parties? How are they accessed?		
2. Can bargaining assistance, direction, process alternatives be initiated other than by the negotiating parties? How and by whom?		
3. Can the parties access bargaining assistance other than provided for by the prevailing labour relations statute?		
Final Matters		
1. When an agreement in committee is concluded by the negotiating parties how is the agreement formalized?		
2. When does the new agreement come into force?		
3. Is there a minimum and/or maximum term of an agreement?		
In Summary, Next Steps		
1. Based on your items 1 to 6 answers and observations what requires further investigation to advance your/our understanding?		

RESOURCE TWO

Collective Bargaining Process (CPB) Checklist

Given the complexity of collective bargaining preparation a process checklist can be of assistance. As a resource, a checklist of this nature will be organization specific. The sources and responsibilities identified in the checklist are for illustrative purposes only.

Item	Sources	Responsible	Due Date
Pre-Preparation Reflection			
1. What is the current state of the union-employer relationship? Why is it *the way it is* and what role did we play? Will this have implications for negotiations and what should we do about it, if anything?		Senior leadership	
2. Consider our enterprise, its mission and vision. What business imperatives with employment implications are evident that may impact negotiations?		Senior leadership	
3. What's our negotiation stance? Traditional/positional, integrative, or . . . And why?		Senior leadership, management	
4. What is the context within which we will negotiate? Economic, statutory, political		Senior management	
A. Establish Collective Bargaining Project Team			
1. Assign Collective Bargaining Project Leader		Senior management	
2. Identify Collective Bargaining Project Team members; assign roles and responsibilities		Senior management, Collective Bargaining Project Leader	
3. Develop a comprehensive Collective Bargaining Plan for the three phases of bargaining: 　i. Preparation 　ii. Negotiation 　iii. Implementation/Administration		Senior management, Collective Bargaining Project Leader	

B. Review the Collective Agreement			
4. Contract language	Collective agreement		
5. Letters of understanding and side agreements	Collective agreement and agreement file		
6. Grievances and arbitrations	Grievance/ arbitration files		
7. Existing practices	Meetings/survey		
8. Operating problems	Meetings/survey		
C. Develop Bargaining Objectives and Proposals			
1. Identification of broad bargaining objectives	Board, senior management, through facilitated meetings, Management staff responsible for human resources through facilitated meetings, Front-line supervisors through meetings/ survey, Senior management, Bargaining Team		
2. Develop specific bargaining objectives	Bargaining Team		
3. Identify/define the interests that are resident in the objectives.	Bargaining team in consultation with key decision makers/influencers		
4. Develop bargaining proposals to be exchanged with the union			
D. External Data			
1. Determine data required	Collective Bargaining Project Team		
2. Collect and review other relevant collective agreements			
3. General information on business conditions, state of economy			
4. Terms of settlement in region/ sector/other similar employers			

5. Pay and benefit surveys • Other jurisdictions • Sectoral • Local			
E. Assemble Internal Data			
1. Review grievance/arbitration history	Grievance/arbitration files		
2. Input from management and front-line supervisors concerning the operation and administration of the collective agreement	Meetings/survey		
3. History of past negotiations	Bargaining resources, bargaining files, bargaining database		
4. Overall compensation per employee • Broken down by regular wages, overtime wages, additional compensation, benefits	Payroll and/or human resources department		
5. Number of employees by classification and by shift	Payroll and/or human resources department		
6. Minimum and maximum pay in each classification	Payroll and/or human resources department		
7. Overtime hours by classification • Amount of overtime worked for each hour, month, shift	Payroll and/or human resources department, previous collective agreement		
8. Shift differential, emergency call out and other special pay • Overall cost • Cost by classification • Cost by shift	Payroll and/or human resources department		
9. Health and welfare plan • Overall cost • Cost per employee • Cost per classification	Payroll and/or human resources department, plan carriers		
10. Other benefits • Overall cost • Cost per employee	Payroll and/or human resources department		

11. Vacation costs • Overall cost • By years of service • Amount of vacation	Payroll and/or human resources department		
12. Stand duration of lunch and other breaks	Payroll and/or human resources department		
13. Absence Rate • Per employee • By classification • By shift	Payroll and/or human resources department		
14. Accident Rate • Per employee • By classification • By shift	Payroll and/or human resources department, occupational health and safety department		
15. Demographic data of bargaining unit by sex, age and seniority	Payroll and/or human resources department		
16. Outline of incentive, progression, evaluation, training, safety and promotion plans	Human resources department		
F. Statutory/Legal Review and Preparation			
1. Legal review of collective agreement (only as required, not typically necessary)			
2. Statutory changes • Minimum/maximum wages • Minimum/maximum benefits • Hours of work and overtime • Holidays • Maternity, paternity benefits under employment standards statutes • Employment Insurance • Pension standards • Termination/severance pay • Human rights • Occupational health and safety			

3. Applicable judicial, arbitration, human rights, and administrative law decisions			
4. Judicial and LRB decisions related to bargaining			
5. Strategy and groundwork for tactical plans (noting statutory limitations) • Nature and extent of employee communications • Steps leading to strike/lockout • Use of management • Approach to threats and intimidation in general • Approach to threats to Employer property • Cross-picketing or picketing by non-employees • Use of employees who cross picket line	Management group		
G. Knowledge of the Union			
1. Organizational structure	Union representatives, constitutions, bylaws		
2. Financial strength of union	Union representatives, employees, internal union publications		
3. Formal and informal power structure	Union representatives, union publications, former union members now in management, media		
4. Internal matters			
5. Union ratification process • Preliminary approvals • When, where, how, who is present			
6. Whether pattern or precedent agreement	Union representatives		
7. Union bargaining team and background information	Union representatives, former union members now in management		

8. Union and employer negotiating practice • Traditional versus problem-solving orientation • Pattern of movement • Method of dropping demands • Last minute demands • Actual settlements vs. demands • How final agreement made—when—who involved—mediator • Bargaining team members' pattern of conduct	Former union members now in management, former bargaining team members, review of bargaining history		
H. Current Business Status and Anticipated Changes			
1. Current business plan and long-range plans 2. Anticipated changes to labour force 3. Technological change 4. Downsizing or layoffs 5. Restructuring 6. Changes in program delivery	Notify finance department of information needed		
I. Costing			
1. Review costs of each applicable item in collective agreement 2. Notify finance department of information needed 3. Prepare total cost and average cost per employee for wages, benefits, and associated leaves (note it is preferable to have a meeting of the minds on the details and content of employment related costs, see earlier comments re efficacy of such as approach)	Senior Management Collective agreement or proposed issues		

J. Bargaining Team			
1. Confirm size and composition			
2. Select members			
3. Determine roles and responsibilities			
4. Formal and informal reporting and outreach standards, processes, practices			
5. Delegation of working committees and expected deliverables			
6. Review the nature and type of bargaining protocol you intend to pursue with the other team			
7. Review and confirm understanding: bargaining context; objectives and associated interests and proposals to be advanced (why, how, when)			
K. Review Bargaining Objectives (broad and specific) and the Associated Proposals			
1. What is (are) the problem(s) you are trying to solve or opportunity you are trying to take advantage of?			
2. For each objective ask why? What interests are resident in each objective? Are there priorities?			
L. Prepare Bargaining Support Resources and Data Base			
1. Confirm form, structure and substance • CB Resource 1: Contextual Data/Information Resource • CB Resource 2: Historical Clause Development • CB Resource 3: Proposal—Counter Proposal—Agreed in Principle Resource • CB Resource 4: Working Resource • CB Resource 5: Bargaining Status Worksheet • CB Resource 6: Bargaining Notes or Minutes			
2. Assign responsibilities for resource preparation and maintenance			

M. Contingency Plan			
1. Review statutory provisions concerning strikes, lockouts, picketing, and the like			
2. Designate Project Manager			
3. Prepare a Contingency Plan (see Chapter 9)			
4. If applicable to the industry, sector, or enterprise review essential services and statutory requirements. Establish policy recommendations and action plan concerning: • Continuation of operations • Determine the level and nature of essentiality • Work by exempt employees • Secondary pickets • Payment of employees on strike			
5. Maintenance and Protection • Organizational assets and equipment • Non-union employees			
6. Notices as required by statute			
7. Potential Liability • Contractual commitments • Insurance review • Steps to minimize liability			
8. Workplace Restoration • Develop a post event return to normal plan (subject to events and timing)			

N. Communications, Public Relations, and the Media			
1. Assign a key communications contact			

2. Consider types of communication media
    • Internal written, Intranet
    • Social media use and monitoring			

3. Given the nature of the enterprise consider the interest and implications of traditional print, radio, and television coverage			
4. Monitoring and response to the other party's internal or public media			

5. Constituent and internal network outreach
    • Primary, secondary, others: when, by whom and in what form and media
    • Develop a feedback loop: you need to know what they are hearing and witnessing as well
    • Do you have a strategy for periodic face to face meetings to update status, hear concerns etc.?			

O. Formal Notice to Bargain			
1. Pursuant to the applicable labour relations statute, issued by the union or initiated by the employer			
2. Copy to the LRB			
P. Logistics			
1. Place			
2. Schedule			
3. How the cost of the facilities will be paid (if applicable)			

4. Pay for union bargaining team members (if any)
    • Regular pay
    • Overtime pay
    • Special pay			

Q. Finalize Approach and Strategy			
1. Review your objectives (broad and specific) and link them to your interests			
2. How do you intend to advance your proposals (form and substance) and how will the other party? How will you proceed from there?			
3. Put yourself in the *other party's shoes*. What are their likely objectives and why would they be pursuing them? How does this inform you? Be prepared to test your assumptions			
4. Have you confirmed with the other team the initial meeting logistics? What do you want to accomplish initially?			
5. Consider the three negotiator orientations, the bargaining history and norms how will you approach bargaining and why? • Review Lewicki, Saunders, Barry, and Tasa negotiator's paradoxes at the end of Chapter 2. How do they inform your approach? • Confirm you approach with constituent influencers/decision-makers and the bargaining team • List the potential matters at issue and identify the contentious or potentially contentious ones			
6. Develop a bargaining agenda for the first meetings			
7. Review and finalize you approach concerning the bargaining protocol. As per past negotiating practice, written, subject of initial discussions, and agreement or . . .?			

RESOURCE THREE

How to Draft a Memorandum of Agreement

A Memorandum of Agreement, also referred to as a Memorandum of Settlement, is a document signed by the union and the employer setting out the terms of the negotiated settlement. At the conclusion of negotiations, the parties need to prepare such a memorandum.

Over the years, employers and local unions have developed practices with respect to the formalization of matters agreed to once negotiations have concluded and an agreement has been reached. The general practice employed is for the parties to sign a Memorandum of Agreement, which sets out the terms and conditions of agreement of the parties with respect to those items that were the subject of negotiations—a brief memorandum referring to separate documents that outline the terms of the agreement reached. Once the formal Collective Agreement has been drafted and executed, it will become the operative collective agreement between the parties and will supersede the Memorandum of Agreement.

The Memorandum of Agreement is not in force until it has been ratified. Once the agreement has been ratified, the parties should immediately provide written notice of ratification to the other party. Then, once both parties have ratified the agreement, a formal collective agreement should be drawn up and signed.

A Memorandum of Agreement requires:

- ☐ The names of the parties to the Memorandum of Agreement are identified.
- ☐ The memorandum is conditional upon ratification by the union membership and the employer.
- ☐ The unchanged portions of the previous collective agreement are continued.
- ☐ The new term is included in the memorandum.
- ☐ All changes are included in the memorandum with express language agreed to, including:

- Wages
- Benefits
- Language amendments
- New provisions

☐ There is confirmation of which letters of understanding continue and which are no longer in effect.

Sample A

Memorandum of Agreement between

[Name of union] (the "Union")

and

[Name of employer] (the "Employer")

The parties agree, subject to ratification by their principals, that the previous collective agreement in effect is to be continued subject to the amendments outlined below:

The term of the collective agreement is from [date] to [date].

Wages are set out in Schedule "A" (attached).

Benefits are set out in Schedule "B" (attached).

Amendments to language and new provisions are set out in Schedule "C" (attached).

Agreed to this..................... day of .... 20.......

.... Employer   .... Union

Sample B

Memorandum of Agreement between

[Name of union] (the "Union")

and

[Name of employer] (the "Employer")

The parties agree, subject to ratification by their principals, that the previous collective agreement in effect is to be continued subject to the amendments outlined below:

The term of the collective agreement is from [date] to [date].

Wages: [set out the changes to wages or any signing bonuses to be paid].

Benefits: [set out any changes to the benefits to the employees].

Amendments to language and new provisions as attached to this memorandum

The Employer and the Union will use their best efforts to ensure the new ratified collective agreement shall be published and distributed as quickly as possible.

The Employer and the Union will use their best efforts to ensure that their principals ratify this memorandum of agreement and will not make any statements or take any actions which undermine the ratification process.

Agreed to this..................... day of .... 20.......

.... Employer   .... Union

GLOSSARY

accommodation conflict style. Also referred to as accommodating, yielding, smoothing, and obliging. Maximizes empathy and minimizes assertiveness. Can be used to set the stage for further constructive actions, but there may be lingering dissatisfaction and building frustration that one's needs are going unmet if nothing emerges from the accommodation.

accreditation. The procedure followed by a labour relations board to designate an organization of employers as the bargaining agent for a group of employers. The parallel term for employee organizations is *certification*.

adjudicator. The term adjudicator includes judges, arbitrators, and employment-related tribunal chair/officials; an arbitrator is the neutral third party chosen by the parties to a collective agreement to render binding decisions on collective agreement disputes. The terms adjudicator and arbitrator are used in connection with conclusions, advice, and considerations resulting from formal employment-related proceedings.

agency shop. See Rand formula.

agreement in committee. Consensus on the part of the union and employer bargaining committees on the contents of a new collective agreement that is intended to be submitted for ratification.

alternative. A choice limited to one or more possibilities, propositions, or courses of action. A selection of one alternative precludes any other possibility.

alternative dispute resolution or **appropriate dispute resolution (ADR).** A range of techniques outside the traditional litigation process (though they may be used in tandem with it). ADR procedures are chosen by parties in conflict to try to resolve the dispute in a less adversarial way. These techniques are usually voluntary and confidential (with some exceptions). ADR procedures range from self-help processes at one end of a continuum to binding arbitration at the other. Except for arbitration, ADR uses non-binding processes that parties can walk away from at any time. Parties remain in control of the process and the outcome. The most common processes are negotiation, mediation, and group facilitation.

analytic frame. An evidence-based framework that informs the issues being addressed and determines what information or research is available and what additional information is required to support informed decision making. Developed collaboratively before formal deliberations or negotiations begin, the analytic frame makes explicit the categories and multiple sub-categories that comprise the issue(s) at hand.

anchor or anchoring. A cognitive bias that describes the common human tendency to attach (or "anchor") our thoughts to a reference point—even though it may have no logical relevance to the decision at hand and rely too heavily on the first piece of information offered (the "anchor") when making decisions. It is considered a bias because it distorts our judgement, especially when matters are unclear or otherwise unexplored.

application grievance. Grievances that involve the application of a collective agreement provision and dispute the facts of the situation being grieved, not the interpretation or meaning of the provision. The most common application grievances are those concerning discipline. See also Grievance.

arbitration. A method of settling an employer-union dispute by having an impartial third party render a decision binding on both the union and the employer. All collective agreements must provide for the arbitration of disputes over the interpretation of collective agreement language—for example, a dispute over the discipline of an employee for insubordination. This type of arbitration, which is referred to as grievance arbitration or rights arbitration, involves the interpretation of existing collective agreement language. It is different from interest arbitration, which is used to resolve collective bargaining disputes. In interest arbitration, an arbitrator awards new collective agreement language for specific matters at issue.

arbitral jurisprudence. The body of labour law developed by arbitrators through their decisions.

back table. Those individuals or entities in the background of a negotiation—advisors, influencers, boards of directors, the board executive, members, public constituents, those who provide direction/approval formally or informally. It's from there, hidden from their counterparts, that direction and approval is provided to their respective negotiators.

bargaining agent. Once a union is certified by a labour relations board, the union becomes the exclusive representative of all the employees in a particular bargaining unit. The employer can no longer negotiate with individual employees over terms and conditions of employment.

bargaining, distributive. Activities and behaviours widely associated with negotiation. A negotiation activity whereby limited resources are divided between the parties—the parties' interests are seen to be in conflict. Because distributive bargaining is based on demands made by the parties or positions taken, it may be referred as positional bargaining.

bargaining, integrative. A form of negotiation or activities in which the parties' objectives are not in fundamental conflict, and there is a possibility of joint gain. It is also referred to as mutual gains, interest-based or collaborative bargaining. In integrative bargaining, the parties focus on problem-solving and the interests of the parties as opposed to the demands they make or positions they adopt.

bargaining, intra-organizational. Activities within the union and employer to build an internal consensus on matters to pursue and how to pursue them. The negotiators for the union and the employer must eventually answer to their respective constituents. As a result, each negotiator must deal with two sets of demands—those made by the other team and those made by their own constituents.

bargaining protocol. The procedure that the parties agree they will follow during collective bargaining. A bargaining protocol can be written or be a verbal understanding, depending on the parties' relationship and practice.

bargaining team. The team at the table that negotiates the collective agreement. The term is used interchangeably with negotiating team.

bargaining unit. A labour relations board will only certify a union to represent a group of employees if the board considers the group to be appropriate for collective bargaining purposes. This group of employees is the bargaining unit. Generally, labour relations boards prefer an all-employee bargaining unit, but they may certify a union for smaller groups under certain circumstances.

Whether any particular employees are properly included in that bargaining unit will be determined by whether those employees and other members of the unit have a "community of interest." A community of interest depends on a number of factors such as similar terms and conditions of employment, similar skills, and similar training.

best alternative to a negotiated agreement (BATNA). The alternative left to a party if the party is unable to reach an agreement—the "walk-away" alternative. It represents one of several paths that you can follow if a resolution cannot be reached. You walk away from the negotiation when your interests are not met. Your BATNA is what you end up with. In general, neither party should agree to something that is worse than its best alternative to a negotiated agreement away from the table. Like its **WATNA (worst**

alternative to a negotiated agreement) counterpart, understanding your BATNA gives you a measure you can use to assess your other options in order to make more informed negotiation decisions.

Most BATNA formulations direct your attention to what you can achieve outside the current negotiation and independent of your counterpart characterized as your walk-away alternative. Your best course of action for satisfying your interests without the other party's agreement.[43] Employment relationships however are interdependent ones. More often than not, parties to problems, contentious matters, workplace negotiations cannot achieve what they need to achieve independent of one another. As a practical matter parties to an employment relationship will remain together and must continue to interact.

bumping. Exercise of seniority rights by employees to displace less senior union employees when business conditions require temporary layoffs or the discontinuance of departments.

business agent. A full-time officer of a local union who handles grievances, helps enforce agreements, and performs other tasks in the day-to-day operation of a union.

call-back pay. Compensation, often at higher wage rates, for workers called back on the job after completing their regular shift. Contract provisions usually provide for a minimum number of hours of pay, regardless of the number of hours actually worked.

call-in pay. Guaranteed hours of pay (for example, ranging from 2–8 hours) to a worker who reports for work and finds that there is insufficient work for him or her to do. Provisions for call-in pay are usually detailed in collective agreements.

Canons of Construction. General rules or maxims used to assist in the interpretation of statutes or written documents such as collective agreements, e.g., where a conflict exists between provisions in a collective agreement, specific clauses override general ones.

certification. Official recognition by a labour relations board of a union as the sole and exclusive bargaining agent, following proof of majority support among employees in a bargaining unit. Once a trade union is certified, the employer must recognize its bargaining agency.

closed shop. A provision in a collective agreement whereby all employees in a bargaining unit must be union members in good standing before being hired, and new employees must be hired through the union. See also Union security clauses.

---

43 William Ury in Getting Past No (1991: 21- 22)

constituents. Members of a constituency; a cohesive body of people bound by shared identity, goals, or loyalty. In the bargaining context there can be a variety of constituents: core constituents with a vested interest represented by one of the parties at the negotiating table, as well as general constituents who are indirectly affected by the outcome or who are interested observers.

collaborative conflict style. May be referred to as collaborating, integrating, or problem-solving. Highly assertive and highly empathetic at the same time.

community of interest. A community of people who share a common interest or passion.

competitive conflict style. Also known as contending, competing, forcing, directing. Maximizes assertiveness and minimizes empathy.

compromising conflict style. Intermediate on both the assertiveness and empathy dimensions of the dual concerns model.

concede. To surrender, yield, or relinquish. Admit, acknowledge, accept, grant or recognize something is true or valid after first denying or resisting it.

conflict. A clash between individuals arising out of a difference in thought process, attitudes, understanding, stated positions, interests, and sometimes even perceptions. Neither inherently good nor bad conflict is an inevitable result of human beings associating with one another. While often viewed as hostile, frustrating, negative, uncomfortable, and "win or lose" in its outcomes it can be seen as being mutually beneficial, facilitating understanding, tolerance, learning, and effectiveness.

conflict mitigation. The act of proactively taking steps to make contentious or potentially contentious circumstances or conditions less disruptive, distracting, or severe.

conflict of interest. A situation that has the potential to undermine the impartiality of a person because of the possibility of a clash between the person's self-interest and professional interest or public interest.

constructive conflict. A type of conflict in which people focus their discussion on the issue while maintaining respect for people having other points of view. It encourages people to present their divergent viewpoints so ideas and recommendations can be clarified, redesigned, and tested for logical soundness.

context. The circumstances that form the setting for an event, statement, or idea, and in terms of which it can be fully understood and addressed; the situation within which something exists or happens, and that can help explain it.

craft. A manual occupation such as carpenter, plumber, or electrician that requires extensive training and a high degree of skill.

craft union. A union that limits its members to a particular craft. However, many craft unions now broaden their jurisdiction to include occupations and skills not closely related to the originally designated craft.

cross-examination. A form of examination during a hearing in which the opposing counsel has great latitude to ask leading questions. The opposing counsel may suggest an answer or ask the witness to agree or disagree with a proposition. Is distinct from direct examination, or examination in chief.

culture (organizational). The combination of shared values and group norms often described as "the way things are done around here." Organizational culture fills the organization with life and ideals; it influences how roles and responsibilities are fulfilled and provides the organization with an external corporate identity. Organizational culture is evident through an individual's words and actions and in the organization's systems and processes.

destabilizers. Bargaining team members who lack commitment to the bargaining table processes and who may feel more comfortable with self-help techniques (such as meeting with others without the authority of the bargaining team), may engage in disruptive behaviour, and may be unwilling to settle at any price.

dovetailing. Term used, especially on the sale of a business or the merger of companies, when two or more seniority lists are combined into one seniority list that credits all employees for previously accumulated seniority.

dual concerns model. Two-dimensional framework that postulates that people in conflict have two independent types of concerns:

- Concern for self: the degree to which you attempt to satisfy your own interests; embodied in the quality of being self-assured and confident without being aggressive (assertiveness).

- Concern for others: the degree to which you attempt to satisfy the interests of others; embodied in the ability to see the world as another person, to share and understand the other's feelings, needs, concerns and interests (empathy).

dues. Periodic fees or payments made to a union by members of the bargaining unit and/or the union.

due process. Procedural fairness; natural justice.

end-tailing. Term used, especially on the sale of a business or the merger of companies, when two or more seniority lists are combined into one seniority list that places employees from one plant or bargaining unit behind those from another, regardless of their previously accumulated seniority.

escalator clause. Collective agreement clause providing for the adjustment of wages in accordance with changes in the cost of living.

estoppel. A principle of law that prevents a party from suffering unfairly or unjustly as a result of relying and acting on representations made by another party by word or conduct. Having made the original representations, the party is compelled to adhere to the conditions assumed as a result of its original representations.

examination in chief. A form of examination, also referred to as "direct examination," during a hearing in which counsel asks open-ended questions and cannot ask leading questions, or questions that may suggest an answer. Is distinct from cross-examination.

expedited arbitration. A dispute resolution mechanism that can be used before a grievance is sent to conventional arbitration, and in which either party can apply to the labour relations board to request resolution of the grievance by expedited arbitration. The board appoints an arbitrator who has strict time limits for hearing and deciding on the grievance. The compressed timelines of expedited arbitration make this approach unsuitable for complex interpretive matters.

familiarization period. A short period of time to which employees are entitled, to acquaint themselves with the particular details and routine of a new job. While arbitrators have held that an employee cannot be denied a promotion simply because a familiarization period is necessary, an employee is not entitled to a trial or training period in the absence of specific language in the collective agreement.

frame of reference. The context, viewpoint, or set of presuppositions or of evaluative criteria within which a person's perception and thinking seem always to occur, and which constrains selectively the course and outcome of these activities. They govern how we think and who we are. Our behavior can be traced to these fundamental values.

grievance. A dispute between an individual and management or between the union and management over the interpretation, application, or administration of a collective agreement. The procedure for dealing with grievances is set out in the collective agreement. If a grievance cannot be settled at the worksite level (where many grievances are settled) or at any of the subsequent steps established in the grievance procedure, it must be resolved by arbitration.

grievance arbitration. Arbitration of a dispute concerning the interpretation, application, or alleged violation of a collective agreement.

human resources. Decisions and activities involving individuals or groups of individuals that are intended to influence the effectiveness of employees and the organization. **Labour relations** is the aspect of human resources concerned with the continuous relationship between a group of employees (represented by a union) and an employer.

integrate. To form, organize, order, coordinate, combine, or blend parties' ideas, suggestions, and resources in ways that creates something of value for both consistent with their respective interests. The potential to integrate to create joint value only exists when there are multiple issues involved and parties are able to adjust, make trade-offs, repurpose resources, and/or meet priorities across issues.

integrative potential. The potential for the parties' interests to be combined or elements incorporated in ways that create joint value. To join forces to achieve something together that cannot be achieved independently though joining several elements, parts into a whole, focused on creating value before claiming value. The following factors indicate the potential for integration:

- The parties cannot achieve what they need to achieve independent of one another.
- More than one issue is involved.
- It is possible to add more issues to the mix.
- The parties' interactions will recur over time.
- The parties have varying preferences across issues.

industrial relations. Social relations among people at work; the nature of all employment relationships in an industrial society; encompasses the role and impact of human resource policies/practices developed by employers and the scope and impact of employment related legislation adopted by governments. Now more commonly referred to as **employment relations**.

industry-wide bargaining. Collective bargaining that takes place on an industry-wide basis. The terms and conditions of employment agreed on cover all or a major number of the organized employees in the industry.

inherent rights. See Management rights.

interest arbitration. Arbitration to establish the terms of a collective agreement where the parties are unable to do so by negotiation.

interests. The things that people want to satisfy or achieve in a conflict or negotiation situation. Unlike people's positions—which are simple statements purportedly that represent their interests—the interests underlying a position answer the question "*Why* do you want that?" or "*Why* do you feel that way?" Interests must be prioritized into needs and wants. Needs are more important and usually must be satisfied before an agreement can be reached, whereas wants may be traded or given away.

interpretation grievance. A grievance where the parties do not agree on the interpretation of the wording used in making a decision. Interpretation grievances involve such matters as the assigning and performance of work, scheduling, layoffs, transfers, workplace safety, wages and benefits, and use of seniority. See also Grievance.

joint bargaining. Two or more unions joining forces to negotiate an agreement with a single employer.

jurisdiction (union). The area of jobs, skills, occupations, and industries or sectors within which a union organizes and engages in collective bargaining. Unions may also define their jurisdiction geographically. For example, a union may state in its constitution that it has jurisdiction over all employees in a particular industry in a particular province.

jurisdictional dispute. A conflict between two or more unions over the right of their membership to perform certain types of work. If the conflict develops into a work stoppage, it is called a jurisdictional strike.

jurisdictional strike. See Jurisdictional dispute.

letter of intent (letter of understanding). Letter by a party to a collective agreement that clarifies or supplements the agreement. Whether a letter of intent forms part of the collective agreement, so that it is enforceable through the grievance and arbitration procedures, depends on the manifest intention of the parties. Where a letter of intent is in writing and signed by both parties, or is referred to in the collective agreement, it will generally be held to form part of the collective agreement.

lockout. The closing of a place of employment, a suspension of work, or a refusal by an employer to continue employing a number of employees, to compel the employees to agree to conditions of employment. A lockout is not permitted during the life of a collective agreement.

management rights. A shorthand expression for the principle, applied in the interpretation of collective agreements, that any rights that the employer has not expressly bargained away in the agreement are retained by management. For example, if the union cannot point to an explicit clause that prohibits management from contracting out union work to an outside company, management can contract out as part of its management rights. Equivalent terms used are inherent rights and residual rights.

master agreement. A collective agreement that serves as the pattern for major terms and conditions for an entire industry or an industry segment. Local terms may be negotiated in addition to the terms set out in the master contract.

mediation. A process that attempts to resolve disputes by compromise or voluntary agreement. In contrast with arbitration, the mediator does not bring in a binding award, and the parties are free to accept or to reject the mediator's recommendation.

modified union shop. A place of work in which non-union workers who are already employed need not join the union, but all new employees must join, and those workers who are already members must remain in the union. Often referred to as a "grandfather clause."

narcotic effect. Parties having an undue reliance on third parties as the mechanism to conclude an agreement.

natural justice. Procedural fairness. Requirement applicable to public bodies and domestic tribunals when making decisions that affect the rights and interests of individuals; the rules of natural justice require that persons affected by a decision be notified of the case against them and be given a reasonable opportunity of presenting their case, and that the body making the decision listen fairly to both sides and reach a decision untainted by bias; the precise content of natural justice varies according to the nature of the power exercised, the decision involved, and the consequences that flow therefrom.

negotiating team. See bargaining team.

objective. Something aimed at or strived for; a goal. In a negotiation, an objective is a statement of what you desire as outcomes or what you hope your settlement position will contain. An objective is not your position, but rather is a description of your desired outcome.

open shop. A workplace in which union membership is not required as a condition of securing or retaining employment.

options. Alternative courses of action. The full range of possibilities on which parties might conceivably reach agreement. Options might be put on the table. A collective agreement is preferable if it is the best of many options, especially if it capitalizes on all potential mutual gain.

picketing. Patrolling near the employer's place of business by union members (pickets) to publicize the existence of a labour dispute; to persuade workers to join a strike or join the union; to discourage customers from buying or using the employer's goods or services; or to serve some related purpose.

policy grievance. A grievance in which the subject matter is of general interest or application. In a policy grievance, the union complains that an employer's action (or its failure or refusal to act) is a violation of the collective agreement that could affect everyone covered by the agreement. A policy grievance normally relates to the interpretation of the agreement, rather than to the complaint of an individual or group. Individual employees may or may not be affected at the time the grievance is filed. See also Grievance.

position. An attitude toward, opinion on, or statement on a subject; a particular stand or stance on an issue or subject. Positions are developed to represent a party's demands.

probation. Initial period of employment during which the employer has an opportunity to assess the suitability of the employee. Ordinarily, a lesser standard of cause is required to discharge probationary employees, and these employees' right to challenge discharge, as well as their seniority rights and benefits, may be further restricted by the terms of the collective agreement.

pyramiding. Usually the practice of providing two or more monetary benefits for the same period—though the term does not have a precise meaning in collective agreements.

quasi-mediators. Usually the bargaining team leaders who are charged with the responsibility for the success of the negotiation, and who see their role as harmonizing the interests of the stabilizers (who may too readily concede) and the destabilizers (who may take extremely impractical or strategically unsound positions).

Rand formula. A provision of a collective agreement stating that non-union employees in the bargaining unit must pay the union a sum equal to union fees or dues as a condition of continuing employment. However, the non-union workers are not required to join the union. Also known as an agency shop.

ratification. Formal approval of a newly negotiated collective agreement by vote of the union members affected.

reciprocity. Responding to a constructive gesture or action with a corresponding one In social psychology, reciprocity is a social norm of in-kind responses to the behavior of others.

recognition. Employer acceptance of a union as the exclusive bargaining agent or representative for the employees in the bargaining unit, without the formal process of certification by a labour relations board. Also referred to as voluntary recognition.

relationship outcomes. The impact of the collective agreement negotiations on the ongoing relationship between the parties. Also known as the spillover effect.

reopener. A provision in a collective agreement that permits either side to reopen the contract at a specified time or under special circumstances, prior to its expiration, to bargain on stated subjects such as wage increases, pensions, and health and welfare schemes. Since the collective agreement is still in effect, failure to negotiate an amendment cannot result in a strike or lockout.

reservation or resistance point. The point in negotiations when the highest price at which someone is willing to buy an item is established, and the lowest price at which a seller will sell the item is confirmed, and the back and forth that occurs between these two negotiators. It's an attempt at reconciling these two, often hidden, goals in negotiation.

residual rights. See management rights.

rights arbitration. See arbitration.

ripe or ripeness. A matter at issue is said to be "ripe" for settlement when it has reached a stalemate or particular point and the parties have determined that their alternatives to negotiation will not get them what they want or need. When so determined, parties are likely ready to negotiate a form of settlement that will attain at least a measure of their interests, more than they are getting otherwise or stand to get if they pursue their force-based options further.

rollover. A collective bargaining expression that means you are prepared to maintain the status quo with respect to an existing article or provision.

rotating strike. See strike.

saving clause. (1) Clause in a statute or contract that exempts special cases from the general provisions; (2) clause in a contract, also referred to as a severability clause, specifying that if any part of the contract is held to be illegal or invalid, the remaining clauses of the contract continue in full force.

seniority. Length of service of employment. Seniority is frequently used in collective agreements as a basis for calculating benefits, such as entitlement to vacation. Seniority provisions (for example, layoff, recall, or promotion clauses) in a collective agreement are terms that give employees preferential job rights in accordance with their relative seniority.

severability clause. See saving clause.

shift differential. Additional pay for a shift worked other than the regular day shift.

shop steward. A union official who represents a specific group of members and the union in union duties, grievance matters, and complaints about employment conditions. Stewards are usually part of the workforce who represent and handle their duties on a part-time basis. Also referred to as a union steward or staff representative.

slowdown. A deliberate lessening of work effort to apply pressure for concessions from the employer. A slowdown constitutes a strike under most labour relations statutes and is legal only when a collective agreement is not in force.

social negotiations. The deliberate interaction of two or more multi-faceted social units that are attempting to define or redefine the terms of their interdependence. Collective bargaining is considered a form of social negotiations.

speed-up. A union term describing a situation in which workers are required to increase production without a compensating increase in wages.

spillover effect. See relationship outcomes.

stabilizers. Bargaining team members who are committed to the bargaining table processes and oriented to reaching an agreement.

staff representative. See shop steward.

strike. A strike includes a cessation of work or a refusal to work or to continue work by employees in combination, in concert, or in accordance with a common understanding. Strikes usually occur as a last resort when collective bargaining and all other means have failed to obtain the employees' demands. Strikes are legal only when a collective agreement is not in force.

A rotating strike is organized so that only some of the employees stop work at any given time, each group taking its turn. A sympathy strike is a strike by workers not directly involved in a labour dispute and is usually intended to show labour solidarity and bring pressure on an employer in a labour dispute. A wildcat strike violates the collective agreement and labour relations statutes.

strike notice. Formal announcement by a group of unionized employees to their employer or to a labour relations board that on a certain date they will go out on strike.

strike vote. A vote conducted among employees in the bargaining unit on the question of whether they should go out on strike.

substantive outcomes. The specific contractual terms achieved through bargaining or otherwise forming part of the collective agreement—for example, terms and conditions of employment, wage and benefit provisions, and codified work rules. Implementation of a collective agreement invariably changes workplace practices and possibly productivity. Substantive outcomes are contrasted with relationship outcomes.

super-seniority. Superior job security under a collective agreement afforded to union officials to ensure continuing union representation in the event of layoff.

surface bargaining. Bargaining that consists of going through the motions without intending to conclude a collective agreement, and therefore amounting to a failure to bargain in good faith.

sympathy strike. See strike.

unfair labour practice. A practice on the part of an employer, union, or employee that violates provisions of the statutes governing labour relations.

union security clauses. Provisions in collective agreements designed to protect the union. Union security clauses include:

- Closed shop—An agreement between a union and an employer that the employer may hire only union members and retain only union members in the shop.

- Preferential hiring—An agreement that in hiring new workers, an employer will give preference to union members.

- Union shop—An agreement that the employer may hire anyone the employer wants, but all workers must join the union within a specified period after being hired and must retain membership as a condition of continuing employment.

- Maintenance of members—A provision that does not require workers to join the union as a condition of employment, but all workers who voluntarily join must maintain their membership for the duration of the collective agreement to keep their jobs.

union shop. A place of work where every worker covered by the collective agreement must become and remain a member of the union. New workers need not be union members to be hired but must join after a certain number of days. See also Union security clauses.

union steward. See shop steward.

value. The regard that something is held to deserve; the importance, worth, or usefulness of something. It is said to be in the eye of the beholder with the result that it varies from person to person. In negotiation value can take a variety of forms, for example: $'s, time, resources, re-purposed resources, contacts, access, support, logistics, components, structured packages, recommendations, referrals.

voluntary recognition. See recognition.

Wagner Act or Wagner Act Model. The 1935 U.S. National Labour Relations Act also known as the Wagner Act established:

- the right of employees to join the union of their choice and be represented in the collective bargaining process;

- the National Labour Relations Board as the administrative agency responsible for the Act;

- a duty on both parties to "bargain in good faith" and a prohibition on "unfair labour practices."

The Wagner Act model was subsequently adopted by Canadian jurisdictions and is the origin of collective bargaining and grievance procedures.

wage-effort bargain. Clauses in a collective agreement that specify hours of work and details of pay.

without prejudice. Expression used to indicate that a person or party making an offer or taking an action does so on the basis that the offer or action does not imply an admission of liability or otherwise adversely affect his or her legal rights.

whipsaw. The process or strategy wherein unions use one contract settlement as a precedent for the next and force the employer to settle all contracts on that basis, effectively playing one employer off against other employers.

wildcat strike. A strike that is not legal, because the collective agreement and the statutes governing labour relations forbid it, but the union strikes anyway.

working conditions. Conditions pertaining to an employee's job environment, such as hours of work, safety, paid public holidays and vacations, rest period, free clothing or uniforms, and possibilities of advancement. Many of these conditions are included in the collective agreement and are subject to collective bargaining.

worst alternative to a negotiated agreement. In a negotiation, your WATNA represents one of several paths that you can follow if a resolution cannot be reached. Like its BATNA counterpart, understanding your WATNA gives you a measure you can use to assess your other options in order to make more informed negotiation decisions.

ZOPA. A "Zone of Possible Agreement" or ZOPA describes the intellectual zone in negotiations between two parties where there is a potential agreement that would benefit both sides more than their alternative options do. Within this zone, an agreement is possible. Outside the zone, no amount of negotiation will yield an agreement.

REFERENCES

Bieristo, B., H.J. Finlayson, and C. Naylor. Proceedings of *Constructive Deliberations*. Vancouver, BC: Centre for the Study of Educational Leadership and Policy (CSELP), 2018–2021

Breslin, J. William, and Jeffrey Z. Rubin, eds. *Negotiation Theory and Practice, the Program on Negotiation*. Cambridge: Harvard Law School, 1991.

Brown, Donald and David Beatty. *Canadian Labour Arbitration,* 5th ed. Aurora: Canada Law Book, 2019.

Bullock, Allen et al., eds. *Harper Dictionary of Modern Thought*. New York: Harper and Row, 1988.

Burrell, Gibson and Gareth Morgan. *Sociological Paradigms and Organisational Analysis: Elements of the Sociology of Corporate Life*. Gateshead, UK: Heinemann Educational Books, 1979.

Cameron, Esther and Mike Green. *Making Sense of Change Management: A complete guide to the models, tools and techniques of organizational change* 3rd ed. London: Kogan Page; Philadelphia, Kogan Page, 2012.

Colosi, Thomas, and Arthur E. Berkeley. *Collective Bargaining: How It Works and Why,* 2nd ed. New York: American Arbitration Association, 1992.

Craver, Charles. *The Impact of Negotiator Styles on Bargaining Interactions*. Washington: George Washington University Law School, and 35 *Am. J. Trial Advocacy* 1, 2010.

Cutcher-Gershenfeld Joel, Robert McKersie, Richard Walton. *Pathways to Change: Case Studies of Strategic Negotiations*. Kalamazoo: W.E. Upjohn Institute for Employment Research, 1995.

Finlayson, Hugh. *When Things Happen at Work: A Practitioner's Guide to People, Circumstances and What to Do Now*: Friesen Press, Victoria, 2019-2021.

Fisher, Roger and Scott Brown. *Getting Together: Building Relationships as We Negotiate*. Boston: Houghton Mifflin, 1988.

Fisher, Roger and William Ury. *Getting to Yes: Negotiating Agreement Without Giving In*, 2nd ed. Boston: Houghton Mifflin, 1991.

Friedman, Raymond A. *Front Stage, Back Stage: The Dramatic Structure of Labor Negotiations*. Cambridge: The MIT Press, 1994.

Gunderson, M., A. Ponak, and D.G. Taras, eds. *Union-Management Relations in Canada*, 5th ed. Toronto: Pearson Canada, 2004.

Holbrook, James, R., and B. Cook. *Advanced Negotiation and Mediation: Concepts, Skills and Exercises*. St. Paul, Minnesota: West Academic Publishing, 2013.

Holbrook, James. "Using Performative, Distributive, Integrative, and Transformative Principles in Negotiation." *Loyola Law Review*, Vol. 56. Chicago, IL: Loyola University, 2010.

Kahane, Adam. *Collaborating with the Enemy: How to Work with People You Don't Agree with or Like or Trust*. Oakland, CA: Berrett-Koehler Publishers, 2017.

Lewicki, Roy J., D.M. Saunders, and J.W. Minton. *Essentials of Negotiation*, 4th ed. Boston: Irwin McGraw-Hill, 2007; Lewicki, Saunders, Barry, and Tasa, 2nd Cdn ed., 2014; 3rd Cdn ed., 2017; 4th Cdn ed., 2020.

Mayer, Bernard. *Staying with Conflict: A Strategic Approach to Ongoing Disputes*. San Francisco, CA: Jossey-Bass, 2009.

McShane, Steven, and Sandra Steen. *Canadian Organizational Behaviour*. Toronto: McGraw-Hill Ryerson, 2012.

Morgan, Gareth. *Images of Organization*. Thousand Oaks, CA: Sage Publications, 1986, 2006.

Phillips, Gerald E. *Labour Relations and the Collective Bargaining Cycle*. Toronto: Butterworths, 1981.

Program on Negotiation. *Executive Education Series Proceedings*, 1994, 1995, 1996, 1998, 2006. Program on Negotiation at Harvard Law School, Harvard University, Cambridge, MA.

The Negotiation Insider, 2016-2021. Program on Negotiation at Harvard Law School, Harvard University, Cambridge, MA.

Sack, Goldblatt, Mitchell. *Words and Phrases: A Dictionary of Collective Agreement Language*. Toronto: Lancaster House, 1993.

Sack, Jeffrey and Ethan Poskanzer. *Contract Clauses: Collective Agreement Language in Canada*, 3rd ed. Toronto: Lancaster House, 2001.

Saxe, Stewart and Brian Maclean. *Collective Agreement Handbook: A Guide for Employers and Employees*. Aurora: Canada Law Book, 1995.

Selekman, B.M., S.K. Selekman, and S.H. Fuller, *Problems in Labor Relations*, 2nd ed. New York: McGraw-Hill, 1958.

Snyder, Ronald. *Palmer & Snyder Collective Agreement Arbitration in Canada*, 6th ed. Toronto: LexisNexis Canada, 2017.

Susskind, Lawrence and Jeffrey Cruikshank, *Breaking the Impasse: Consensual Approaches to Resolving Public Disputes*. New York: Basic Books, 1988.

Susskind, Lawrence. *Good for You, Great for Me: Finding the Trading Zone*. New York: Public Affairs, 2014.

Tidwell, Alan C. *Conflict Resolved? A Critical Assessment of Conflict Resolution*. New York: Continuum, 2003.

Ury, W. L. *Getting Past No. Negotiating Your Way from Confrontation to Cooperation*. New York: Bantam Books, 1993.

Ury, William L., Jeanne M. Brett and Stephen B. Goldberg. *Getting Disputes Resolved Designing Systems to Cut the Cost of Conflict*. Cambridge: Program on Negotiation at Harvard Law School, 1988.

Walton, Richard and Robert McKersie. *A Behavioral Theory of Labor Negotiations: An Analysis of a Social Interaction System*. New York: McGraw-Hill, 1993.

Weiler, Paul C. *Reconcilable Differences: New Directions in Canadian Labour Law*. Toronto: Carswell, 1980.

Williams-Whitt, Kelly, Michael Begg, Terrance Harris, and Kathryn Filsinger. *Employment Law for Business and Human Resources Professionals: Alberta and British Columbia* 3rd edition. Toronto: Edmond Montgomery Publishers, 2017.

INDEX

A

ability to pay, and wage determination, 99–100
accommodation conflict, 41
accommodation model of emergent relationships, 34–35, 36, 38
actual cost, 100–101
administration phase, stages in, 7
advance notice, of strikes and lockouts, 148–49
adversarial process in traditional collective bargaining, 23–25, 161–62
agreement. *See* collective agreement
ally picketing, 150
alternatives
   BATNA, 63, 63n25, 124–28
   to collective agreement, 123–28, 170
   definition, 123n33
   mediation and other paths, 126–27
   and *no deal* reality, 123–24
analytic frame
   for contentious matters, 58, 170
   description, 48n16
   and informed decisions, 166–67
   in positioning, 49–50
   use as tool, 58, 137, 170, 174
anchoring, description and in positioning, 44–45
antecedent determinants (predetermined factors), in union-employer relationship, 32–33
approach, in organizing concepts of collective bargaining, 38–39
arbitration
   final offer selection (FOS) and variants, 157–59
   inclusion in provisions, 104
   interest arbitration, 159–60
   mediation-arbitration (Med-Arb), 157
arbitrators

    and first agreements, 122–23
    interpretation of provisions, 110–13
    role, 158
articles. *See* clauses in agreement
assistance (bargaining assistance)
    conciliation, 154
    as continuum, 153, 170
    final offer selection (FOS) and variants, 157–59
    inquiries and statutory commissions, 156–57
    interest arbitration, 159–60
    mediation, 154–56
    mediation-arbitration (Med-Arb), 157
assumptions, 15, 25, 130
attitudinal structuring (or relationship), 30
avoidant conflict, 41

B

bargaining
    assessment of environment, 84–85
    impasse remedies (*See* assistance)
    learning from results, 166–67
    need for proposals, 83–84
    objectives development, 78–81
    proposals development, 82–83
    questionnaire example, 75–76
    as social negotiations, 27–30
    stages, 7
    stance, 167
    status/summary worksheet, 94–95
    use of term, 17
    See also negotiation; specific topics
bargaining, collective. *See* collective bargaining
bargaining assistance. *See* assistance
bargaining notes or minutes (CB Resource 6), 95–96
bargaining phase, stages in, 7
bargaining protocol. *See* protocol
bargaining status worksheet (CB Resource 5), 94–95
bargaining table. *See* table
bargaining team. *See* team

bargaining unit clauses, 103
bargaining zone model, 27–28
Barry, Bruce, 19
BATNA (Best Alternative to the Negotiated Agreement), 63, 63n25, 124–28
benchmark settlements, 71
Berkeley, Arthur, 72
Best Alternative to the Negotiated Agreement (BATNA), 63, 63n25, 124–28
British Columbia (BC), 121–22, 148, 157
Brown, Scott, 48, 58
Burrell, Gibson, 13–14
business reimbursement, 102
by-issue selection, 158

C

caucus, 88, 115, 131
CB Resources 1–6, 90–96
checklist
   in collective bargaining process, 180–90
   for mediation, 155–56
   for negotiation and bargaining table, 139–40
clauses in agreement
   groups of, 103–4
   historical development data, 92
   for management rights, 84
   mandatory provisions, 104
   new clauses inclusion, 83–84
   and objectives development, 79–80
   other clauses, 104–5
   wording, 106
   See also provisions
coalitions, definition and types, 10
cognitive biases, 163
collaborative conflict, 41
collective agreement
   alternatives to, 123–28, 170
   appendices, 104
   awareness and biases, 163–65
   clauses (*See* clauses in agreement)
   constructive engagement points, 162–72

    crafting of language, 105–9
    drafting, 105–8, 113
    duration, 104
    elements in, 103
    existing agreement information, 70–71
    first agreement, 121–23
    framework for, 173–74
    "good" agreement, 61–66
    good faith in, 141–46
    language interpretation, 110–13
    mandatory provisions, 104
    and Memorandum of Agreement, 187
    other side as opponent, 161–62
    re-orientation of reactions, 167–69
    and statutes, 108
    time in between, 57, 58, 59, 172–73
collective bargaining
    change in, 56–60
    checklist for process, 180–89
    configurations, 8–10
    and continuous improvement, 56–61, 174
    definition (as process), ix, 3, 26
    description, main concerns, and role, ix–x, 3–4, 6, 17
    and ideological frames, 15–16, 163
    importance, 17
    information for (*See* information for collective bargaining)
    interests in, x, 1, 17
    main ideas in, 1–6
    organizing concepts, 38–39
    outcomes, 2, 3, 5–6
    phases and stages, 6–7, 172–73
    relationships in, x, 4, 26
    as representative process, 1
    as social negotiations, 27–30
    subjects of, 103–8
    traditional process, 23–25, 161–62, 172
    way of doing bargaining, 22–25
collusion model of emergent relationships, 35, 36
Colosi, Thomas, 72
commissions of inquiry, 157

"common site" picketing, 150
compensation, 97, 101–2
compensation trade-offs, 102
competitive conflict, 41
competitive negotiations, and positions, 53–55
compromising conflict, 41–42
conciliation, 154
confirmation bias, 164
conflicting interests in negotiation, 1
conflict in workplace
    and assumptions in ideological frames, 15
    and dual concerns, 39–42
    styles and outcomes, 39, 40, 41
    and third side concept, 171
conflict model of emergent relationships, 34, 35, 36, 38
conflict of interest, definition, 35n11
constituents and constituent groups
    description and types, 8–10
    place in negotiation, 9–10
    in team, 8, 9, 11, 170
constructive behaviour and approach
    advantages in relationships, 61, 162, 170–71
    in collective agreement, 162–72
    as pursuit, 166–72
    in self and our team, 162, 166
    in working relationship development, 58–60
containment-aggression model of emergent relationships, 34, 35, 36, 38
contextual data/information resource (CB Resource 1), 90–92
contingency plans, 128–29, 184
contingent agreements, 127, 127n36
continuous improvement, in collective bargaining, 56–61, 174
"controlled strike," 150–51
cooperation model, of emergent relationships, 35, 36, 38
cooperative negotiations, and positions, 51–55
costing of proposals
    checklist, 182
    definitions and principles, 100–102
    method and objectives, 97–98, 101–2
    wage determination in, 98–100
cost of living, and wage determination, 100

costs, 77, 97
Cruikshank, Jeffrey, 63, 64, 65
Cutcher-Gershenfeld, J.E., 56

D

data. *See* information for collective bargaining
deadlock, and mediation, 155
de minimis rule, 111
destabilizers, in team members, 72
direct costs, 97
discussion of parties and duty to bargain in good faith, 143–44
dispute resolution. *See* assistance
distributive approach, 38–39
distributive bargaining
   description, 27–28, 29, 30
   and positioning tactics, 44
dual concerns
   and conflict, 39–42
   in organizing concepts of collective bargaining, 38
   and strikes and lockouts, 152
   types, 38, 39
dual total package, 158
duty to bargain in good faith
   definition and description, 141
   guidelines, 142–45
   and LRB, 141–42, 145–46
   tests for, 141–42

E

efficiency, in a good agreement, 64, 66
emergent relationships
   definition, 34
   models, 34–36
   test for, 37–38, 162
employee relations, definition, 3
employees, wages as bargaining members, 116
employer
   contextual data as resource, 90–92
   duty to bargain in good faith, 142–45

knowledge about, 69, 70
  management rights, 84
  in statutory framework, 5
  See also union-employer relationship
employment, three-way terms and conditions, 3
end cost, 100
equitable positioning
  and orientations, 38, 42, 43
  as position, 28, 44, 46, 51–52
essential services, in strikes and lockouts, 150–51

F

fact finding, in bargaining assistance, 156–57, 158
"fair and reasonable" in first agreements, 122
fairness, in a good agreement, 63–64, 66
faith. *See* good faith
false consensus effect, 164–65
"final no," 125
final offer selection (FOS) and variants, 157–59
first agreement, 121–23
Fisher, Roger, 48, 58, 62–63
5 Whys Root Cause Analysis technique, 18, 20
frames of reference
  description and role, 2n2, 13, 133, 163
  at initial meeting, 133
  and orientations, 38, 42–43, 51, 58
  types, 13–14
  See also ideological frames
Friedman, Raymond, 23–25
fundamental attribution error, 165

G

General Negotiation Framework (GNF), and objectives development, 78
glossary, 190–205
good faith in collective agreement
  duty of, 141–46
  guidelines, 142–45
  remedies, 145–46
  tests and conditions, 141–45, 169

good faith in integrative approach, 47
"good" settlement (or agreement)
   characteristics, 63–66
   overview, 61
   and win-win outcome, 62–63
"go to the balcony" metaphor, 167–69
grievance provisions, 104
grievances, analysis in objectives development, 80

H
historical clause development (CB Resource 2), 92

I
ideas, use of, 22n9
ideological frames (or theories)
   assumptions in, 15
   as management control, 15–16, 163
   types, 13–14
   in union-employer relationship, 15–16, 33, 163
   See also frames of reference
ideologies of management control, 15–16, 163
imagination, failure of, 59, 152
impact (or "roll-up") costs, 97
implementation/administration phase, stages in, 7
incremental cost, 101
information for collective bargaining
   checklist, 85, 180–89
   contextual data, 90–92
   data collection and analysis, 67–68
   and existing agreement, 70–71
   importance, 67–69
   last negotiation summary, 73–74
   notes and minutes, 95–96
   objectives and limits of the organization, 71–72
   and the organization, 69–70
   organization systems during bargaining (CB Resources 1–6), 90–96
   and the other team, 68, 72–73, 77
   outreach for, 74–76
   probable demands and costs, 77

 status worksheet, 94–95
initial session, preparation and strategy, 132–34
instability, in an agreement, 65–66
integrative approach (in negotiation)
 and a good agreement, 61
 interest- or position-based, 52–54, 55–56
 in orientations, 39, 43
 in positioning, 38, 46–53
 transition to, 56–57, 58
integrative bargaining and potential, 28–29, 30
intention to enter into agreement and duty to bargain in good faith, 144–45
interest arbitration, 159–60
interests
 in collective bargaining, x, 1, 17
 conflicting and common, 1
 and a good agreement, 61–66
 integrative approach and interest-based negotiations, 52–56
 in mixed-motive dynamic, 26
 observations about, 19–21
 questions about, 20
 satisfaction as goal, 10
 surfacing interests, 20–21
 at table, 130, 137
 as term in collective bargaining, 18
 types, 18–19, 20
"interests as principles," 20
intractability
 awareness of and solutions, 166–71
 institutionalization of, 59, 166
intra-organizational (or internal) bargaining, 8, 30
intrinsic interests, 19

L
Labour Board or Labour Relations Board (LRB)
 and duty to bargain in good faith, 141–42, 144–46
 and first agreements, 121–22
 involvement in negotiations, 141
 and picketing, 150
 role, xiv

    in strikes or lockouts, 148–49
labour relations, definition, 3
language
    in agreement, 70
    in crafting of collective agreement, 105–9
    interpretation issues, 110–13
    in proposals, 82
    and provisions, 110–13
    in union-employer relationship, 22–23
    use of, 22n8
"laundry list," 24
legal framework. *See* statutory framework
Lewicki, Roy, 19
lockout, 147, 148
    See also strikes and lockouts
lump-sum payments, 102

M

MacPhail, Bryn, 172n41
management rights (also inherent or residual rights), 84, 84n29
Marcus Aurelius, 172
maximalist positioning
    and orientations, 38, 42, 43
    as position, 28, 44, 45–46, 51–52
"may," interpretation as term, 112
McKersie, Robert, 27, 29
mediation
    description, 154
    guidelines checklist, 155–56
    reasons for, 154–55
mediation-arbitration (Med-Arb), 157
mediators, 126, 154, 155–56
meeting of parties and duty to bargain in good faith, 142–43
meetings location, timing, and length, 115
Memorandum of Agreement (or of Settlement), description and samples, 190–92
metaphors, 22–23, 22n9, 167–69
minutes. *See* notes or minutes
modified final offer selection (modified FOS), 159
Morgan, Gareth, 13–14

multiple-offer final selection (multiple-offer FOS), 159

N
natural coalition, 10
negotiating phase, stages in, 7
negotiating team. *See* team
negotiation
   approaches for a good agreement, 61–66
   change in, 56–60
   checklist, 139–40
   closing of, 138
   concerns and interests in, x
   configurations, 8–10
   description and goal, ix
   dynamics change, 172
   frames of reference, 2n2
   initial session, 132–34
   internal bargaining, 8, 30
   main ideas in, 1–6
   metaphors in, 23, 167–69
   next round preparation, 73–74
   non-traditional concepts, 55–56
   opening meeting, 135–36
   positions in, 28, 43–44
   principles, 59–60
   in private, 8
   proceedings decisions, 116–17
   stages, 7
   time in between, 57, 58, 59, 172–73
   timing in, 2
   understanding in, 136–37
   use of term, 17
   See also bargaining; specific topics
negotiators
   knowledge about the organization, 69–70
   and mediation, 155–56
   in representative process, 1
   role and objectives, 10, 11–12
   and satisfaction of interests, 10

See also spokespersons; team
"no" and alternatives to proposals, 124–25
no deal reality, 123–24
non-wage impacted benefits, 102
no strikes/no lockouts provision, 104
notes or minutes (in bargaining), 95–96
"no to re-set," 124

O
objectives
   broad and specific objectives, 80–82
   description, 78
   development for bargaining, 78–81
   as term in collective bargaining, 18
objective test of duty to bargain in good faith, 142
opening meeting, 135–36
organization
   information about, 69–70
   team in, 11
   understanding of context and values, 11–12, 16–17, 69–70
   visible *vs.* "shadow," 16–17
organizational culture
   change in, 57–60
   description and role, 13, 16
   knowledge about, 69–70, 162–63
orientations (or stances)
   as approach, 38, 42
   frames for, 38, 42–43, 51, 58
   in organizing concepts of collective bargaining, 38
   and positioning, 38, 42–43, 51–52
   in proposals, 83
other team
   information for collective bargaining, 68, 72–73, 77
   as opponent, 161–62
outcomes in collective bargaining, 2, 3, 5–6

P
parties in duty to bargain in good faith, guidelines for, 142–45
personalities, in union-employer relationship, 32–33

picketing, 149–50
   See also strikes and lockouts
plan manager, 129
pluralist ideological frame, 14, 15
positions and positioning
   anchoring in, 44–45
   as approach, 43–51
   and cooperation, 51, 52–53
   cooperative *vs.* competitive negotiation, 53–55
   and economic situation, 59
   features and limitations, 45–46
   and integrative approach, 38, 46–53
   in negotiations, 28, 43–44
   and orientations, 38, 42–43, 51–52
   as term in collective bargaining, 18
   traditional approach and position-based negotiations, 52–54
power, and ideological frames, 14
predetermined factors (antecedent determinants), in union-employer relationship, 32–33
preparation
   awareness in, 163–65
   checklist, 180–89
   and contingency plans, 128–29
   focus on future, 80
   foundations for, 68–69
   for initial session, 132–34
   for next round of negotiation, 73–74
preparation phase, stages in, 7
primary constituents, 8
principles, role and examples, 18–19
process-based (procedural) interests, 18, 19
productivity, and wage determination, 99
professional development, allowances, 102
proposal—counter proposal—agreed in principle resource (P-CP-AiP) (CB Resource 3), 93
proposals
   categorization, 71–72, 95
   costing (*See* costing of proposals)
   development, 82–83
   exchange of initial proposals, 120
   information for bargaining, 93–95
   need for, 83–84

"no" and alternatives to, 124–25
presentation method, 82–83
protocol (bargaining protocol)
considerations and rules, 114–15, 117–19
exchange of initial proposals, 120
formal agreement example, 118–19
meetings (location, timing, length), 115
wages for members, 116
Provis, ttt, 20
provisions
and change over time, 105–6
drafting, 105–8, 113
interpretation, 110–13
mandatory provisions in agreement, 104
matters to include, 109
meaning and language, 110–13
non-mandatory provisions in agreement, 104–5
See also clauses in agreement
pyramiding of benefits or penalties, 112

Q
quasi-mediators, in team members, 73
questions and questioning, 20, 134–35, 136

R
radical (critical or Marxist) ideological frame, 14, 15
recognition clause, 104
relationship–others, concerns for, 38, 39
relationship outcomes, 6
relationships
in collective bargaining, x, 4, 26
constituents–spokespersons–team, 8, 9
constructive behaviour advantages, 61, 162, 170–71
emergent relationships, 34–38, 162
employer–union–statutory framework, 5
factors in, 32–34
and ideologies of management control, 15–16, 163
and metaphors, 23
See also union-employer relationship

repeated-offer selection, 158
replication principle, 122
ripeness, 2, 170
"rules of construction," and language, 110–11

S

Saunders, David, 19
Sebenius, James, 125
secondary constituents, 8
security, in work stoppages, 129
self-serving bias, 165
"shall," interpretation as term, 112
single-issue coalition, 10
social beliefs, in union-employer relationship, 33
social negotiations, 27–30
spokespersons, 8–9, 10, 88
    See also negotiators
stability, in a good agreement, 65–66
stabilizers, in team members, 72
stances. *See* orientations
status quo, 16, 59, 151–52
statutes, and collective agreement, 108
statutory (or legal) framework
    in bargaining assistance, 154, 156–57
    checklist for review, 177–79
    duty to bargain in good faith, 141, 145–46
    employer and union in, 5
    and essential services, 150–51
    examples in collective bargaining, 4
    main points in Canada, xiii–xiv
    and objectives in collective agreement, 147
    and strikes and lockouts, 148, 149, 150–51
strikes and lockouts
    advance notice, 148–49
    and benefits, 149
    causes of, 151–52
    in contingency plans, 129
    description and purpose, 147–48
    and duty to bargain in good faith, 145

   and essential services, 150–51
   and interest arbitration, 159
   and picketing, 149–50
   preconditions, 148–49
   remedies (*See* assistance)
   and statutory framework, 148, 149, 150–51
   unlawful strikes and lockouts, 149
subjective interests, 18–19
subjective test of duty to bargain in good faith, 141
subjects of collective bargaining, 103–8
substance–self, concerns for, 38, 39, 40
substantive interests, 18, 19
substantive outcomes, 5
Susskind, Lawrence, 62–63, 64, 65

T

table (bargaining table)
   alternatives at, 123–28, 170
   approaches to interactions, 130–32
   checklist, 139–40
   contingency plans, 128–29
   guidelines for bargaining, 132–38
   movement toward agreement, 137–38
   understanding at, 136–37
"tactical no," 124
targeted adjustments, 102
Tasa, Kevin, 19
team (bargaining or negotiating)
   attributes of members, 87
   authority to bargain, 117
   checklist, 177, 180
   in configurations, 8–9
   constituents in, 8, 9, 11, 170
   constructive behaviour, 162, 166
   exchange of initial protocol, 120
   internal bargaining, 8, 30
   number of members, 86
   for organization, 11
   responsibilities, 117–18, 134

    roles and objectives, 11–12, 88–89
    selection, 86–89
    signals and code words, 88, 89
    types of members, 72–73
    for union, 11
    wages, 116
    See also other team
third party assistance. *See* assistance
third-party processes, 3
third side concept, 171
Tidwell, Alan, 62, 63
time in between (interim period), 57, 58, 59, 172–73
timing in negotiation, importance, 2
total labour costs, 100
training allowances, 102
tri-offer selection, 158

U

unconscious biases, 163
unilateral determination, 3
union
    and assumptions in frames, 15
    bargaining questionnaire example, 75–76
    and benefits, 149
    checklist for review, 180–89
    and duty to bargain in good faith, 142–45
    exchange of initial protocol, 120
    knowledge about, 69, 70
    in statutory framework, 5
    team, 11
    See also union-employer relationship
union-employer relationship
    attitudes, 30–31, 32
    change in, 57–60
    evolution in, 25, 30–31
    factors, 32–34
    framework for, 173–74
    and ideologies, 15–16, 33, 163
    as interdependent, 124

    language and metaphors in, 22–23, 167–69
    as mixed-motive dynamic, 26
    at table, 131
    understanding of, 26–30, 87
    unitarist view, 27
unionized environment, and emergent employment relationships, 31
unitary/unitarist ideological frame, 14, 15, 27
universal concerns (substance, process, relationships), x, 130
    See also relationships
Ury, William, 62–63, 167

V

value
    creation and claiming, 57–58
    as notion, 29n10, 47n14
values, 12–13, 69–70, 87

W

wage criteria, determination, 98–100
"wage-effort bargain" clauses, 103
wage-impacted costs, 102
wage rate, comparability, 98–99
wages, for bargaining members, 116
Wagner Act, as model of legislation, xiv n1
Walton, Richard, 27, 29
Weiler, Paul, 150–51
what you see and hear / what you don't, 10, 22–23
"wildcat" strikes or lockouts, 148
win-win bargaining, 62–63
wisdom, in a good agreement, 64–65, 66
working resource (CB Resource 4), 93–94
workplace conflict. *See* conflict in workplace
workplace organization, ideological frame types, 14
workplace relations, and assumptions, 15
work stoppage, and contingency plans, 128–29

Y

Yarrow Lodge Limited, as seminal case, 121n31, 122

Z

"zero-sum proposition" issue, 25, 43–44, 161

zone of potential agreement (ZOPA), and anchoring, 45

ABOUT THE AUTHOR

Hugh J. Finlayson

Hugh J. Finlayson is a Chartered Professional in Human Resources (CPHR) and a faculty member in the School of Business, Human Resources Management Program at the British Columbia Institute of Technology (BCIT). He is also an Affiliated Scholar with the Centre for Educational Leadership and Policy (CSELP), Faculty of Education, Simon Fraser University.

His current research and teaching builds upon his 35-year career in human resource leadership and management across multiple roles, from practitioner, manager, and director to chief executive officer. Responsible for collective bargaining at the local, sectoral and provincial levels he is the author of numerous collective bargaining resource and discussion papers about collective bargaining processes, structures and practices, negotiator professional development initiatives, and the comprehensive human resource practitioner's best practices resource, *When Things Happen at Work: A Practitioner's Guide to People, Circumstances and What to Do Now.*[44]

Hugh is an Honorary Life Member of the CPHR British Columbia & Yukon in recognition of his contribution to the field of human resources and designated a Fellow CPHR, a title that recognizes the most exceptional CPHR holders in BC and the Yukon.

---

44 Hugh J. Finlayson, *When Things Happen at Work: A Practitioner's Guide to People, Circumstances and What to Do Now*—3rd edition. Victoria, BC: FriesenPress, 2020.

NOTES

Printed in the USA
CPSIA information can be obtained
at www.ICGtesting.com
LVHW071147050124
768154LV00006B/787